UNMASKING FOR LIFE

PRAISE FOR
UNMASKING FOR LIFE

"Devon Price is the most exciting, revolutionary voice in autism advocacy today."

FERN BRADY, COMEDIAN AND AUTHOR OF
STRONG FEMALE CHARACTER

"Devon Price has written an essential and practical guide for autistic people to live as their full and authentic selves. *Unmasking for Life* should be read not only by autistic people, but their loved ones to ensure they facilitate a truly fulfilling life."

ERIC GARCIA, AUTHOR OF *WE'RE NOT BROKEN:*
CHANGING THE AUTISM CONVERSATION

"Dr Devon Price is a voice of compassion and transformation for autistic people everywhere. *Unmasking for Life* is deeply insightful and empowering, illuminating a path for those of us searching for authentic connections and relationships in a world of ableism, trauma and misunderstanding. This is the book I desperately needed."

EMILY KATY, AUTHOR OF *GIRL UNMASKED:*
HOW UNCOVERING MY AUTISM SAVED MY LIFE

"An essential roadmap for autistic people to be themselves."
NPR

PRAISE FOR
UNMASKING AUTISM

"Reading this felt like being at home – I didn't realise how much I masked. What an incredible book that I know will be re-read many times over."
DR CAMILLA PANG, AUTHOR OF *EXPLAINING HUMANS: WHAT SCIENCE CAN TEACH US ABOUT LIFE, LOVE AND RELATIONSHIPS*

"*Unmasking Autism* is at once a most deeply personal and scholarly account of the damage caused by autistic (and all) people leading masked lives, and how unmasking is essential to creating a self-determined, authentic life... This is a remarkable work that will stand at the forefront of the neurodiversity movement."
DR BARRY M. PRIZANT, AUTHOR OF *UNIQUELY HUMAN: A DIFFERENT WAY OF SEEING AUTISM*

"Price's accessible and compassionate writing shines, and readers will feel encouraged to embrace a new understanding of themselves. Its potential to help masked autistic adults, especially those from systemically marginalized backgrounds, makes this book essential for most collections."
LIBRARY JOURNAL

DR DEVON PRICE

UNMASKING FOR LIFE

A GUIDE TO
EMBRACING YOUR AUTISM
IN A
NEUROTYPICAL WORLD

monoray

First published in Great Britain in 2025 by Monoray, an imprint of
Octopus Publishing Group Ltd
Carmelite House
50 Victoria Embankment
London EC4Y 0DZ
www.octopusbooks.co.uk

An Hachette UK Company
www.hachette.co.uk

The authorized representative in the EEA is Hachette Ireland, 8 Castlecourt Centre, Dublin 15, D15 XTP3, Ireland (email: info@hbgi.ie)

Text copyright © Devon Price 2025
Published by arrangement with Harmony Books, an imprint of Random House, a division of Penguin Random House LLC. First published in the United States in 2025.

All rights reserved. No part of this work may be reproduced or utilized in any form or by any means, electronic or mechanical, including photocopying, recording or by any information storage and retrieval system, without the prior written permission of the publisher.

ISBN (hardback) 978-1-80096-291-0
ISBN (trade paperback) 978-1-80096-292-7

A CIP catalogue record for this book is available from the British Library.

Printed and bound in Great Britain

3 5 7 9 10 8 6 4

This FSC® label means that materials used for the product have been responsibly sourced.

This is a work of nonfiction. Nonetheless, some of the names and identifying details of individuals discussed have been altered. Any resulting resemblance to persons living or dead is entirely coincidental and unintentional.

For Tay, and for all the other Autistics
who live life completely unmasked

CONTENTS

Introduction: From Unmasking Autism to Unmasking Life   xi

1. **Five Core Skills for Unmasking Your Life**   3
2. **Friendship**   44
3. **Family**   85
4. **Work**   133
5. **Love and Sex**   173
6. **Life**   212

Acknowledgments   263
Notes   267
Index   283

INTRODUCTION

From Unmasking Autism to Unmasking Life

I first found out that I was Autistic in 2014, when I was twenty-five years old. I'd known very little about Autism up to that point, despite having completed a PhD in psychology. I mostly viewed the disability the same way the average person did: a condition of three-year-old boys who were obsessed with baseball statistics or trains. Even in some graduate-level clinical classes, I'd heard ignorant, stereotypical myths about Autism: that Autistic people lacked any interest in forming friendships, for example, and that they were incapable of compassion. I'd heard that Autism was always a very obviously debilitating burden, and that there was essentially no hope of Autistics ever leading fulfilling lives. Though I'd struggled to form healthy relationships, live independently, and experience happiness of my own, I'd never considered that the Autism label had anything to do with me.

What I didn't realize then was that Autism is actually a complex developmental disorder, one that shapes every aspect of how a person processes information and makes sense of the world around them. I didn't understand, for example, that Autistic people take in sensory data in a bottom-up fashion, rather than the efficient top-down way many non-Autistics (also known as *allistics*) do. For example, laboratory studies have used eye-tracking technology to observe that Autistic people, when presented with a photo of a person's face and asked to judge what emotion the person in the photo is feeling, look at *all* the individual components of the face equally, and carefully: their gaze darts from the mouth to the nose to the eyes, forehead, and chin, processing each feature and trying to piece together what the person might be feeling. Non-Autistic people, in contrast, look at the face as a whole, and recognize emotions on an intuitive level at a glance.[1] Because Autistics typically can't see this top-down "picture" of an emotion, we instead have to memorize what specific arrangements of face parts might mean (for example, that wide eyes could mean either fear or aggression).

This bottom-up processing style also explains why we Autistics find it so much more stressful to be in loud or visually busy spaces compared to most allistics, whose brains instinctively filter out unwanted distractions in ways ours cannot. It is also the reason Autistics need far more time to figure out how to behave in an unfamiliar situation. But sometimes our processing style works to our advantage: studies show that we make fewer errors than non-Autistics when faced with complicated logic problems.[2] I didn't know my brain processed things more effortfully, precisely, and slowly than many other people's brains when I was growing up. All I knew was that other people seemed to move so quickly, driven by instincts I couldn't follow. By my teenage years, I chalked up my confusion and detachment to my being a misanthrope.

I also didn't understand that many Autistic people desperately crave close relationships but have trouble forming them, because many of us cannot read facial expressions, hear differences in tone of voice, or comprehend the indirectness of sarcasm and small talk. I'd just figured other people were worse communicators than me, and I had no time for their irrationality.

I had no clue that my childhood inability to ride a bike or write in cursive could be linked to Autistic fine motor deficits, or that the furious rage I felt when a meeting dragged on longer than expected was due to an Autistic need for predictability and structure. Finally, I didn't understand that my inability to recognize my own emotions or bodily needs (such as hunger or tiredness) was because I'd been masquerading as neurotypical for my entire life, stuffing down all the voices inside me that were constantly clamoring for softer clothes, darker rooms, less cluttered spaces, more intense flavors, and an explanation for what the hell was going on around me at all times.

Introduction

I spent many years of my life believing that I was an unfeeling robot who could never love or be loved by other people, and camouflaging every moment of discomfort and confusion I ever experienced. Then I finally received the gift of learning I was Autistic, after a relative's diagnosis set off a chain reaction of self-examination, research, and embedding myself within the Autistic self-advocacy community. I realized then that my grumpy, misanthropic exterior was how I'd survived in a painfully unaccommodating world. All my anger, all my coldness and judgment, the aloof walls I put up to keep people from taking advantage of my naivete—it was all *masking*, an attempt at hiding my disability that many undiagnosed Autistic people take part in.

As I learned more about Autism and got to know myself as a disabled person a bit better, decades of emotional repression and complex trauma burst from deep within. Suddenly I became a person who called in sick to work for the sake of my mental health, and cried myself to sleep at night while clutching stuffed animals. I stopped wearing painfully tight skirt suits and chopped off my long, scratchy hair; I began working alone in the dark at odd hours and climbing underneath the bed to hide when ambulances blared too loudly on my street. These were things I had always craved doing but had feared would make me seem pathetic, childish, or attention-seeking.

Discovering that I was Autistic gave me the freedom to behave in a more obviously Autistic way, and my life improved immensely. My chronic anemia went away, as I learned to feed myself the heavily seasoned, burnt-to-a-crisp meals that my palate could tolerate. The quality of my writing got better, as I stopped trying to hide what made my thinking unique. I started dressing the way I'd always wanted to dress, sitting the way I wanted to sit, and I became more outgoing and expressive about topics that interested me. I took a more active interest in other people, finally asking them *why* they felt the way they did and believed the things they believed. I didn't have to pretend to naturally understand other people anymore. By being so openly curious, I found it far easier to make friends. I worked less, I slept more, and I started trying an array of new hobbies and experiences just for the sake of better knowing myself and studying how other people behaved. Slowly, a well-balanced life came together for me, and I actually *liked* the person I was as I lived it.

This long journey of *unmasking* and embracing my authentically Autistic self took the better part of a decade. The first few years were devoted entirely to learning about what Autism truly was, and examining what an Autistic identity might mean for me. I engaged in a lot of research and deep introspection during this period, and quietly experimented with sensory accommodations and self-stimulation ("stim") toys to regulate my stress. I reflected on my past and the neurodivergent traits that others had punished or judged me for, and tried to repair my self-concept. I also interviewed countless other Autistic people, including many who were coaches and therapists themselves, and I developed exercises designed to help me and other Autistics get to know ourselves better. The fruits of this labor appeared in *Unmasking Autism: Discovering the New Faces of Neurodiversity*, one of my previous books.

Getting to know myself as an Autistic brought me incredible relief and empowerment. But in order to truly unmask, I had to venture beyond myself and forge new relationships with other people whose ways of thinking, feeling, and behaving didn't conform to the neurotypical norm. I also had to learn to explain my needs to my existing friends and family, who had only ever known the masked version of me. I started to think strategically about advocating for the accommodations I needed within my workplace. I noticed that over time, my energy levels and degree of functioning were flagging, so I started to contemplate what a sustainable long-term future would be like, assuming that I wouldn't always be able to work. I threw out the old scripts of what a meaningful adult life meant by neurotypical standards—marriage, single-family home ownership, retirement at age sixty-seven, 2.5 children—and really thought about what I wanted to accomplish and how I might safely grow old.

I had already unmasked my Autism. But after I'd done that, I still desperately needed to unmask my entire *life*—carefully planning and building my relationships, my family, my means of survival, my living space, and even my preparations for the future to revolve around my genuine needs, rather than neurotypical expectations. It wasn't easy work. Often it was quite unpopular with others who didn't "get" me, or who were deeply invested in conformity to the neurotypical ideal. Powerful institutions like the federal government, the education system, and my employer had created policies that rewarded people for living in conventional ways, so I was systematically discouraged from diverging from the "normal" path. Still, I knew I had to keep at it. There was no returning to the state of ignorance and self-hatred I'd been in when I was masked.

To build an existence that worked with my Autism rather than against it, I needed extensive self-advocacy tools, scripts for negotiating with other people, resources for taking care of myself and those I cared about, and the courage to believe I genuinely deserved any of it. Today, in my late thirties with a steady support system, a plan for the future, and vast reserves of self-acceptance that I'd never believed were possible for me, I can say all this planning and self-advocacy was completely worth it. I wasn't able to fully *live* when I was masquerading as a neurotypical person and quietly hating myself for my difference. Now I am vibrantly alive, and connected, and I get to author the rules for my own existence.

In my research as a psychologist and my work as an Autistic thinker and advocate, I've encountered countless neurodivergent people who have had to embark on similar journeys. Some of them are Autistic like me; others are ADHDers, or they have Tourette's Syndrome, Bipolar Disorder, Narcissistic Personality Disorder, a traumatic brain injury, Down Syndrome, or any number of other stigmatized mental and emotional diversities. Others don't identify with any psychiatric label at all, but recognize they suffer from society's pressure to *neuroconform*[3]—to make ourselves behave in accordance with the neurotypical standards of our time—all the same. We've all felt the need to bury crucial parts of who we are—how we think, feel, and behave—but after doing that for entirely too long, and at great personal cost, many of us are ready to dig our long-hidden selves up and find a secure, nourishing bed in which we can be planted and grow.

Many of us spend years trying to live up to a neuroconformist ideal and failing. We try to get full-time jobs when we truly don't have the energy for them; we form romantic relationships that look pleasing to the outside world, but which are filled with turmoil; we accept mistreatment from our friends and judgment from our relatives; and we get by with great difficulty and no positive vision of what might be waiting for us at the end of the road. Most of us eventually become burned out or disillusioned and conclude we can't keep on living in this way. This often coincides with us falling ill, and then finding out that we're Autistic or otherwise different. But even after we've discovered that our struggles were never our fault, we remain trapped in a world that demands we lead a neurotypical life. We need to do more than simply accept ourselves as disabled in order to survive. We have to construct a radically new and proudly disabled way of living—and that is where this book begins.

This book is a call to action for neurodivergent or otherwise proudly nonconforming people who have begun their personal unmasking journeys but need additional support bringing their private revelations into their public realities. It's a collection of tools for those who struggle to identify and push for the supports and accommodations that they need. And it's also a potential road map toward an unrecognizably better life for those of us who've never been afforded the right to dream of a contented and comfortable existence because we've been so focused on merely trying to survive.

Lifelong unmasking is made possible through the practice of several key skills, which can be applied to nearly any practical or interpersonal struggle in our lives. But before we dive into developing these skills, let's briefly consider *why* the act of masking is so destructive to our wonderfully nonnormative bodies, minds, and defiant inner spirits.

Masking: When Internalized Ableism Becomes Your Way of Life

When an undiagnosed Autistic (or otherwise neurodivergent) person grows up unaware that they are disabled, the only source of meaning they have to reach for is the neurotypical script for what a worthy life is. If making eye contact is painful but socially required, they assume that doing so must be painful for just about everybody—then they force themself to go ahead and give eye contact anyway. If they can't follow verbal instructions during class or at work, they learn to nod along and figure things out on their own, believing that everybody else must have to put that much effort in, too. If all the food available makes them retch and most conversations strike them as bafflingly superficial, they may conclude life is just supposed to be joyless. If their relationships feel hollow and performative and their existence is a strenuous slog through discomfort and unfulfillment, they may conclude that's just what being an adult in the world means. For the disabled person who is struggling desperately to neuroconform, there's no way to understand why a conventional life doesn't fit. There's only the pressure to match with what's "normal," and the enduring loneliness of never really succeeding at it.

Masked Autism is what results when an entire population of disabled people grows up not being allowed to be openly disabled. Typically, masked Autistics belong to the groups that mainstream psychiatry has most overlooked: transgender people, women, and other gender minorities, as well as people of color, people who grew up in poverty, queer people, and older adults who grew up in a period when Autism was still quite poorly understood. These groups are underdiagnosed as Autistic to an overwhelming degree,[4] being far more likely to be misdiagnosed with other conditions first (such as Obsessive-Compulsive Disorder, Oppositional Defiant Disorder, Borderline Personality Disorder, Narcissistic Personality Disorder, Social Anxiety Disorder, or Bipolar Disorder). When they do get diagnosed, it happens at much later ages than for white cisgender males from wealthy backgrounds.[5] This means that they miss out on the potentially positive childhood experiences of being assigned a support team, receiving disability accommodations, being understood by their peers and caregivers as in need, and finding a place for themselves within the disabled community. Instead, undiagnosed Autistics learn to stop asking for the help that is never provided to them and to stop behaving in ways that make them stand out—in other words, they learn to mask.

A study published in 2023 in the journal *Autism* found that Autistic college students who had been diagnosed when they were young fared far better than those who arrived at an Autistic identity later in life.[6] An early diagnosis was associated with a higher quality of life and higher life satisfaction. Autistics who were diagnosed early in life reported that they were able to process any complex or negative feelings they had about their disability at a younger age, alongside parents and caregivers who were busy learning more about Autism at the same exact time. As a result, many had come to feel proud of or joyful about their disabled identity. They and their families were able to find support groups and social groups with the aid of their diagnosis, and had the language to explain to schools, doctors, and other institutions that they needed help and what help looked like for them.

Additional research suggests that when Autistic people grow up knowing about their disability, they are more able to view their neurotype as a neutral or even positive aspect of themselves that can be discussed and even joked about freely.[7] Later discoveries of Autism, in contrast, are more strongly associated with shame and concealment, and hesitation to request disability services.[8] Early diagnosis of Autism can also come with genuine risks to a child's well-being, by marking them with disability stigma, for example, or by increasing the odds that they will be pushed through unhelpful "treatment" programs such as Applied Behavior Analysis therapy (also known as ABA, which focuses on behaviorally conditioning a child to fake a non-Autistic personality). But on balance, knowing who one is, being able to articulate that identity to the world, and recognizing oneself within a community of disabled people have net benefits early in life.

Unfortunately, marginalized Autistics are rarely afforded this opportunity. Instead of being identified as disabled and receiving services, they are viewed as a problem and punished for their nonconformity and any challenge they present to their teachers and parents. This has a far-reaching impact on how the undiagnosed relate to other people, what kind of treatment they learn to expect from the world, and even how they feel about themselves.

Here's a simple example: if an undiagnosed ten-year-old Autistic child thrashes and screams as they enter the doctor's office, their parent may criticize them, the staff at the front desk may roll their eyes at them, their doctor may be curt and impatient with them, and all the other patients in the waiting room may stare and view them as a spoiled brat. But if that same child is diagnosed as Autistic, they *may* be granted a far gentler transition: their parent may give them a soft-voiced warning about the upcoming appointment, maybe even with a narrative about what to expect. The doctor's office might allow them to wear noise-canceling ear defenders and a hat to manage the noise and brightness of the clinic; staff might let them enter the office from a side door and go directly into a dimly lit private room with a doctor who speaks gently to them.

Without helpful environmental and social adjustments like these, Autistic children suffer from confusion, overstimulation, and fear. They may be seen as spoiled, bratty, overly sensitive, or violent simply because they express the pain of living in a world that's hostile to them. In time, the Autistic child will tend to internalize this, viewing themself as antisocial or difficult to deal with. They also may lose faith in other people and withdraw from the world, believing that most public spaces are not "for" them. The expectation that they think, feel, and behave in a fully neurotypical way slowly becomes a protective mask they wear everywhere, ensuring that they are never stared at or insulted again.

Each one of us masks our disability a little bit differently. Some of us wear masks of compliance and agreeability to prevent ourselves from being seen as stubborn or difficult. Others become class clowns to hide how unmoored we feel in a social world governed by unspoken rules we cannot understand. Some masked Autistics lean into our intellectual achievements, or become compulsive people-pleasers, hoping to earn acceptance by defining ourselves by the few socially approved skills we have. And some of us pull away from other people entirely, slipping into a dissociated, extremely passive state because even our best attempts at fitting in have failed. Although each of these survival strategies presents in a different way, they are all motivated by the same underlying goal: to avoid detection and further ostracism, and to hide the reality of how deeply we are struggling, sometimes even from ourselves.

Masking comes at an immense personal cost. Empirical research shows that masked Autistics are lonelier and more socially anxious than their unmasked Autistic peers,[9] and experience depression at elevated rates.[10] Maskers frequently use substances to numb the constant pain that they are in,[11] or engage in compulsive self-harm,[12] disordered eating behaviors, or other acts of self-destruction.[13] Hard-core maskers can't form authentically loving relationships because it is impossible for anyone to truly get to know them or for them to express what they really want. In its most extreme form, masking is a dreadful act of self-negation, and so it's no wonder maskers experience a heightened risk of suicidal thoughts and suicide attempts.[14]

Eventually, many masked Autistics and other neurodivergent individuals hit a period of burnout, during which they function far more poorly than they were able to before, and can no longer maintain their masks. It is during this dramatic shift in abilities and priorities that people typically find out they are disabled. Then they may begin to question the harsh societal standards that led them to such a miserable and effortful existence and start to imagine what a life that accommodates their way of functioning could be like. This is often the first real stage of a person's unmasking journey—learning that the intense social pressures of being neurotypical might not be inevitable, but in fact are a constructed social bias that a person can question and unlearn.

The Pursuit of Neurotypicality

Shuài grew up in China in the 1990s, within a family and community that knew very little about Autism. When he experienced meltdowns, his parents' and grandparents' solutions were to try to take care of his basic needs by feeding him or putting him to bed early. In time, Shuài came to view offers of food and a nap as a punishment intended to silence him. He enjoyed certain repetitive household chores, such as washing vegetables and putting clean clothing away, so he often self-soothed by performing them for hours at a time. He was very shy, and had no interest in playing sports and games, going outside, or talking to girls, though he was often expected to try these activities. Still, he says that if he hadn't moved to the United States for graduate school and then found the adjustment to be incredibly difficult, it's likely he never would have figured out that he was Autistic.

"Even then it took a while for anybody to suggest it," he says to me. "Because of the stereotyping of Asian men in the United States, it was not super noteworthy for me to be keeping to myself and leading a relatively simple life focusing on completing school." But his roommate, who was a social work student, did notice Shuài's repetitive cleaning rituals, and that he walked on his tiptoes (a common motor difference in Autistic individuals)[15]—and he introduced Shuài to some online videos about Autism. A multiyear process of Autistic self-discovery then followed.

Taking on an Autistic identity emboldened Shuài in a couple of ways. He has the power now to distinguish between social expectations and what he personally wants. "I met a girl at an Autism social group on Meetup.com, and like me she wants to be child-free and thinks having a lifelong romantic commitment is risky and irrational. This is the first time I've ever had a real interest in dating, or been able to tell a girl I believe these things."

Still, Shuài's afraid to seek out a formal diagnosis and ask for help at school, such as having the verbal presentation requirement for his thesis be waived. "I'm afraid of how it will look for an international student to not have to give a presentation in English," he says.

He's also concerned that his family will view a diagnosis as a threat to his professional success and visa status—which is a reasonable concern. Many countries still ban the immigration of Autistic people and their families or turn them away as visa-seekers or refugees. In 2019, then-president Donald Trump enacted a "public charge rule" that limited immigrants' ability to access disability services, and restricted Autistic immigrants from entering the country.[16] Autistic people are also banned from immigrating to countries like New Zealand[17] and the United Kingdom,[18] and Canada only lifted its ban on Autistic immigrants in 2018.[19]

Living in a college town in a country that's a bit more knowledgeable about Autism[20] has benefited Shuài in some ways. On campus, he can wear cozy clothing, give himself simple haircuts, and get by without driving and never stand out. He turns down invitations for parties or university networking events, knowing that they're just not his speed. Still, there's a stigma to his multiple marginalized identities that follows him and makes him feel more visible now than he ever did in China. And for all the positive changes he has been able to make in his life, he worries that he'll lose that freedom when he graduates and must enter the "real world."

"Sometimes," he says, "I worry that doing things my way now is just making me too weak for the future"—a future where he will be expected to work, dress up, live independently, and perhaps settle down and raise a family.

Because they never received disability accommodations or any understanding of themselves as members of an oppressed group, many masked Autistics cope by hiding behind a façade of neurotypicality. Neurotypicality refers to the standards of behavior, emotion, and thought that people in the broader culture view as healthy, safe, and socially acceptable. People who meet these standards are more likely to be judged as "sane," though the behaviors and traits that are seen as signs of sanity vary widely across cultures and time periods.

In America, for instance, it's considered socially desirable to smile at complete strangers and casually chat with co-workers as if they are friends, and so neurotypical people are those who do exactly that. Anyone who falls short of this expectation runs the risk of being seen as pathologically shy, socially anxious, suspicious, or antisocial. We're also expected in the United States to be quite openly emotional, at least when it comes to positive emotions, and to show that we are "confident" by staring people in the eye and giving them a firm handshake. In a country like Germany, in contrast, it's far more normal to avoid looking at strangers and to take years to befriend a new person. There, an overly friendly, socially pushy way of relating might not be neurotypical at all. Instead, it might come across as histrionic.

Neurotypical standards are a moving target: even people without a diagnosable disability may fail to live up to neurotypical ideals if they can't work full-time, live independently, form gender normative romantic relationships, control their emotional expressions, and "contribute" to society in typically expected ways. And when we consider how common difficult experiences like depression and anxiety are,[21] as well as conditions like Alzheimer's, it becomes clear that very few human beings actually live up to the standards of neurotypicality for the whole of their life. According to the neurodiversity perspective, no single person is ever truly neurotypical, in fact. We all just vary in our ability to neuroconform.

Autistic people find it especially difficult to neuroconform. We generally have a hard time picking up vague, unarticulated social guidelines and rules, so we often manage to stick out as strange no matter the culture we're in. We struggle to hold full-time jobs, to initiate relationships, and to articulate our feelings in ways others respect or find understandable. Our bodies move differently than allistic bodies do, and research shows that non-Autistics find our emotions difficult to read.[22] Even when we attempt to mask, we are a tiny bit slower to process than other people are, and our performances are ever-so-slightly, subliminally "off," and non-Autistic people dislike us for it.[23]

Though many Autistic people initially believe that our masks will protect us from ostracism, in time we come to realize that to be masked is not to be freed from judgment but to be imprisoned by it. Masking is a labor-intensive, largely unsuccessful process that cleaves us from our bodies and our true feelings, and engaging in it can actively prevent us from forging real relationships or building happy lives. Losing faith in the power of the mask can come as a relief—but learning how to venture into the world without a mask brings its own set of challenges.

The Rewards and Challenges of Unmasking

For many masked Autistic people, discovering that we are disabled comes as a world-shaking revelation. In my case, I learned that I was never really an antisocial creep with rage issues; it was just that crowded spaces sent me into sensory overload mode. As a teen, I hadn't failed to sign up customers for my retail job's predatory credit card because I was a coward, or lazy; it was just that lying to people and pressuring them felt simply *wrong* to me. Once I had a clear vision of the person I was, I could finally stop beating myself up for failing to be somebody else.

For many late-realized Autistics, our entire life histories up to the moment we found out we are Autistic are cast in a new light: the friends we lost, the family members we disappointed, the classes we dropped, the jobs we've been fired from, the expected life milestones we never seemed to reach, and the seemingly "strange" tastes and dreams that we have all suddenly make sense. The many difficulties we have faced are revealed as a mismatch between our neurotype and what society has conditioned us to be. Piecing together a new identity as a disabled person and unlearning an entire culture's worth of anti-Autistic stigma take years for many of us. But even after we come to know and accept who we are, there remain the practical problems of paying the rent, feeding and clothing ourselves, pursuing our passions, and finding appreciation or even love within a society that primarily treats us as defective.

One unmasked Autistic woman I spoke with, Aisha, told me that after figuring out she was Autistic, she had to confront the fact that her elderly mother and sister were most likely masked Autistics, too. Both Aisha's relatives are still absolutely devoted to the respectable, serious, high-achieving façades they had adopted to get by as Black women with undiagnosed sensory issues, social difficulties, cognitive processing differences, and other Autistic traits. They judge Aisha harshly for becoming a more relaxed, openly flawed person with a messy house, a part-time job, a sometimes-foggy short-term memory, and a wardrobe filled with sensory-friendly pajamas and fluffy socks. They even question Aisha's fitness to parent her kids. "They keep bullying me to do exactly what helped them survive, and I don't know how to fight it without them getting defensive," she told me. "They don't believe it's possible to ever show weakness and be okay, and so they hate that I'm openly weak."

Another Autistic that I spoke to, Bill, explained that he spent the first forty-five years of his life being so ashamed of his disability that he never allowed himself to explore any new interests or try meeting any new people. "I was so afraid of saying or doing the wrong thing that I never tried any hobbies or even visited a concert on my own. There are so many things that I want to do, like checking out the local punk music scene or getting a tattoo, but I wonder if it's too late for me." Bill has come to believe that he deserves a place in public life as an Autistic person, and after a few years of unmasking in his home and around his family, he has a pretty firm sense of who he is and what he wants. But he doesn't have much practice engaging with unfamiliar people or trying new things out in the world.

My book *Unmasking Autism* was largely tailored to newly self-realized Autistic people who were hoping to get back in touch with their authentic disabled selves—as well as the loved ones and allies who wanted to learn how to support us. It was a book I wrote to educate people about what Autism really is, and how starkly that reality contrasts with the myths we've been told about Autistic people being antisocial, uncaring, and fundamentally broken. It was exactly the kind of book that I wished had existed back when I was first grappling with an Autistic identity myself at the age of twenty-five. Now, years after *Unmasking Autism*'s release, I find that readers still crave more knowledge and tools for better understanding Autism, and for creating a more fully unmasked existence. Once they know their own sensory needs better, for example, unmasking Autistics have questions about how to get those needs met in the workplace. After abandoning the uncomfortable social "mask" of agreeability, they've lost some (bad) friendships, and they want to know how to rebuild their social lives from a more genuine place. Or they've got a relative they're pretty sure is also a masked Autistic, and they want to know what steps they can take to also help that person find themselves.

Parents, therapists, and teachers who work with Autistic people have also asked me for more resources so they can better support the disabled people they care about. In a world where the only insurance-approved "treatment" for Autism is ABA therapy, which the Autistic community widely rejects as traumatizing and abusive,[24] the need for practical, compassionate resources on accommodating us is quite urgent. But today, even if a parent or caregiver wants to embrace the way the Autistic child in their life actually functions—rather than conditioning them to mimic a neurotypical person—they don't have many places to turn in order to learn how. Even most "social skills" groups created for Autistic children and teens teach them that they must neuroconform and vie for neurotypical people's approval, rather than encourage them to build fulfilling connections with other people like themselves.

Embracing an Autistic identity brought me incredible relief, but it also forced me to face certain truths about myself that were difficult to grapple with while living under capitalism. When I found out I was Autistic, I was in the middle of recovering from a yearlong period of burnout that had ravaged my physical and mental health. I came out the other side of this experience recognizing that full-time, in-person employment would never truly be feasible for me, and that if I wanted to be healthy and happy, I'd have to figure out some alternative means of survival. For a while, this came in the form of teaching online classes part-time and doing light consulting work that I picked up from freelancing websites. I didn't own a car, and I pared down my possessions so that I could live in a very small, cheap space. I walked everywhere and ate very modest meals at home. These kinds of adjustments were possible for me, especially when I was young and felt indestructible, and eventually one of my online teaching gigs turned into a more permanent job. But not all Autistics have the good fortune or privilege that I have. With some estimates putting the Autistic unemployment rate at as high as 80 percent[25] (and many other studies documenting a rate at least as high as 30[26] to 50 percent),[27] it's clear that many of us do not have the means to exist easily as ourselves, or even to get by at all.

Several Autistic people that I spoke to for this book shared with me that the only period in their lives when they'd ever been able to thrive was the early months of the COVID-19 pandemic. They were comfortably at home, freed from any expectation that they might socialize or work, and receiving federal aid money that covered their bills, with a little left over for fun pursuits and donating to causes they believed in as well. For the first time ever, their doctors' appointments and classes were entirely online, their grocery store had no-contact pickup, and they had full control over their temperature, attire, and daily rhythms. Beyond that, other people were in a compassionate mindset during that time, and were flexible toward their unique ways of being. Nobody stared at them for making twisted-up faces underneath their surgical masks. Loved ones were more than happy to bond over online games rather than elaborate family dinners. In the midst of a nightmarish international mass death event, they got a taste of true disability justice and felt peace.

It shouldn't have to take a global crisis to get us there, but the early response to the pandemic reveals that building a different world is possible, and that accommodating neurodiversity and other disabilities can yield numerous benefits. It wasn't just Autistics who, ironically, thrived in 2020. Research shows consistently that worker productivity and job satisfaction went up across the board for those who were able to work from home,[28] and many people who were sheltering in place felt more connected to their children and spouses and more fulfilled in their personal lives.[29] Sadly, all these benefits dissipated the moment many of us were dragged back into physical workplaces and asked to take on the impossible burden of busy, "independent" adult life once again.[30] Those of us who can't easily neuroconform felt that loss the most.

Autistic people are in desperate need of help in order to build comfortable, neurodiversity-accepting futures. We need support if we struggle to complete tasks like doing the laundry, brushing our teeth, paying our taxes, or driving to doctors' appointments. Because of our position of economic precarity, we often need financial support from the social welfare system or loved ones who recognize our lives as innately valuable. We must build robust communities for ourselves if we are to survive. But at the same time, we must also be able to assert ourselves, point out ableism where it happens, and engage in healthy conflict with people when they do not respect who we really are.

Unmasking for life requires a ton of planning and self-advocacy skills. And assisting Autistics and other neuro nonconformers in building up those skills is one of the major projects of this book.

The Five Skills Needed to Unmask

Accepting oneself as a disabled person cannot be a solely interior journey. No amount of pride or self-acceptance can undo the fact that Autistic people are systematically overlooked and disadvantaged at school, in the workplace, in our bureaucratic systems, and even just walking down the street. As a teen, I was fired from that retail job I mentioned earlier because I was Autistic; my bosses hated that I didn't know how to chat up customers, and that I was incapable of faking enthusiasm about a high-interest-rate credit card. That reality doesn't change the moment I take more pride in myself as a stubbornly honest Autistic. Confidence doesn't stop strangers from staring at me on the street. I (and other unmasked Autistic people like me) need more than internal healing. We need practical, interpersonal tools to navigate our unmasked lives in a world that would often prefer we be repressed.

To lead a truly unmasked life is to fight regular battles with abusive authority figures, dismissive family members, uncaring governmental structures, and even fellow neurodivergent people who still have a great deal of stigma to unlearn. I've conducted extensive research on Autistic people's adjustments and unmasking processes and interviewed dozens upon dozens of members of our community. I also hear from hundreds of Autistic and otherwise neurodivergent people each year, in private messages, in emails, and at conferences. When I synthesize the whole of these experiences and questions, I find that these are the areas where our community struggles the most:

First, we need help making friends who truly respect us. Most of us have spent a lifetime failing to follow unspoken social rules and missing out on social opportunities because of it, which has trained us to settle for unbalanced, unfulfilling relationships that don't provide us with the support we truly need. If we've been abused and disregarded for long enough, we might not even know what we want in a friendship, or how wonderful true acceptance could feel.

Second, we need to reset fraught family dynamics that were established long before anyone knew about our accessibility needs. Our loved ones have often judged us for seeming lazy, difficult, or incapable because they didn't understand that we were disabled. Some of our family members are also fighting internally with hidden neurodivergence themselves, and their complex feelings about their disabilities bleed into how they view us, creating legacies of shame and family dysfunction. If we are parents or caregivers to neurodivergent kids, we also may wonder how to best celebrate their differences and raise them to be confident and proud of themselves in a society that works constantly to stifle them.

Third, since the vast majority of us cannot find stable work, we must form a plan for surviving in a capitalist system that doesn't value nonconformity and divergence. We have to learn to navigate the challenging world of job applications, interviews, and diplomatic assertiveness at work—or if working is not possible, we have to interface with the social welfare and disability service systems and find ways to reduce our expenses and pool our resources with others so that we can get by. Since the dominant culture praises work as the primary source of life's meaning, embarking on this process means reinventing a life's purpose for ourselves as well.

Fourth, we want to express our sexualities and form attachments that reflect our real desires, not traditional roles that have only ever felt like a performance for many of us. The data is abundantly clear that Autistics are far more likely to be queer and kinky than other groups of people, and many are asexual or aromantic as well. The dominant culture doesn't provide anyone with tools to develop relationships that reflect their unique preferences and modes of being—especially not Autistics, who already face discrimination in dating.[31] Even if we do have loving relationships, the trauma of being masked may have made us deeply averse to conflict or incapable of conversing frankly about consent—and so we need support in building healthy, secure partnerships where we can openly communicate.

Finally—and perhaps most important of all—we all want to reclaim a place in society that has long been denied to us, forming strong, empowering social networks and chasing after the passions and fulfilling pursuits that will make all this effort worthwhile. This means learning how to try new hobbies and meet new people, contemplating our long-term legacies, and even planning for old age as a disabled person who will always need others.

Because most Autistic people fear change, struggle to process unfamiliar situations, and have trauma histories that have conditioned us to avoid making anyone upset, we don't always know how to chase after these goals. But we can become more assertive and effective in building a fully unmasked life for ourselves, so long as we develop the following key skills:

1. Acceptance of change, loss, and uncertainty.

    Change can ignite panic within the Autistic person's nervous system, and the fear of change closes us off from new experiences. In order to survive in an unpredictable world, we have to develop the ability to resiliently weather change.

2. Engagement in productive conflict, discussion, and disagreement.

    For fear of seeming disruptive or stubborn, masked Autistics become passive to a fault. It is impossible for us to pursue the things we want or build respectful relationships if we lack agency, and so we must learn to approach other people, speak up when we are unhappy, and engage with reality actively.

3. Transgression of unfair rules, demands, and social expectations.

    Autistic people can't help but be nonconforming, though many of us desperately try to fit in. We are marked as the "other" from the moment someone meets us, and we seem to naturally find many oppressive rules baffling. The Autistic capacity to break rules and question unjust policies is one of our greatest, most revolutionary abilities, and those of us who are masked need to learn to harness it, rather than suppress it.

4. Tolerance of distress, disagreement, or being disliked.

    When you live vibrantly as your authentic self, you take up space and project your perspective outwardly into the world. It is inevitable that some people will not agree with what you have to say. As we learn to self-advocate more effectively, we have to make peace with all the possible consequences. Sometimes when you set a boundary, others will have a problem with it, but that doesn't mean you don't get to continue enforcing it. Approval is not always worth chasing after.

5. Creation of new accommodations, relationship structures, and ways of living.

    The world was not built for people like us. Public spaces are so busy and boisterous that they cause us sensory meltdowns that require hours of rest to recover from; most workplaces demand more social and cognitive energy than we are capable of providing on a daily basis; and unspoken, impossible-to-parse rules govern how everyone around us acts. If we are going to get by as authentically Autistic people, we have to be bold enough to rewrite the rules. If a conventional life defined by work, marriage, and property ownership is not right for us, we need the creativity and courage to define for *ourselves* what a life well lived means.

In this book, we will examine how Autistic people can develop these five skills and apply each of them to the five areas of life where we struggle the most: Friendship, Family, Work, Love, and Life. Within each of these sections, readers will find the latest academic scholarship, wisdom from experts, profiles of ordinary Autistic people, and an array of exercises and scripts for self-advocating, building relationships, and living more genuinely and boldly in everyday life.

Autistic self-discovery can be a kind of rebirth. When each of us learns that we are not "broken," just disabled, an entire new way of life opens up before us. Through our own unmasking experiences and by meeting other Autistics like us, we learn that existence doesn't have to be defined by social rejection and unfulfilling conformity to an incredibly narrow neurotypical standard. We don't have to aspire to be high achieving to somehow "make up" for our disabilities. We aren't failures if we require regular support in order to stay housed, fed, bathed, and healthy. We aren't pathetic or clingy for wanting to be around only a small handful of trusted people for the rest of our lives, and we aren't crushing disappointments to our parents if we never want to be married, have kids, or get rich. We can live with our friends, subsist on the handful of "safe foods" that we love, half-ass our part-time jobs while devoting our real energy to hobbies, cry openly when we're hurting, and go to sleep in a race car bed the whole rest of our days if we want. In the pages to come, we will explore how to make such a vibrantly Autistic life possible—and how those same skills can benefit anyone else who has found themself stifled and oppressed by the neurotypical standard. Neuroconformity is imprisoning—but unmasking is for everyone.

UNMASKING FOR LIFE

Five Core Skills for Unmasking Your Life

This is a book of social skills exercises for Autistic people, but not in the typical meaning of that term.

Most social skills trainings for Autistic people focus on the normative qualities we supposedly lack: we are asked to make eye contact, feign polite interest in other people's lives, avoid talking about our interests and ourselves, and put a sharp filter upon any information that might strike other people as private or "oversharing." We are told not to be too loud, to only self-stimulate in non-distracting ways that will not draw negative attention toward us, and not to make statements that are too provocative or rude.

Many of these programs are created with the very best of intentions: the non-Autistic people who organize them believe that by explaining normal social rules to us, they are helping us to be more interpersonally effective and accomplish our goals—and they assume that being liked by a large number of non-Autistic people should always be our goal.

Unfortunately, this supposedly benevolent goal was also the goal behind Applied Behavior Analysis therapy, which punishes Autistic children with hot sauce on the tongue or electric shocks when they behave too strangely.[1] The creator of ABA therapy, O. Ivar Lovaas, also was the creator of anti-gay conversion therapy designed to cure "feminine boys," and both "treatments" had the same outcome in mind: to take young children who violated the norms of the day and repeatedly condition them like trained dogs to conform and behave. Lovaas believed that he was doing good for both Autistic patients and the "feminine boys" he conditioned to behave more masculinely. In actuality, he was unleashing a mental and emotional torment that would go on to cause post-traumatic stress symptoms, social anxiety, depression, a vulnerability to abuse, and even suicide in thousands of neurodivergent and queer people.[2] Members of both groups live with the legacy of Lovaas's projects today. We've been told that our lives will improve once we learn to behave "normally"—but we know better. We understand that living bravely in our difference will be our liberation.

Recently, I was at a conference for therapists who treat disorganization, and I spoke to a woman whose young nephew had been placed into a social skills group for Autistics. This woman shared with me that compared to his previous school's treatment, which had been ABA therapy, the nephew's new therapy group seemed to genuinely be pretty good. Instead of being hidden away from the other kids at school, he was deliberately included in clubs and group projects. His teachers allowed him to rip up bits of paper to stim and take breaks to stretch his legs in the hallway. Still, he also had mandatory socializing classes where teachers had him act out grocery store trips or imaginary playdates, and instructed him to always acknowledge the people around him and to ask them polite questions.

"He has the chance to ask why certain social rules are important, and to practice them free of judgment, but he's still expected to *do* them," the boy's aunt said to me. "And so, I'm wondering, is that really better than ABA? They're still teaching him that in order to be liked, he has to do certain things."

My answer to this boy's aunt was that honestly, I didn't see a fundamental difference. Social skills trainings might feel more benevolent and gentle than an ABA therapy session where a child is forced to sit still in a chair and is not permitted to speak to anyone or use the bathroom until he parrots a prewritten conversational script. But in both therapies, the child's autonomy and sense of ease in his body are disregarded, his freedom of movement treated as a privilege he will only sometimes be "allowed." He's still being trained to become socially hypervigilant, scanning his surroundings for unacknowledged people so that he can be certain to greet them in an approved-of way, and to do so quickly enough that he doesn't ever seem rude. And his social success is still being measured by his ability to appeal to the neuroconforming majority. But what about the other kids who, like him, want to wander around in the hallway not looking at anybody, ripping up paper and chattering excitedly about their favorite *My Hero Academia* episode? Why can't it be a social success for this boy to find more people like him? Why does preparing him for adult life require training him to make small talk, participate in commerce, and obsess over others' approval?

Social skills trainings exist for both Autistic children and adults, and they're widely adopted worldwide. In a meta-analytic review of more than fifty-five social skills interventions, psychologist Scott Bellini and colleagues report that these programs mainly treat the following Autistic "social skills deficits":[3]

Initiating interactions

Maintaining reciprocity

Sharing enjoyment

Taking another person's perspective

Inferring the interests of others

You'll notice that every single one of these supposed social skills targets how the Autistic person treats someone else, or how they make someone else feel—there is no consideration of how the Autistic person feels, or the skills they might need to advocate for themself. Autistic children and adults alike are encouraged to start conversations with other people, to ensure they are being fair toward others, to share things with other people, to think from another person's point of view, and to put a great deal of effort into mind reading another person's interests and emotions. Where do the Autistic person's interests, perspective, and need for attention come in? What about the important social skill of speaking up for yourself?

By the end of these social skills training programs, Autistics are expected to be emotionally even-keeled, discreet, cheerful, and chatty toward other people, and to seem mature. In other words, they are expected to *mask*—that is, to conceal the parts of them that are overly excitable, easily emotionally wounded, socially confused, slow, wacky, and obsessive about any number of odd or niche things.

It's small wonder, then, that in a meta-analysis of more than fifty different interventions for Autistic people, researchers have concluded that social skills trainings do not work.[4] Generally speaking, the studies evaluating social skills interventions for Autistics fail to find significant positive effects, and suffer from overly inflated statistical effect sizes, one 2022 meta-analysis reports.[5] The only outcome where social skills interventions appear to make a difference is in the Autistic person's *social responsiveness:* Autistic people do tend to become more attentive toward others after undergoing a battery of trainings that teach them to prioritize neurotypicals' reactions above their own feelings. But an increase in social responsiveness does not translate into an Autistic person being able to communicate more honestly with people, or more persuasively, nor does it lead to them having more genuine friendships or locating people that they actually like. Paying more attention to others doesn't necessarily make them feel more supported or understood. All it does is make them better at disregarding themself.

Social skills interventions fail for the exact same reasons that early interventions for Autism such as ABA therapy fail: they painstakingly destroy the ability of an Autistic person to remain emotionally and psychologically present around another person. The true social skills that Autistic people need help developing are not ones of acquiescence or attentiveness. Rather, they are the ones that will allow us to actively demand the accommodations and just treatment we need.

In order to unmask for life, we have to get more comfortable with unfamiliarity and *change* so that we can explore the social spaces, workplaces, educational facilities, and other realms of public life that have long shut us out. We have to be able to *engage* with other people in an authentic way, rather than attempting to appease them. We must be willing to *transgress* the social norms and scripts that restrict and harm us—everything from narrow gender roles to rules of politeness that dictate that we can't ever say that we're feeling uncomfortable and that we must jump to acknowledge every single person that we meet. We also need to be able to *tolerate the discomfort* of other people disliking us at times, and make peace with the fact that no matter what we do, sometimes others will be wrong about us, but that this doesn't make us failures. Finally, we require *the courage to create our own ways of life*, finding new modes of loving, living, and being that center our neurotype rather than conceal it.

We can contrast the five skills that most social skills groups impart to Autistics (which basically train them to mask) with the five core skills for unmasking, which instead are designed to help us self-advocate.

The Five Core Skills for Unmasking

1. **Acceptance** (of Change, Loss, and Uncertainty)
2. **Engagement** (in Conflict, Discussion, and Disagreement)
3. **Transgression** (of Rules, Demands, and Social Expectations)
4. **Tolerance** (of Disagreement, Discomfort, and Being Disliked)
5. **Creation** (of Accommodations, Relationship Structures, and New Ways of Being)

Whereas conventional social skills trainings for Autistics condition us to attend to the needs of other people more, these skills will help us tune back into ourselves. And where conventional social skills aim to foster agreement and minimize conflict or awkwardness, the core skills for unmasking instead assume that a healthy degree of conflict is actually necessary to assert oneself in the world.

The five core skills of acceptance, engagement, transgression, tolerance, and creation will support the reader through the process of unmasking for life. Exercises throughout the book will call back to these skills and challenge you to deepen your use of them as you go about finding the friendships, family bonds, means of survival, relationship structures, and ways of life that suit you. But first we will take a look at what each of those skills entails, define them, begin to practice them, and come to understand why they are essential to proud, comfortable neuro nonconformity.

Accept (Change, Loss, and Uncertainty)

"What will people think about me, seeing a balding middle-aged man acting all shy at his first hard-core show?" wonders Bill. "Will anybody ever want to talk to me, or will they all think I'm a creep?"

Bill is the forty-five-year-old Autistic who worries that he's wasted too many years masking to be able to lead an interesting life. When I speak to him, his head traces the floor and he claps his shoes together repeatedly, laughing to himself in a Tourette's tic. None of that is a problem for Bill, nor is it an issue with Bill's sister and her husband, with whom Bill lives. But Bill is convinced it will be a problem for others. In high school, Bill was transitioned to an online education program because he was bullied so severely it made him suicidal. He completed an associate's degree online, and took up a job as a content writer at home. He relies on his sister and brother-in-law for housing, but they have a comfortable arrangement where he helps out in the yard and looks after the dogs. His day-to-day life, he says, isn't all that bad. But he dreams of something more.

"I want piercings, I want tattoos, I want to get a van and trick it out and drive it to all my favorite bands' shows across the tri-state area, but the idea of even going to get one terrifies me." He rubs at his pant seams. He feels positive about being Autistic but tells me, "I feel pathetic about how much I still don't know."

Autistic people *loathe* change, the old stereotype goes. Since we process new information in a more effortful, detailed way than non-Autistic people do and don't take many assumptions for granted, this stereotype has some truth. Change takes us more time to adjust to than it does for others, and we rely upon certainty and predictability as anchors when life does not make sense.

On top of having a mental processing style that is unfriendly to change, we're also a group of people who are largely traumatized. A study published in 2016 noted that 90 percent of Autistic children surveyed had experienced at least one significant life trauma,[6] with more recent research suggesting that between 45 and 61 percent of Autistic adults have PTSD.[7] Sudden, unexpected rejections and losses render us hypervigilant, assuming that anything new on our horizon can spell only doom. We're also incredibly sensitive people, as a group, and some researchers theorize that repeated experiences of sensory overwhelm cumulatively traumatize us.[8] The discomfort of the unfamiliar can register as an active threat, and most transitions from one place to another or from one social context to the next happen entirely too fast.

When faced with an unfamiliar situation, most Autistics desperately want to know everything we possibly can about it in order to prepare: when it will start and how long it will last, how we will get there, who will be there and how those people will behave, what we're supposed to do and say, how things will end, and everything that will happen after that. We crave the security of a set schedule and easy-to-process, familiar information, but we'll settle for the certainty of knowing *everything* to expect instead. But real life isn't friendly to our demands for structure and "all the information." And so we often panic at the prospect of change.

Loss and change are inevitabilities in life, however. The familiar prepackaged sandwiches we rely on for lunch every day can, at any moment, be discontinued; the best friend we've relied on since we were ten years old may slowly evolve into another person as they mature and life changes them. I've often felt unmoored by the fact that for other people, romantic relationships naturally change; a boyfriend who wanted to have sex every single day eventually only wants intimacy a few times a week, and regular date nights reduce in frequency over the course of the typical relationship. Instinctively, I feel kind of betrayed or bait-and-switched by things like this. To me, it seems intuitive that the activities a person enjoys are ones that they will always enjoy, and that the way we present ourselves at the start of a relationship should represent who we generally are. It took more than a decade and a half of dating for me to internalize that non-Autistic people just aren't that consistent. I crave consistency, but people are allowed to change, and if I want to be respectful of others' boundaries and stop seeing rejection in places where it doesn't exist, it serves me better to accept this.

We might viscerally dislike it, and we can take all the steps we want to limit unwanted change in our private lives, but each one of us must learn to accept loss and tolerate uncertainty to a degree. And for the unmasking Autistic, cultivating a healthy *acceptance* of change can bring us considerable benefits. When we recognize that some amount of change is nonnegotiable, we can prevent some of the meltdowns and feelings of threat we would experience if we felt entitled to permanence. We can be more patient with our loved ones and supportive of exciting developments in their lives if we recognize that one day they might move away or treat us differently no matter what we do. Accepting change also empowers us to venture into new spaces where we can forge new friendships, and makes it possible for us to develop new skills. Fortunately, the more practice we have encountering the unfamiliar, the greater faith we will have in our ability to weather change.

What does it mean to really accept change? It begins by trying something new and acknowledging that we might feel uncomfortable, crave more information, or wish to have greater control over what will happen—but then persisting in doing the unfamiliar thing anyway. When we dwell in the unpleasant (yet manageable) feeling of discomfort instead of fleeing, our familiarity with the unknown slowly improves. Over time, with repeated, tolerable exposures to a variety of new situations and people, we build a diversity of life experiences, which provides us with evidence of our resilience. The more things we try, the more we develop a useful internal database about how to handle unexpected events. This empowers us to grow in all kinds of new directions.

Here's what the process of accepting change looks like in action:

Five Core Skills for Unmasking Your Life

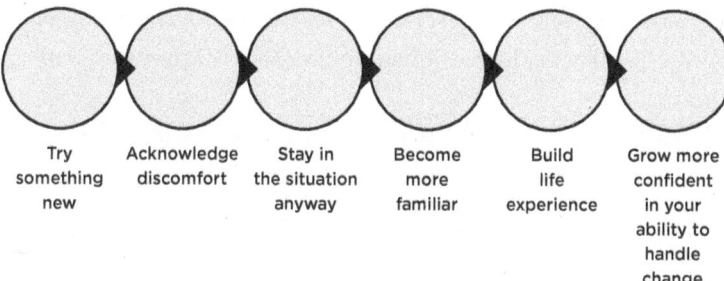

For many unmasking Autistics, getting better at accepting change can be as simple as trying activities that are appealing but mildly anxiety-provoking, which puts them in the tolerable "challenge zone." For those of us who are socially anxious, entering the challenge zone might involve visiting a bookstore we've never been to before and asking a few questions of the staff instead of looking information up online. The next time we visit that same store, we may challenge ourselves to ask questions that are more complex—for example, requesting a recommendation for a book based on our general tastes, or inquiring into whether the bookstore offers any book clubs or other events. Over time, and with repeated interactions of increasing depth, our minds will slowly learn that asking for help does not always lead to being reprimanded (even if we have been reprimanded in the past!), and that we have as much right to express ourselves in public as anyone.

For Bill, one way to accept change that is firmly within his challenge zone is getting into the habit of greeting his neighbors. An unstructured social interaction with an unknown person can go in any number of possible directions, and that uncertainty is frightening. But Bill's learned he can use his sister's dogs as a conversational entry point—and even an escape route, if need be.

"I just blurt out, 'Hi there!' and let the dogs take it from there," Bill says. Usually, his neighbors ask to pet the dogs, and then spend a few moments speaking with him about local events or the weather. Small conversations have deepened slowly into budding friendships, and now Bill knows most of his neighbors' names and a few facts about them.

Through repeated, low-stakes exposures that he's in control of, Bill is gradually reducing his fear of uncertainty and widening his community.

The blogger David Cain is a formerly socially anxious person who has written a lot about how people can work to become less shy. I've seen numerous Autistic people pass along his advice, because it's broadly applicable to many of our experiences. In one entry on his blog, Cain writes about the importance of acknowledging the discomfort of many social situations—and then remaining present in spite of it.

"Fleeing from social situations makes future get-togethers more difficult," he writes.[9] "Shyness begins to reinforce itself when you believe that the pain of embarrassment or self-consciousness can never be allowed to happen, that it's damaging to you."

Instead, he recommends taking note of the fact that you are uncomfortable but choosing not to leave.

"Stay at the party," he says. "Let those feelings linger inside you, but don't leave . . . You need to demonstrate to your brain that nervousness is just a passing feeling. It's not an emergency, and it's not an identity."

Sometimes an unexpected situation will arise, or a conversation will not progress perfectly. This, itself, is actually a blessing for those of us who want to become more adaptable and resilient in the face of change. A fresh challenge that we have not planned for is an opportunity for us to gather really rich and informative social data—and a hard moment is one that we can look back on in the future, to remind ourselves of all that we are capable of. The first time you're at a restaurant and your dinner partner pukes in front of you, your social scripts probably will short-circuit, and you'll be at a loss as to what to do. But after you've taken a moment to process things, and then jumped into action to comfort them and help them clean up, you'll know in the future that handling unanticipated bodily functions and supporting another person through their embarrassment are things you can do.

The same principle applies to other stressful interactions, such as shutting down racist comments or informing a medical provider that you don't wish to be weighed. The first time you have to respond to a

Five Core Skills for Unmasking Your Life

scenario like these, you will feel clueless and helpless. But as Cain recommends, stay at the party. Allow yourself to feel shy. Allow yourself to have doubts. Take the action you desire anyway. With your actions, you have made yourself into a person who can handle wild, upsetting situations.

For many masked Autistic people, one of the major drivers of social anxiety and resistance to change is the need to prevent any negative outcome from ever occurring. And so another productive way to get more comfortable with change and loss is to turn this impulse on its head, and actively *expect* that a negative scenario will come to pass, and plan for it. What if instead of avoiding feelings of social anxiety at all costs, you assumed that you *would* have an anxiety attack at the conference? Could you accept that as the cost of a new experience? How would you plan to deal with it when it occurs? If you stopped being terrified of having nothing to say to people and instead assumed there *would* be moments of silence and uneasy dead air, could you be okay with it?

To think about it more broadly, what would happen if you entered into every relationship acknowledging that one day it would probably change or end? Could you appreciate the wonderful moments without any assurance that they would last? Could you believe that you would find friendship again, since you were able to do so in the past? And if not, how much more experience and practice would you need before you could really believe you are capable of being socially skillful and true to yourself?

On the following pages is an exercise designed to get you thinking about the social changes and losses you've endured in the past—and reframing how you think about them to help build greater acceptance of change.

Accepting Change
When Social Dynamics Shift

Over the course of our lives, some of our relationships will inevitably change. Friends move away, romances cool, social groups restructure themselves, and people go through major shifts in their identities and outlooks. This can be terrifying, but usually it's not a reflection of any problem within us. It's simply a fact of life we can get better at accepting.

Use this exercise to help you reflect on how you make sense of changing social dynamics.

1. Think of a time when a friend or acquaintance suddenly changed how they behaved or treated you. Describe that experience briefly here.

   _____

   _____

   _____

2. How did you know that something had changed in your relationship? Describe what you noticed or felt.

   _____

   _____

   _____

3. Jot down any worries or negative thoughts you had about the experience here (for example, "I must have said something wrong that made them angry with me.").

   _____

   _____

   _____

Five Core Skills for Unmasking Your Life

4. Think for a moment of the friends you've unintentionally lost contact with over the years, perhaps due to a move, leaving school, or because you stopped practicing a hobby. List some of the friends you still feel fondly about here.

   _____

   _____

   _____

5. List any new people you have met over the course of the past year whose company you enjoy.

   _____

   _____

   _____

6. Here are some affirmations to help you remember that it's normal for friend groups to shift and change over time:

   "I haven't met every person who is going to play an important role in my life yet."

   "Most people's problems are not about me."

   "I've gotten to know all kinds of people, and this year I'll get to know even more."

   "I get to decide who I spend time with."

   "I can make choices that broaden my social sphere."

7. Finally, contact at least one person whose name you listed in #5.

Many of us will always dread large life changes, such as moving into a new house or beginning a new job or educational program. We can allow that dread to happen without seeing it as a problem or a reason to turn back on our decisions. In fact, we can expect that it will show up and view it as a necessary side effect of growth. Even if we hate change, we can still learn from every new encounter and experience and draw confidence from our growing body of knowledge.

Becoming more resilient in the face of change and loss can grant us the inner security to take actions that may risk alienating some people, particularly people with ableist outlooks or who do not respect us. The next core skill that we will examine involves initiating hard conversations and welcoming healthy conflict with others.

Engage (in Conflict, Discussion, and Disagreement)

Autism was first "discovered" by psychiatrist Eugen Bleuler in 1911, and for the next century, Autistic people were seldom included in any academic conversation about our disability. Bleuler saw Autism as a disorder of profound isolation, and for decades afterward psychiatrists parroted the (completely untested) truism that people of our neurotype had absolutely zero desire to connect with others. Researchers theorized that Autism was caused by a person possessing an "extremely male brain," ignoring that countless women and trans people were also Autistic, that numerous Autistics aren't especially masculine, and that in fact, there's very little neuroscientific evidence that "male brains" even exist.[10]

For more than fifty years, psychiatrists didn't even realize that Autistic people suffered from sensory issues—one of the most fundamentally painful parts of being Autistic in the world—until Autistic scientist Temple Grandin took the public stage and began writing about her inner experiences. This means that for decades, whenever an Autistic patient at an institution complained about the air-conditioning humming too loudly or an Autistic child ran in distress from their church's Bible study room because the chairs were too scratchy, their concerns were taken as completely unserious. Entire generations of Autistic people lived their lives being told that their pain didn't exist.

For these and so many other reasons, many Autistics lack the skills to actively engage with others and fight for what we believe and want. Clinicians frequently view Autistic children as overly "passive" and "inhibited," yet when they *do* attempt to play by stacking and organizing their belongings or staring at a stuffed animal and imagining a fictional story about it, therapists penalize them for not playing in a neuroconforming way.[11] If an Autistic person cannot speak, or temporarily loses speech because of exhaustion, their attempts to communicate through writing or technology use are largely ignored by non-Autistic people who immediately doubt their competence[12]—robbing them of the ability to engage with the world and advocate for themself. Numerous school psychologists, early childhood interventionists, and other paraprofessionals have devoted their careers to solving the problem of Autistic "noncompliance" to abled people's instructions,[13] and yet when we examine the long-term mental health outcomes, we instead see a problem of *over*compliance, with many Autistics exhibiting intense agreeability, deference toward other people, and susceptibility to manipulation and abuse.[14]

Moving through life, Autistics face a maddening predicament: if we give voice to our needs, ask questions when we're confused, seek help with hard tasks, or make any kind of move to address our sensory complaints, we are accused of being obstinate troublemakers. Yet when we internalize society's message that our bodies and minds are a problem, and not to be trusted, we're viewed as overly passive nonhumans who lack any agency worth respecting, and our needs still don't get addressed.

There is an entire sub-profile of Autism that embodies this impossible, ableist Catch-22: called the *pathologically demand avoidant* (or PDA) profile of Autism, it describes us as incapable of complying with instructions. PDA Autistics may throw "tantrums" when expected to endure painful hair-brushings as a child, or may find it impossible to submit to the authority of a boss or teacher who has been unfair or showed signs of incompetence. Though PDA Autistics are described as passive to a fault, the creator of the concept, psychologist Elizabeth Newson, has also written that she sees PDAers as "manipulative" and highly "socially skillful," because we try to argue with demands that we disagree with, or ask others to help complete difficult tasks for us.[15]

PDAers are frequently accused of pretending to be less capable than we actually are, or of neurotically "letting" our worst fears get in the way of us taking action. The simpler interpretation of PDA behavior, however, is that we're just disabled and stressed by not being believed. Disabled people are rarely trusted to accurately gauge our own abilities, and so, when we state that we cannot follow someone's instructions, do not have strong motor control, or can't stay on task without reminders, we are called manipulative and punished for it.

Neurodivergent people repeatedly receive the message that our assertions of agency are completely unacceptable inconveniences, and that we don't have an accurate gauge of what's going on within our own bodies and minds. Collectively, these experiences take on the effect of a kind of society-wide act of gaslighting. We think that we are bad people for ever experiencing a feeling that inconveniences others, and we don't even believe *ourselves* to be genuine when we're stuck and need help.

Unmasked Autistics have to be able to name our sensory needs, to refuse demands that harm us, and to let other people know how we feel even when those feelings might be unpopular. In order to accomplish these things, we must target the important social skill of *engagement*, the ability to initiate hard conversations, articulate past harms and current demands, ask for help, and take agency in our own lives.

Engagement is the polar opposite of overwhelmed, self-doubting passivity. It encourages us to bring our impressions forward and share them with others. Engagement works against the impulse we often have to never be a bother, and challenges us to voice concerns. It is also the skill of engagement that empowers us to speak out when we witness acts of injustice, correct others' ignorance, and reorient relationships that have become unbalanced.

When a person is used to harshly censoring their every reaction and feeling, jumping into action can feel impossibly hard. It's likely for reasons of trauma that Autistics so famously struggle with starting conversations or approaching other people, for instance—we simply do not trust our ability to not screw up interactions. We also tend to become dissociated from our own body's sensations and emotions, after years of repeatedly being told we are hearing things that no one else can hear, noticing scents that no one else can smell, and yet also missing social cues that everyone else can see.

Being able to engage actively with reality and other people requires getting back in touch with our true feelings and working to give a name to our experiences, even when others might doubt them. Here are some common steps to practicing the skill of engagement, particularly if it's not already comfortable for you:

1. Notice what is wrong or lacking about your current situation.

    Instead of trying to argue this problem away or come up with reasons *not* to voice it, try to accept that the experience is there, and remind yourself that it deserves attention.

2. Name what you need.

    Put the problem into words or convey it in some other form of message to others. You do not need to have a potential solution in mind yet. Simple declarations such as "I'm tired," "I'm thirsty," "I don't like wearing this," "Being here feels bad," or "I don't like the way he talks to me" are perfectly fine.

3. Identify conflicting perspectives.

    Your needs might not be compatible with another person's. That does not mean your needs should be erased. Conflict is sometimes necessary when two people's perspectives are hard to reconcile. If you're hungry but the person by your side can't stand to hear you chewing, you two are experiencing conflicting needs that both should be discussed.

4. Ask questions about others' perspectives, or the situation.

    Masked Autistics are frequently discouraged from asking questions because many allistics communicate in covert, symbolic ways and expect us to do the same. But you deserve to understand the situation you are in, any expectations a person has put upon you, or why a rule is what it is. A powerful way to stay engaged rather than passive and checked out is by asking directly when something isn't clear. This may surprise some people who see asking questions as rude—do it anyway.

5. Enlist another person to help you, if possible.

    Make a specific request that could reduce your discomfort. Even a slight improvement is worth seeking out. Ask for the lights to be dimmed, for a private place to go eat a snack, for a break to take a walk, for a blanket, for a sympathetic ear, or for the topic of conversation to change.

6. Take action to address anything that still isn't working.

    After expressing yourself and requesting support, identify any steps you might take to continue to improve your well-being. Can you step away, end the conversation, approach someone new, or directly work on the problem yourself? Are there new concerns that you also want to voice? There's no limit on the number of times that you "get" to assert yourself. In fact, we *have* to do it constantly, every single day.

Engagement is a strategy of approach, meaning that it requires we take action of some kind—which many of us will find incredibly difficult at first because we tend to process and move more slowly than other people, take a lot of time to choose our words carefully, and have stepped on many hidden social landmines in the past that leave us understandably shy. Being a bit slow to react is completely fine, and communicating when you are ready in an email or letter is a proud act of neurodivergent defiance in its own right. At the same time, many unmasking Autistics find that as they get more practiced in self-advocacy, they begin jumping into action more quickly because they're no longer questioning their every feeling and how every behavior looks.

A few years ago, I enlisted the help of my friend Dio, an Autistic trans man, in getting better at correcting people when they misgendered me. People still regularly used she/her pronouns for me back then, and though it bothered me massively, I hesitated to ever bring it up because I could understand why people viewed me in that way. I didn't want to interrupt them or seem rude. I focused so strongly on the other person's perspective that there was no room left for my own.

This is what Dio advised me to do: "You have to treat your gender as a *fact*. It is a fact, and it's helpful and right to correct someone when they're wrong on the facts." Later that same day, a random acquaintance misgendered me, and sure enough, Dio cut in with my correct pronouns immediately, as easily as if he were telling someone the date. There was no reason to feel guilty about asserting the truth of who I was. I could only have meaningful relationships with people if I actively engaged with them and gave them the information needed to respect me.

Developing the skill of engagement requires that we start speaking up at moments when we traditionally would have silenced ourselves, and that we broaden our notion of which forms of discomfort deserve to be voiced. Exercises throughout the book will challenge you to identify times when you are unhappy with how another person is treating you, or when your environment is painfully unpleasant, and to bring that discomfort out into the open, rather than hiding it away. Here's an example.

Engage in Conflict

Articulate Your Discomfort

Many Autistic people believe they do not "deserve" to voice their needs unless they are in unfathomable pain. To challenge that instinct, practice articulating very mild forms of discomfort the moment they arise using this exercise.

1. Identify at least one feature of your current surroundings that is making you uncomfortable. For example: the room might be too cold, your neighbor's music might be playing too loudly, or your partner might have left a distracting pile of dirty clothes on the couch.

2. Express this discomfort aloud, no matter who might be around to hear it. "It's too cold in here, and it's making it hard for me to focus"; "I can't sit on the couch because it's so covered with clothing."

3. Make a request to have this problem addressed. "Could you please turn down your music?" "Could you please put away your clothes when you get home?" If you need to make the request in writing or via text rather than in words, that is completely okay.

4. Take at least one proactive step to improve your own comfort. For example: putting in earbuds, changing into a sweatshirt, or moving to a more comfortable space.

Challenge yourself to follow this sequence every time you enter a new space. Work to find at least one thing that is making you uncomfortable, no matter how small. Make a game out of getting better and better at noticing your discomfort, expressing it, and taking steps to improve it.

In addition to engaging in healthy conflict with other individuals, we must also become willing to push up against unfair societal expectations—because many of our preferences and opinions as neurodivergent people will inevitably go against the grain. This brings us to the next core skill.

Transgress (Rules, Demands, and Social Expectations)

One of the aspects of being Autistic that most readily identifies us to others is just how unusual and socially transgressive we can be. We can't really help it: our unique, bottom-up processing style and tendency to take nothing for granted mean that we see the world from a different angle than most. What perplexes us seems obvious and unquestionable to most neuroconforming people; what we love and find exciting often strikes others as painfully dull and vice versa. And research shows that even when we strive to mask our differences, our nonconforming mannerisms and thought processes still leak out.

The nonconformity of Autistic people is one of our great strengths, but we're taught to believe it's one of our worst qualities. It makes us excellent whistle-blowers, outspoken crusaders for justice, and predisposes us to being more openly queer, kinky, polyamorous, or nontraditional than neuroconformists are. When we collectively refuse to follow unjust rules, our revolutionary potential is nearly limitless—and we help free other non-Autistic people to live as they desire to as well.

But standing firm in our uniqueness is a skill that must be developed, as many of us have winnowed away our capacity to be socially challenging because we fear the consequences of being too odd. This is where the skill of *transgression* comes in. Unlike acceptance and engagement, which are generally more approach-motivated skills that involve confronting newness and difficulty head-on, transgression is more of a lateral move, a sidestepping of all the judgments and social rules that discourage us from being openly ourselves. To boldly transgress norms is to recognize society's dominant path, see the ways in which people are forced upon it, and choose to diverge from it anyway.

It is important for unmasking Autistics to recognize society's dominant path, so that we can understand the many ways in which we have been quietly pushed onto it. Forms of covert social pressure are typically treated like untouchable third rails, the electrified tracks that run along the middle of a subway and supply them with a current of (potentially lethal) power. But unlike literal third rails, the elaborate systems of pressure and ostracism that society runs on are not actually deadly for us to make contact with. Noticing and naming them can remove their power.

For example, a common way that teachers, parents, peers, and therapists pressure Autistic people into neuroconformity is by telling us that our behavior is unusual. For instance, when I was a nine-year-old child, my best friend and her parents sat me down in their house's garage to let me know that it was not normal for a kid to be running around the neighborhood snarling and pretending to be possessed by a demon. That year I'd become obsessed with horror novels and stories about the occult, and my new favorite pastime was playing at casting spells and summoning spirits. But with their simple declaration that what I was doing wasn't normal, they dried that tendency right up. I became embarrassed and not only stopped with the demon role-playing but began hiding all my pretend games from others.

There was an unstated assumption lurking behind my friend and her parents' statements. When they declared my actions were not *normal*, they meant they must be *bad*, and looking back, I no longer agree. Now that I am an unmasked Autistic adult, I can recognize when someone is demanding that I be normal, and I have the clarity of mind to ask myself whether what's normal is always what is good. It's *normal* to look the other way and do nothing when a parent strikes their child in public. It's *normal* to never discuss money or sex, creating a culture where such high-stakes topics are shrouded in mystery. It's *normal* to hate the beginning of every single week because you hate your job, and it's *normal* to smile through that pain so you don't enrage your boss. Many of us would strongly prefer to be abnormal and be quietly satisfied in our weirdness instead.

Another common way that Autistics experience covert social pressure is through instructions to not behave *inappropriately*. Darcie is an English Autistic woman who's frequently heard that she isn't behaving appropriately. She's very high energy and fidgety, and a sensory seeker, particularly when it comes to interesting visuals and soft textures. Darcie loves to dash from room to room to burn off her excess energy, and doesn't enjoy sitting on furniture, preferring instead to spread out on soft rugs and hold pillows and blankets against her skin. She also self-soothes when experiencing distress by rubbing at her legs and stomach, which always left her family members completely aghast.

Darcie's family responds to all of her self-soothing sensory behaviors as if they are shameful and inappropriate, even in the comfort of her own home. "When Mom comes into the apartment and sees me on the floor, she screams, *Stop that! Nobody can see you doing that! It's not appropriate!* and all I'm doing is just rolling around trying to chill," she says.

When an Autistic person hears that our actions are inappropriate, it's worth contemplating who has declared them so. We can ask ourselves questions like the following:

> Is this rule really universal?
>
> Who says I can't behave this way?
>
> Where did these rules come from?
>
> Am I hurting anyone?
>
> Is anyone really in charge of me right now?
>
> Do I agree with this rule?

If Darcie were to examine her behavior by asking these questions, she might recognize that there is no logical reason that she can't cover herself with pillows and blankets while lying on the floor. There's also no harm in her rushing from one side of the room to the other, so long as she keeps a lookout for other people's bodies and doesn't break anything that isn't hers. While Darcie's actions might embarrass her mother or confuse other people, Darcie can't see any sensible reason not to engage in them.

"People are allowed to be comfortable. Or excitable," she says. "If someone sees me touching my body to self-soothe and gives me a funny look I can explain it to them, but it's not my job to make them feel okay about it."

The skill of transgression enables us to see clearly that the values of our culture and time period are in fact open to questioning, and that violating rules is often possible. Most of the time, conformity is enforced with negative glances, throat-clearing, comparisons to other people, and maybe some social avoidance—and none of this will kill us. While there are situations where Autistic people must filter our actions for the sake of safety, we generally can maintain our own inner sense of what we believe in, and work to surround ourselves with people who do respect how we function.

When unmasking Autistic people seek to build lives and relationships fully honoring our disabilities, we have to be ready to choose the unusual path. Masking, after all, is motivated by a desire to not seem unusual—and to not desire anything too strange or nonconforming as well. Scientists can't quite explain why so many of us seem so weird, but the simple fact remains that we are—we fall in love with buildings, dream of making love to cable cars, collect taxidermized animals, cover our wrists in dozens of rubber bands, sleep in bathtubs, eat couscous covered in mustard, and forget to wipe the crumbs off our faces. In fact, there is no need for research to ever account for why we are the way we are because we are not a problem to be solved—human diversity does not need a "cure." All we need is the space to be ourselves, and the recognition that we are part of what makes humanity so dynamic, fascinating, and lovable.

A variety of exercises throughout this book will shore up your ability to transgress social norms for the sake of building a more fully unmasked life. Here's one to get you started, to help you grow more comfortable with stimming and being visibly odd in public.

Transgress Expectations
Stimming in Public

Masked Autistic people have many good reasons to fear self-stimulating (stimming) in front of strangers, but being able to regulate our nervous systems is absolutely essential to our healthy functioning. Here's how to feel a little less ashamed of how your neurodivergent body works, while still being mindful of safety.

Five Core Skills for Unmasking Your Life

1. List at least five of your favorite stims that you engage in privately at home (for example, spinning around in a chair, tugging at your hair, singing along to music, rocking in place, chewing on your fingers, jumping up and down):

   _____
   _____
   _____
   _____

2. Place an X next to any of the stims in the previous question that you currently do not allow yourself to perform in public. What might happen if you were to engage in this activity at a party, a coffee shop, or a doctor's office, or in a public park?

   _____
   _____
   _____
   _____

3. Try to identify two to three stims from your list that you *could* participate in publicly without hurting anyone or being targeted for violence.

   _____
   _____
   _____
   _____

4. List a few public settings where you could try engaging in these stims. (Some ideas: a public park, a concert, a crowded bar, the library, a party at a friend's house, the grocery store, church, a support group, a classroom, walking down the street, a coffee shop, the movie theater.)

_____

_____

_____

_____

5. Plan for contingencies: expect that some people will notice you stimming and be curious or surprised by it. Think of how you will manage to keep stimming despite this. For example:

If someone <u>stares at me</u>, I will <u>give them a nod, then look away and keep stimming</u>.

If someone <u>asks me what I'm doing</u>, I will say <u>"I'm doing this because it helps me focus."</u>

If someone <u>makes me feel threatened</u>, I will <u>leave the area and come up with a new plan.</u>

If someone _____,
I will _____.

If someone _____,
I will _____.

If someone _____,
I will _____.

Making oneself visibly Autistic and socially transgressive in public will introduce feelings of unease and discomfort at times. For all the work she's done embracing her distinct form of movement, Darcie still has to cope with her family's shameful messages that her body's movements look "wrong." That's why the next core skill for unmasking is building one's tolerance for discomfort, and even for being actively disliked.

Tolerate (Distress, Disagreement, and Being Disliked)

Masking turns Autistic people into inveterate people-pleasers who scan every social interaction meticulously for any sign of looming social threat. Some of this hypervigilance is born out of the trauma of repeated social rejections; many Autistics who describe themselves as "empaths" or "highly sensitive persons" believe they have an almost magical-seeming intuition for how other people are feeling and what they might need. In reality, we've just taken on the cognitive load of thinking about everybody else's motivations long before we even consider our own. Though it's sometimes framed as an "Autistic superpower," it's really an immense burden that can lead to us having unbalanced, exploitative relationships and no true sense of self. It also conditions us to view others' negative emotions as our personal failure—even though varied reactions from other people are an inevitability in life, and are neither good nor bad.

From the early days that Autism was documented by researchers such as Leo Kanner, the disability has been linked to elevated anxiety levels. In published studies spanning decades, the anxiety disorder and phobia rate among Autistics has hovered around 40 to 50 percent, with some studies placing it as high as 79 percent.[16] Some of this can be attributed to the sensory unfriendliness of our world—repeated exposures to startling, unpleasant stimuli that we cannot control and cannot escape can erode our psychological well-being and feelings of safety. This is an important form of distress that Autistics unfortunately have to learn to manage on our own. Nobody teaches us to drown out the smells of other people's bodies in the elevator by rubbing a patch of scented lip balm under our nose, or that there are mock "dress pants" sold online with elastic waistbands that are almost as comfortable as pajamas. We have to concoct our own ways of making life bearable. Typically, this involves a lot of avoidance—of untrusted places, unfamiliar people, and any situation where we can't make a quick modification to the environment or beat a hasty escape.

Of course, a massive part of our anxiety and distress reactivity is linked to social fear as well. Any sign of disagreement or potential ostracism can send masked Autistics spiraling into a panic—to such a degree that merely being around another person can provoke us to lose all sense of ourselves. The Autistic writer Attlee Hall calls this tendency *memory-foaming*: much like people trapped in a codependent relationship, or anxiously attached individuals with a history of abuse, many Autistics reflexively shape our identities around the tastes, mannerisms, and opinions of the people we see every day.

"[Memory-foaming] often involves excessively conceding, bending, conforming and acquiescing to someone, either actively or passively, either as a reaction to specific feedback, or in anticipation of a certain response," Attlee writes.[17] They clarify that it is a deeper form of compliance than people-pleasing because it involves actually anchoring your identity to the perspective of someone else. "It often involves the actual adoption and internalization of someone else's perceptions and desires, and therefore often involves not knowing the difference between 'mine' and 'theirs,'" they say. Memory-foaming can lead to the Autistic person eliminating all trust in their own instincts and having absolutely no clue what it is that they want in the moment, or even out of life in general, beyond the reassurance from other people that they are worthy and good.

I regularly hear from Autistic people who cannot fathom alienating anyone, or even setting a boundary that another person might not like to hear. Considering embarking on an unconventional life path can call forth emotions of terror, shame, or guilt because it threatens the status quo, where they put impressing and soothing others first. But managing authentic, unmasked relationships demands that we voice unpopular truths—and that we recognize where one person's desires for us end, and our own vision of our lives begins.

Engaging in discussion or conflict is useful when another person respects us, values our well-being, and is open to changing their mind, but when it comes to immovable people or the opinions of strangers, we have to be able to tolerate the distress of rifts that can't ever be mended. We also need to be able to draw a firm line between our opinions and others' and stand by our values even when it makes others dislike us.

In a word, we need to work on our distress *tolerance*. If we can allow someone to frown at us, insult us, talk about us behind our backs, or even outright reject us without folding, we have won back an important part of ourselves. We also become more resilient in confronting difficult situations when we learn how to regulate our distress.

Improving our distress tolerance comes down to four steps:

1. Separate your perspective from someone else's.

2. Disregard opinions that you do not respect.

3. Check in with your own values and feelings.

4. Self-soothe and regulate your anxiety.

The first step to boost our distress tolerance is grabbing hold of our perspective, which might currently be all wrapped up in the feelings and reactions of somebody else, and carefully extracting it so that it can exist on its own. There is a psychological measure of interpersonal closeness called the Inclusion of Self in the Other Scale (or the IOS)[18] that I think illustrates this well. This is what a fully enmeshed sense of self looks like in the IOS:

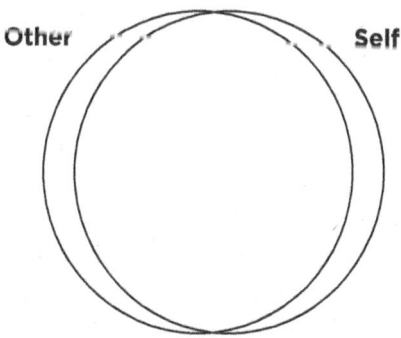

We may feel that we are this deeply connected to another person when we're in the midst of memory-foaming. When Jennette McCurdy described herself and her abusive mother as completely connected in her memoir, *I'm Glad My Mom Died*, this is what she meant. And in psychological research on relationship functioning, this degree of closeness is consistently found to be unhealthy because even a slight rift between the two parties feels like an unfathomable loss, a ripping apart of the self. If you're distressed at even the *idea* of your parent, partner, or close friend disagreeing with you, you may want to slowly work to extract your self-concept until your felt closeness looks more like this:

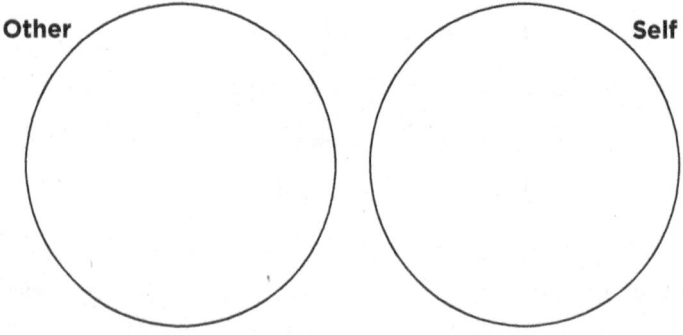

When you are allowed to be a whole person separate from someone else, you have the freedom and privacy within your own mind to really consider what you think. The other person's thoughts and feelings are busy brewing away inside them, but what you think and feel is happening inside *you*—and you can watch these inner reactions form and change shape as if you were gazing into a glowing, moving lava lamp. Nobody is harmed by your having your own inner world. It is fascinating and private, and belongs completely to you. Even negative or scary thoughts are allowed to happen there. Thoughts and feelings are completely morally neutral and cannot harm anyone. It is only our actions toward others that have an impact on the world.

This brings us to the second stage of boosting our distress tolerance: disregarding opinions that aren't useful to us or that come from a person we don't respect. When you're in the throes of people-pleasing and memory-foaming, any disapproval is an attack on your worthiness. But once we exist firmly within ourselves, we can ask whether another person's take on our lives even makes sense to consider. We can never win the approval of everyone, and we shouldn't aim to impress people whose actions sharply contradict our values. Having integrity means embracing being disliked by the right people.

For a long time, Henry hung on his best friend Jake's every last word. Jake was a popular, blond-haired jock type who acted like he ruled the world, and Henry was a shy Indigenous kid with foster parents and a bunch of disabilities, like Autism and Epilepsy, that he was trying not to be ostracized for. Jake was always telling Henry what to do to seem cool—to drink and stay out late at night driving around—and when the two grew older, Jake pressured Henry into working at his corner store when Henry really didn't want to. Through years of manipulation, Henry clung to the friendship, thinking that he owed Jake everything.

Henry says, "It dawned on me that I didn't want any of the things Jake set up for me. The friends he introduced me to were terrible people. The clothes he told me to wear were tacky. The job he'd so 'kindly' given me was third shift and was horrible." Since childhood he'd been terrified of losing his closest friend—but were they really that close? All Jake did was insult him and tell Henry that he knew better. "I was like, wait, is he really just a big asshole?"

Numerous unmasking Autistics that I've spoken to have left careers, ended marriages, gone no-contact with certain family members, moved across the country, downsized their homes, or started families after discovering who they really are. After we begin separating our mindsets from people who mistreat us and make us feel detective, we gain a new ability to check in with our own beliefs. Then, instead of constantly asking ourselves if somebody is mad at us, or trying to think up ways we can prevent any conflict before it begins, we get to take the next step and ponder questions like these:

- If I could go anywhere right now and do anything that I wanted, where would I go?

- How would I spend my days if I didn't have to worry about anyone watching and judging me?
- Which important values that I hold dear have I been neglecting?
- Who do I miss spending time with?
- What possibilities feel forbidden yet exciting to me?
- What do I really like?
- What do I want to try?

No matter how thoroughly we work on our own self-concepts, disregarding other people's judgments and choosing to take actions that will be criticized will still often cause anxiety to rise up in us. It is important to remember that the existence of these feelings is okay. These feelings are a sign that we have pushed ourselves past another person's controlling influence and into the realm of the unknown, where we can learn more about ourselves and grow. We do need to be able to soothe that anxiety, however, which is where the final step of practicing distress tolerance comes in.

There are numerous ways to reduce anxiety and lessen the impact of distress, and we will be reviewing a great many options for doing so throughout this book. Not all these exercises will work for everyone, and it may take some experimentation and practice to figure out the ones that best suit you. But to get us started, here is a tool kit of common, empirically supported distress regulation strategies that do show some promise of working for neurodivergent people. I've taken care here to avoid strategies that tend to backfire on us, such as the Cognitive Behavioral therapy practice of cognitive reframing. Most of us don't need help wondering if we have assessed a situation incorrectly and trying to view it in a new way. Years of invalidation have already left us constantly doing that. Instead, we need help relaxing our bodies and trusting in our *own* perspectives.

Five Core Skills for Unmasking Your Life

Distress Tolerance Toolbox

Feeling anxious, guilty, or overwhelmed?
Try a few of these activities:

Take a deep breath that raises your belly up, hold it for five seconds, breathe out slowly, pause for three seconds, and then repeat.	**Seek pressure:** Dig your nails into your palms, curl up with your knees against your chest, hug your arms, tighten your belt, or lean your body against a hard surface.
Focus on an item with a small, detailed texture, like a piece of furniture with an intricate wood grain, a complex work of art, or the veins on the back of a leaf. Zoom your attention in closer and closer, and see what the smallest, finest details you can perceive are.	**Get your energy out:** Throw a balled-up pair of socks against the wall, rip up paper or bar coasters, break the handles off pens, vigorously brush a rug, chew on ice, or pull apart gummy candy or taffy.
Get some distance: Remove yourself from the room you're in or step to the far edge of it. Take a long walk, explore hidden passageways or corners. If you can't physically escape, try imagining a comforting, familiar space or explore an imaginary realm within your mind.	**Organize and sort objects:** Clean out a cluttered closet or help collect dishes and silverware. Line up spare coins, office supplies, or other small items into neat piles or lines. Throw unwanted items away or donate them.
Distract your mind: Play a mentally taxing game like chess, 2048, or sudoku, or a stimulating one like a first-person shooter. Focus your attention on practical problems: planning your meals for the week, for example, or putting fun plans into your calendar.	**Seek comfort:** Picture a location (real or imagined) where you feel safe. Imagine yourself moving through it. Message a trusted friend and tell them how you are feeling. Look at photos or treasured mementos, cuddle with a stuffed animal, or listen to a sad song and cry.
Observe other people or your surroundings. Try to direct your focus away from yourself and instead study other people. Who looks excited? Who seems bored? Is anything interesting going on? Pretend you are a researcher from an alien planet.	**Find the humor** in the situation. Make a game of thinking of the strangest reply you can give to a question. Notice other people's awkward moments—see if you can find the overall goofiness of humanity to be lovable.

After we've gotten better at accepting change, engaging actively with other people, breaking unfair social rules, and tolerating some of the distress and social judgment that comes with each of these steps, we can finally embark on the most positive and empowering side of unmasking: the lifelong project of creating our own neurodiverse realities. Learning to invent and create such ways of life for ourselves is the final of the five core skills.

Create (Accommodations, Relationship Structures, and Ways of Living)

There's a big difference between merely surviving ableism and actually thriving as an Autistic person whose physical, emotional, and social needs are met. My first book on the subject of neurodiversity, *Unmasking Autism*, largely focused on Autistic people finding some escape from social judgment—at least within the safety of our own heads. When we are assumed to be neurotypical from birth and never given an alternative script for what a healthy disabled life could be like, we are essentially born with an imprisoning mask forced onto our faces. As we begin the early stages of the unmasking process, we learn more about what Autism really is, and how our way of functioning differs from neurodivergent expectations—we learn to identify that the mask has been placed on us, and we can start to distinguish between the person society required us to be, and who we really are.

But this book is about actually living freely in the world with that mask off—being authentically Autistic in our friendships, our family, at work, in love, and throughout all other elements of our lives. And so, the final of the five core skills is the ability to *think creatively* and even idealistically about what we long to be free *to do*—not just the oppressions we need to be free *from*.

Despite the stereotype that we're all unfeeling robots, Autistic people are actually incredibly creative. A recent systemic review of Autistic creativity published in the journal *Cognitive Processing* found that though Autistics often struggle with flexibility of thought (probably because we have been so conditioned to fear the unfamiliar), Autistics actually demonstrate a higher degree of originality than our more neuroconforming peers.[19] In particular, researchers Paola Pennisi and colleagues found that Autistics are more highly detailed in our creativity and original in our thinking when we have the privacy and time to dream up ideas on our own. We also tend to exhibit a great deal of creativity with language, in spite of the widespread belief that we're "poor communicators."

When groups of Autistic people come together to vent about our shared frustrations and trade tips for meeting our needs in a roundabout way, the incredible depth of our creativity is on full display. Recently, for example, a friend of mine posted on Facebook that they needed far more physical human contact in order to remain emotionally regulated. They didn't just want to ask friends to come over and cuddle or give them more hugs. They also wanted practical tips for naturally working more touch into their daily schedule.

"The 155 bus route is almost always packed with people west of the Loyola stop," shared a mutual friend of ours. If they were to ride the bus heading west during rush hour, it would be like being in "a mobile mosh-pit." Other friends recommended contra and ballroom dancing classes or volunteering at an animal shelter to pet bunnies or dogs. Another suggested *contact improvisation,* a form of expressive movement that isn't quite dance and isn't quite yoga or cuddling either, but instead a dynamic, fluid form of touch.

There are no prescriptions that psychiatrists can write for the touch-starved, and very few Autistic-supporting organizations produce these kinds of resources. We have to invent them on our own and then share them to better care for ourselves and our community. Autistic people are already well-versed in having to compensate for the abilities that we lack or the accommodations that we require but have never been given. When we get to freely harness our creativity, we can do more than just get by—we can explore sides of the human experience that few neurotypicals ever know.

Developing one's creative abilities (and confidence in one's creativity) is therefore a skill that we will practice throughout this book. Psychologists have attempted to quantify what it means to be creative many times—usually, they define creativity as generating an idea that has elements of both *novelty* and *usefulness*.[20] But usefulness is in the eye of the beholder, and what an Autistic person finds worthwhile might not always be what neurotypical society regards as a productive use of one's time. For some of us, having a spreadsheet that perfectly organizes every attribute of our Warframe miniatures collection is the height of usefulness. It doesn't matter if such a creation seems pointless to anybody else.

Some studies examine how to boost creativity, and typically conclude that looking at a problem in a new way, learning new information, and reflecting upon a problem without external pressure are major creativity boosters.[21] That general finding is likely true for Autistics as well, but keep in mind that we're more attuned to social pressure and judgment than others. We may need *lots* of time alone before we feel safe being creative and may need reassurance before we share our inventions with others. This is not a sign that we are sick with *rejection sensitive dysphoria*, as many psychiatrists might have it.[22] It's just us accurately recognizing that we have frequently been rejected, often with catastrophic results. Time in nature,[23] meditation,[24] or time spent stimming may also help improve our creativity by helping us to feel soothed and stimulated while also breaking us out of repetitive-thinking patterns. But nothing beats enthusiastic social support.

Research shows that teams are more creative when they have a chance to brainstorm without any censorship or harsh criticism of their ideas,[25] and on an individual level, being able to play freely with ideas without first having to worry about practical concerns has been shown to be beneficial, too. Autistics may particularly benefit from exercising creativity with unbridled play: by role-playing fictional characters or using improv, for example, or by imagining an idealized way of doing things, and only worrying later about how to bring that ideal into reality. We may also wish to consume huge amounts of information on a subject before exercising our creativity—allowing our penchant for "special interests" and for systematizing knowledge to beautifully unfurl.

As a tool for lifelong unmasking, our creative thinking and problem-solving can be further expanded by taking the following steps:

1. Connect with other disabled people. Observe how they live their lives, ask them questions about problems they encounter, and visit their homes and workspaces to get a better sense of life's possibilities.

2. Compile resources for your community. Trade advice, compile information into shared databases, write cheat sheets and scripts for tricky interactions, or share skills. This may mean pooling financial resources too: multiple Autistic neighbors may share a single car or live together to cut down on living expenses, cook meals together, or collectively share childcare. Any move away from capitalistic "independence" is a creative solution.

3. Research alternative options and modes of being. Collect information on social welfare benefits and aid provided by nonprofits or charities; learn new skills that may make your home life easier, such as sewing or basic repairs. Also consider looking for cross-cultural and historical sources of inspiration: study how humans have organized themselves in other eras and societies. Participate respectfully in other cultures.

4. Dream of something better than your current reality. All too often, Autistics are told that we're asking for too much and being too picky to stop us from requesting anything at all. Let yourself really think big. Do you want to knock out all the walls and live in a giant circus tent of a room? Do you want to live in a van tricked out with a gaming PC and a soft, cozy bed? Does your heart yearn to be part of a large, loving nonmonogamous family? Do you never want to have to speak verbally again? Really grant yourself the room to dream without being ashamed of how large or impractical a desire might seem.

5. Invent new solutions and next steps. After you've gathered a lot of inspiration and resources, and given yourself some time to dream, try to identify a few positive steps you can take. Focus on small actions you can take now that will bring you closer to the future you desire. For example, if you want to settle down on a big farm with a bunch of your friends, take some steps to research possible locations, and schedule some quality time with those friends to help deepen your relationship and commitment to one another.

Autistic people truly are more resilient and solutions-focused than we get credit for. Because we're so adept at synthesizing and systematizing information, we can do incredible things once we've had enough life experiences and accumulated a little knowledge. Numerous neurodivergent people that I know open their homes to community members who are injured or in need, or have created support groups or mutual aid funds that serve to buffer people during the hardest times of their lives. They author how-to guides that demystify everything from requesting an extension from a college professor to negotiating a good price on a car so that other disabled people can become more confident and capable. And they organize protests and letter writing campaigns, take their elderly neighbors to doctors' visits, or block boats to prevent weapons from being delivered to colonized lands overseas. Being different and frequently ostracized is a heavy load to carry, and by no means an Autistic "superpower"—but together, with a little mutual support, we can do heroic things for one another.

Here's a brief exercise for broadening our creative abilities—and breaking free from neuroconforming conventions.

Creating an Autistic Life
Reimagining Your Routine

When we are still actively masking, we allow social norms to guide how we structure our days and which obligations we prioritize.

Use these reflection questions to reimagine how you might actually want to spend your days.

1. *Productivity:* Many neurodivergent people find they are not alert during the standard "work hours" of 9 A.M. to 5 P.M., and instead are most active early in the morning or late at night.

    Which times of day do you find that you feel the most active and focused?

    _____

2. *Rest:* Similarly, many neurodivergent people's sleep-wake cycles differ from what's currently considered normal.

    Which times of day do you find yourself feeling the most sleepy and tired?

    _____

    How many hours of sleep do you need in order to feel refreshed?

    _____

3. *Rejuvenation:* Some of us don't find traditionally "relaxing" activities to be all that relaxing. We may need stimulation or a rewarding activity to quiet our minds instead.

    Which activities leave you feeling inspired, and distracted from life's problems?

    _____

    Do you ever find it hard to relax? What makes it difficult for you to feel at ease?

    _____

4. *Priority:* In the present culture, most adults are expected to treat work as their number one priority. But what really matters to you most?

> Which life pursuits feel the absolutely most meaningful to you?
>
> _____
>
> If you could spend your day doing exactly what you'd like to be doing, what would that day look like?
>
> _____

5. Most of us aren't in full control of how we spend our days because of duties like school, doctors' appointments, family obligations, and work. What are some steps you could take to make your schedule more closely resemble your ideal one right now?

> _____
>
> What are some ways you could work to change your routine over the course of the next year?
>
> _____

Each of us is the sole expert on our interior experience and what is best for us, no matter how many times others have told us that we're overly sensitive, seeing things that aren't real, demanding too much, or are simply built "wrong." Autistic and otherwise neurodivergent people have spent our entire lifetimes being told how to behave, how to carry ourselves, what to feel, and how to live. But with this book, I will never impose a set value system or ideal outcome onto you. The goal of every life is not the same. As disabled people, none of us should have to justify our existence. We each have the power to decide what we need out of life. We can trust in our ability to select the right path for us. We just need support and a strategy to help us get it.

As we work our way through the rest of this book, we will return regularly to the five core skills of acceptance, engagement, transgression, tolerance, and creation, applying them to the numerous areas of life where neurodivergent people commonly experience difficulty. In the next chapter, we will start off by tackling one of the most basic and yet most pervasive sources of difficulty in the masked Autistic's life: friendship, an area where we often struggle to find belonging or even to believe that our real selves are worthy of love.

Friendship

Delilah's primary engagement with the "Autistic community" so far has happened online. She started questioning whether she was neurodivergent at the start of the pandemic, when being alone for long stretches of time allowed deeply buried parts of her personality to finally come into the foreground. She stopped wearing makeup, tore up her office to make a dark, quiet reading nook, and talks to herself and makes faces as she paces through the house. She's read all the books about Autism she can find, spends a lot of time on Autistic Instagram and Autistic TikTok, and has quietly attended virtual community events—but the idea of actually meeting anyone terrifies her.

"I already had bad social anxiety before COVID started," she says, "and now I haven't been active at a large social thing for nearly half a decade."

Delilah tells me that almost every form of social connection she enjoys right now involves passively observing what other people are doing, or consuming and posting content online. She reads, she watches videos, and she pines for a connection like the ones she sees others forming, but she struggles to envision herself taking steps of her own to form such bonds. She knows of lots of cool neurodiversity advocates, but nobody really knows her.

Many Autistic people rely on what psychologists call *social snacking*:[1] we soothe loneliness by forming attachments to influencers or fictional characters, simulating connection by getting invested in depictions of other people's lives. During a brief moment of sadness, social snacking has been found to improve mood. There is no harm, for instance, in looking over old photos of good times that you spent with your friends and reveling for a bit in the fond memories, or listening to other people share a conversation across the bar or in a podcast and quietly appreciating their closeness. But ultimately, Autistic people like Delilah need reciprocal relationships with people who know and care for them, not just comforting content on their feeds. In its most extreme form, relying on stand-in connections to public figures can morph into a parasocial relationship, wherein a person imagines that they share a real connection with another person because of the intensity of their feelings, but where no mutual knowledge or investment actually exists.[2]

Forming supportive social connections is one of the most difficult parts of many Autistic people's lives. Young Autistics often attempt to forge friendships in ways that confuse their more neuroconforming peers, for example by excitedly "info dumping" about subjects that interest them, regardless of whether their new friend shares an interest, or by simply standing next to a person and playing near them, hoping that the other party will make the choice to engage. This often inspires bullying and ostracism in an attempt to "punish" Autistic kids for their perceived misbehavior.[3] One study found that only 34 percent of Autistic children had what their parents judged to be a "good friend," compared to 71 percent of other disabled children and 93 percent of abled children.[4]

We should consider that what a non-Autistic parent judges to be a close bond for their kid will be skewed by society's neurotypical lens—they may be missing friendships that aren't as vocal or expressive in their connection as other kids' friendships are.[5] Still, it's undeniable that Autistic people report desiring more and deeper social connections than they are currently experiencing; one foundational study by Gael Orsmond and colleagues found, for instance, that only 8 percent of Autistic adults and adolescents reported having a close friend.[6]

A 2022 study in the journal *Autism* authored by Kana Grace and colleagues was one of the first to explore the full dimensions of Autistic people's loneliness.[7] That Autistic people are lonely is broadly well-documented[8] and entirely taken as fact within the published literature, but what does loneliness really mean? The authors specified that Autistic people's feelings of isolation occur along at least three dimensions:

1. Collective loneliness (i.e., a lack of belonging in society)
2. Relational loneliness (a lack of closeness and acceptance in friendships and family relationships)
3. Intimate loneliness (a lack of close romantic or sexual connection)

Addressing collective and relational loneliness will take up the bulk of this chapter. We will further consider relational loneliness in the chapter on unmasking in families, and intimate loneliness in the chapter on unmasking in one's love and sex life.

Because we take steps to conceal our stigmatized sides and learn to imitate neurotypicals, masked Autistics tend to be more successful in making friends than our less-masked Autistic peers. However, the bonds we form are often superficial and not genuinely supportive. We often make friends by imitating other people, allowing others to approach us, or by hiding our true feelings.[9] In a study published in the journal *Intellectual and Developmental Disabilities*, authors Margaret Mehling and Marc Tasse noted that even when Autistic people participate just as actively in our communities as non-Autistic people do, we experience lower friendship quality with the people that we meet. There's still a greater distance between us and others due to anti-Autistic biases and because we're masking so much of ourselves.[10] As we grow older, the separation between our true personalities and the false selves we project to the world only widens, and we often lose the few, unsatisfying friendships that we were able to make through the incidental contact of school or work. This is particularly concerning because the research shows that having a robust and genuinely loving support network is essential to well-being as we age.[11]

A majority of Autistic adults report elevated levels of loneliness compared to non-Autistics, and our social isolation is linked to numerous adverse health outcomes.[12] We also tend to feel far less socially competent and more socially anxious than non-Autistics.[13] Our past social traumas lead us to further withdraw, so we don't develop the more complex social skills of conflict resolution and boundary-setting that many other people learn to master in their teens and twenties, and which are absolutely essential to maintaining enduring friendships that can weather life's many changes.

Even after a masked Autistic person learns they are disabled and realizes that they never deserved the bullying, exclusion, and other cruel "corrections" they received in their past, old wounds linger, and they may spend decades not knowing how to go about making true friends. In fact, one of the areas of life where I receive the most questions from Autistic readers is in the realm of managing friendships: how to form new ones, how to stand up for oneself when a friend crosses the line, how to cope with people's prejudices against Autistics while trying to make new friends, how to adapt when the dynamic of a friendship changes, and even how to simply exist in public on your own when you've been taught you don't belong.

Contrary to the widely held belief that we completely lack the social skills necessary to ever be liked by anyone or to ever find people we like in return, the reality is that we've been excluded repeatedly from public life, and our unique social needs have been obscured by poorly done ableist research. Recall that for decades, psychologists and psychiatrists alike believed that Autistic people had no desire to make friends; in my own clinical coursework as a psychologist, I heard professors declare that people like me had absolutely zero social drive and would prefer to be alone forever. One of the leading theories of Autistic friendlessness, Social Motivation Theory, *still* holds that our alienation is caused by us failing to show enough interest in others.[14]

Autistic people are not actually socially defective or incapable of connection, though. We can accept the challenge of venturing into new social spaces, engage intentionally with other people, transgress unhelpful norms of politeness when they don't serve us, tolerate the discomfort of sometimes being seen as strange, and even invent new ways of socializing that are completely our own. Once we develop the true social skills of advocating for ourselves and living more authentically, we can find the close, supportive connections that so many of us crave, and work to ensure that those friendships aren't unbalanced or based on a neuroconforming lie. Here's how.

Meeting New People

"How does anybody meet new people, if not from work or school?" Delilah wonders. "How does that happen?" As a stay-at-home mom and a heavily masked Autistic whose primary camouflage strategy has been extreme shyness, she can't quite wrap her head around it. At times, it seems to her about as inexplicable as magic.

Due to the dual traumas of coping with anti-Autistic ableism and spending a lifetime masking, many Autistics feel helpless and hopeless about our own social prospects. Any friendships we've found were the ones that were set up for us by some external force: the placement of lockers and desks in elementary school, the sudden presence of a stranger who wanted our help. Even those of us who can mask as more outgoing and gregarious may find it impossible to really be "seen." Our struggles with loneliness are only amplified in a moment that the U.S. Surgeon General has deemed an *epidemic* of loneliness:[15] people of all ages and disability status are increasingly friendless these days due to the social erosion caused by the pandemic, the decline of public spaces that allow strangers to meet and interact, increased reliance upon digital technology, rising fear of crime, longer work hours, and more. If it is prohibitively difficult for even the most neuroconforming and socially skillful to build deep connections now, for Autistics it can feel like we don't stand a chance.

I have observed that many masked Autistic people harbor a fantasy of finding their belonging within an already-existing, vibrantly supportive community without having to take the risk of creating new friendships themselves. According to this fantasy, all a person has to do is place themselves in the exact correct space at the right time, or locate the exact right group of people, and they'll be able to find warmth and belonging instantly. Perhaps this fantasy exists because we can't follow the subtle dance of intimacy-building that non-Autistics are trained to

Friendship

participate in, and so friend-making looks like instant magic to us. Maybe we believe in it because media depictions don't show the messy, yearslong work that goes into building every single relationship a real person will ever have. I think that a legacy of colonialism and capitalism also have conditioned us to see ourselves as individuals who need to simply "claim" the social territory we require, rather than as members of a culture, a family, and a neighborhood that we must invest our effort into. But regardless, in actuality a community must be created from the ground up, one ongoing relationship at a time, and there is no possibility of being accepted and loved for who we really are if we don't make a change and take the risk of allowing them to know us.

In other words, making friends is a whole lot of newness and coping with uncertainty, and a lot of confronting potential rejection. It's unsurprising, then, that masked Autistics often feel frozen, incapable, and totally overwhelmed by the enormity of it. But we can break down this massive, looming task into manageable steps, growing in our skills all the while.

Lately, Delilah has begun researching more interactive social opportunities online. She has joined a few Discord channels run by her favorite social media creators, and in some of them, there are regular book clubs, gaming sessions, or movie-watching nights. She's also looked up volunteering opportunities at the local historical society, particularly administrative tasks that will put her in an office with a couple of other volunteers per week. She recognizes that she needs to start small because she really hasn't had a lot of meaningful contact with other people these last few years.

The first step to making new friends as an Autistic person is accepting that you'll need to find and venture into new social spaces. I recommend setting aside at least an hour per week to research upcoming events, local groups, online communities, volunteer positions, and other public spaces where it might be possible for you to interact with people. During this research period, fill your calendar with the most promising options you can find: events that are physically accessible to you, and where you can imagine yourself having a good time. If you know that you have very limited social batteries and that introducing new events on your calendar causes stress (it does for most of us!), don't overwhelm yourself with too many obligations. You may only want to add one extra social engagement per week (or month) to start. As we'll discuss later on in this section, consistency is key to establishing a rapport with new people, so it's better to commit to one book club that you will attend faithfully every single month than it is to cram your calendar with woodworking classes and clothing swaps and potlucks that you're not really going to show up to.

If you're not sure how to get started, here are some spaces to visit to potentially make new friends.

Accepting Change
New Events to Visit and Places to Make Friends

Public Libraries: Readings, workshops, and book clubs	**Park Districts:** Classes, crafts, restoration work, and intramural sports	**Eventbrite.com:** Concerts, parties, film showings, online events	**Meetup.com:** Social groups for Autistics and socially anxious people, LGBTQ events, biking or running groups, cooking groups, clubs, hobby groups, and more
Museums and Public Gardens: Guided tours, volunteer work, clubs	**Local Theaters and Comedy Clubs:** Open mics, improv classes, volunteering, backstage or back-of-house work	**Tabletop Gaming Stores:** Open role-playing sessions, card game nights, tournaments	**AutisticAdvocacy.org:** Autistic Self Advocacy Network (ASAN) chapter meetings, online events

Accepting Change
New Events to Visit and Places to Make Friends

Places of Worship and Spirituality: Worship services, study groups, meditation groups, community support groups	Community Centers: Support groups, group therapy, clothing swaps, classes, volunteer opportunities	Reddit.com and Discord: Video game groups, movie watch parties, role-playing groups, hobbyist communities, geek communities	Conventions and Conferences: Panels, mixers, networking sessions, tournaments, after-parties
Performance Venues: Concerts, comedy shows, plays, raves, DJ sets, and film showings	Public Sporting Spaces: Skate parks, running paths, fishing areas, beaches, volleyball courts, tennis courts, basketball courts, hiking trails, fire jams	Gyms: Weightlifting classes, aerobics classes, Pilates, yoga, dance classes, self-defense classes, contact improv groups	Neighborhood Groups: Community gardens, mutual aid groups, food banks, activist groups, "buy nothing" groups, potlucks

I've made decades-long, meaningful connections at a variety of the spaces outlined in this list, and so have many Autistic and neurodivergent people that I've surveyed. I made numerous new friends after a stint volunteering in the box office of one of my favorite local theaters, and then asking to contribute to one local director's plays. The monthly comic book club that I attend via the Chicago Public Library has led to my making a handful of new friends in the past couple of years, and I really cherish the time we get to spend together. Two of my very closest friends are a married couple from Michigan who approached me during a Dorian Electra concert in 2019 to compliment my outfit and ask if I minded them dancing and singing alongside me.

I had no expectation that I'd find people who would one day be deeply important to me when I first ventured into these spaces. In fact, most of the time when I show up to an unfamiliar space, I walk away having enjoyed a new experience and a brief conversation with a stranger and nothing more. Establishing new friendships comes slowly, and accepting change means knowing there's no assurance any single attempt to broaden one's social sphere will pay off. But we can learn to appreciate these small moments of connection on their own merits because they help the world to feel less menacing and make it possible for something deeper to take root. The possibility itself can be enjoyable.

With this list, I've made sure to include both in-person and digital options for socializing. Some Autistic people have no desire to socialize in person or are unable to do so because of physical disabilities or a high risk of long COVID. That is completely fine, and research shows that Autistic people do find meaningful social support through our online friendships.[16] Unmasking for life means finding creative ways to meet your needs that truly work for you, and you don't have to socialize in neuroconformist ways if you don't want to. It wasn't all that long ago that dating someone you met online was considered completely unusual in mainstream society, but today it's the primary way that people meet their partners.[17] By creating remote and unconventional options for socializing, Autistic people help create a more accessible world. As long as your modes of socializing are based in genuine interaction rather than passive consumption of content, doing everything online can emotionally and psychologically benefit you.

After identifying one or two new social opportunities, your next challenge is to actually attend them. There are many barriers to successfully trying a new thing as an Autistic person, though. You'll probably be filled with questions about how the event functions, what the space looks like, and even how to behave. You can reduce some of your anxiety by doing additional research in advance of the event—looking up particulars of the space, reading the event description, and even by googling how people typically behave at events of its kind. When Delilah was invited to a ground-breaking ceremony for a new building at the historical society, for example, she prepared for it by watching videos of similar building openings online. This helped her guess how long the event might take, and understand what its symbolic purpose was. You can also minimize uncertainty by planning your route to the event and making sure to give yourself recovery time so that you don't accidentally come to associate the event with panic or exhaustion.

You can further cope with change through consistent, repeated visits and attempts. Because unfamiliar spaces present a massive data overload for Autistics, we often perceive the discomfort of a new activity as dislike of the activity itself. But with time, repeated exposures, and use of distress-regulation tools, you'll have a clearer view of things. As a general rule, it's worth visiting a new space at least three times before you dismiss it as simply not for you—that should give you enough data and familiarity to begin to make a judgment. And by showing up to the same space numerous times in a row, we make ourselves more familiar to others, and thus increase the chances of them feeling comfortable around us and approaching us, too.

A few years ago, my dear friend Mel decided to branch out in her dating and social life. Mel began regularly attending local dungeon nights, meetups for local kinksters, and queer mixer type events—but she sometimes found these busy spaces to be quite a lot to adjust to. She also felt the weight of expectation, beating herself up at times for failing to integrate into the group or to be sufficiently "fun." That's when she invented something I now call Mel's Rule, an affirmation that any neurodivergent, shy, traumatized, or introverted person can recall whenever they enter a new, potentially uncomfortable situation.

Transgress Expectations
Mel's Rule

You don't have to do shit, say shit,
or feel shit that you don't want to.

Mel is a quiet, sometimes enigmatic person. Many people are attracted to her, but she doesn't always know what she wants from her romantic or sexual life. So when Mel first started venturing out into dungeons and kinky meetup events, she reminded herself that she didn't owe anybody any kind of emotional reaction, interest, or participation in activities that she did not truly want to give. She told herself that she didn't even need to *enjoy* the new social experience at all. Merely getting out of the house and trying a new thing was enough. Ultimately, Mel did make numerous close friends in the Chicago kink scene—and they were genuine friendships, rooted in a true appreciation of her darkly witty, dry personality and tendency to carefully think things through.

"If I were an animal," Mel's dating profile says, "I would be a vulture." Those of us who are lucky enough to have Mel in our lives love her for the elegant, foreboding scavenger bird that she is—and we don't expect her to be a chirping, enthusiastic parakeet. As an unmasking neurodivergent person, you deserve to grant yourself those same freedoms.

Once you've actually gotten yourself out into a new social environment a few times and have begun to acclimate to it, your next task is to engage meaningfully with other people on your own terms. You've given yourself permission not to do anything you don't want to do, and so now you have space to ask yourself which activities you do wish to pursue. Who seems approachable or interesting? What catches your eye? How can you get more involved in an organization in a meaningful way? What skills or knowledge bases do you have to contribute to an event?

Delilah has gotten more involved by proposing that her local historical society offer outdoor and child-friendly events, as it would make ongoing involvement easier for her and her family. There seems to be a genuine interest, so she's started assisting with the planning.

"I don't know how to be a person sometimes, but I am good with kids," she says. By offering short day-camp activities on the historical society lawn and teaching local children about the history of the community, she hopes to make some more parent friends. "It's much easier for me when I'm given a task," she explains. So now Delilah's assigning fulfilling tasks to herself.

There are a variety of ways that we can challenge ourselves to engage with others and deepen our social contacts, even if we feel intensely socially inhibited. Asking clarifying questions and introducing new, helpful information are both ways many neurodivergent people engage. As a group, we tend to be highly detail-oriented, so we can anticipate issues in the planning of events that others might overlook. We may enjoy taking on the role of documenting the group's activities by taking photographs or keeping meeting notes. Approaching newer members and explaining group processes to them or trying to welcome those even more shy than ourselves can also be beneficial. Sometimes, the very best way for us to engage is to just remain present and respond to our environment—moving our bodies to the music, nodding along eagerly to the conversation, building the Jenga tower, joining the chants at the protest, or simply applauding the group's collective work.

Here are some ways that you can try to engage with a group more deeply, once you've become a part of it.

Engage with Others
Ways to Get More Deeply Involved Within a Social Group

Ask a question	Offer to help with a task	Share information and resources
Bring food or refreshments	Offer to tidy the space or organize materials	Request a change to make the space more accessible for you
Compliment someone's performance or work	Express appreciation for the group	Organize a separate event or hangout
Identify a problem others may also be experiencing	Propose a solution to a shared problem	Welcome someone new
Validate someone else's perceptions (if you agree with them)	Express your disagreement or a competing point of view	Share something you've made or done with the group
Ask someone in the group about their life	Share personal news with the group	Trade in-jokes or references to past events
Let people know that you notice them and value them	Ask for help	Suggest a new activity

It can be difficult to get outside our heads and really interact with other people in these ways. And once we take a risk, we might experience rejection, mockery, or a dread-inducing blank stare. But this is not a reason to retreat from social interaction—instead, we must learn to discern between a moment of harmless awkwardness and a real threat. We also need to distinguish between people we can safely open up to more fully, and people who we can't win over no matter what we do and whose opinions we therefore should not worry about. We need a variety of self-advocacy tools to navigate this minefield—so our next section is all about balancing the liberating act of unmasking against the tough reality of the world's ableism.

Coping with Anti-Autistic Bias

Delilah's hesitation around other people doesn't come from nowhere. Since she was a child, she has repeatedly incurred painful social wounds, and encounters in her daily life still regularly reopen them.

"I was in integrated special-ed for a while, and some of my teachers would shame me in front of the class because I didn't like bathing, and sometimes had a bit of a smell," she says. Other kids squealed in disgust when she came near them on the playground, sometimes even covering their noses and demanding she go bathe. Delilah's first few adult jobs weren't any better. Working at a sandwich shop, she would incur her boss's wrath for taking too much time to arrange orders and for letting customers speak to her for too long. When she tried befriending coworkers, Delilah says, "People called me creepy, because I'd ask them things like where they lived and their relationship status . . . but these were topics other people could bring up with no issue. I didn't see what I was doing wrong."

One of the biggest barriers to making new friends for the Autistic person is the pervasiveness of anti-Autistic bias in society. Empirical research has repeatedly shown that non-Autistic people viscerally dislike Autistics within mere seconds of meeting us, even when they have no idea we are disabled and we have behaved in a completely socially

Friendship

acceptable way.[18] This is due to the rigid standards of neuroconformity, which dictate what it means to think, feel, and act normally within a very narrow scope.

Many masked Autistics feel powerless to overcome neuroconformity, because even if they perfectly memorize social rules and learn to carefully read the nonverbal signals of other people, something about them still creeps strangers out.

Delilah tried for much of her twenties and thirties to shake off the stigma of being the girl in special education who did not bathe by masking as an agreeable, unremarkable person who was always helpful and clean, and didn't stand out. She complimented everyone that she worked with, always took a person's side when they complained to her about their problems (even if this meant telling both people involved in a fight that they were right), took extra shifts at the sandwich shop whenever someone asked her, and tried ingratiating herself to her boss by tidying up his desk in the back room and bringing him coffee. This attentiveness was rewarded with Delilah being passed over for a promotion because she wasn't "leadership material," and being repeatedly forgotten when co-workers sent out invitations for parties. By the time she got married and started having kids, Delilah had concluded that there was no point in trying to get people to like her.

"The more I try, the more others pull away," she laments.

It may sound like a dark realization, but in concluding that masking frequently backfires, Delilah might really be on to something. The mental and physical health costs of hiding one's disability are well-documented, and we reviewed some of its consequences at the top of this book (and you can also read far more about the negative health effects of masking in *Unmasking Autism*). However, there's a real social cost to conforming to neurotypical standards that we might not always realize we're paying, too.

Like Delilah, I used to try obscuring my neurodivergence by making myself smaller around other people. I was so afraid of being seen as a freak that others could sense my reflexive mistrust of them, and so they kept their distance. My behavior was highly practiced, and I was incredibly guarded, so in retrospect it was no wonder I couldn't make friends. But once I came out as both transgender and Autistic, and became far more openly vulnerable and weird, other freaky people started flocking to me.

When we're masking, we might believe that we are following the social rules that are guaranteed to make us seem normal and likable, but in reality we are just reinforcing the very standards that exclude us. A 2020 study conducted by Sarah Cassidy and colleagues found that in addition to contributing to psychological distress and suicidality, Autistic college students who masked also experienced less belongingness than Autistics who didn't.[19] Research on Autistic adults shows that many maskers feel deceptive and guilty about not showing their true selves to other people, and that camouflaging their disability frays their interior sense of self as well.[20]

There are times, of course, when a person must mask for their own safety. Black and brown Autistics use masking to protect themselves from arrests and killings at the hands of the police.[21] Autistics attempting to access medical or psychiatric care often have to mask to be treated as competent by doctors.[22] And as we'll discuss in later chapters, it's perilous to be openly Autistic while we are at work. Sometimes, masking is necessary. But the fact that it is necessary does not make it good—and the fact that masking may bring us some short-term relief from bullying doesn't mean it's compatible with leading an actually liberated life. To get free, we must escape the social conditions that demand that we mask as often and as fully as we can.

One way to do this is by actively centering Autistic (and other disabled) people in our lives. Recall that the goal of most social skills trainings for Autistics is to condition us to behave in ways that non-Autistic people find easy to be around. We can powerfully transgress that goal by instead prioritizing people who are unconventional, stigmatized, or strange just like us. Rather than trying to meet neurotypical standards and failing, we can aspire to be as openly weird as our circumstances possibly allow. We can also rethink any unfair biases that might have kept us from seeing other divergent people as worthy of being liked. To mask is to treat difference as a shameful secret, and in most cases that attitude does bleed into how we regard others who move oddly, take a long time to speak, can't work, or can't bathe. By creating lives for ourselves that center disability and nonconformity, we flip the power dynamic in our existing relationships too, which makes it far easier to self-advocate.

Reham is a lab manager who used to get criticized by co-workers for having an emotionally "flat" face and for sitting so perfectly still during meetings that people called her the Ice Queen. She internalized this and put energy into making herself move and emote to seem more "alive," but doing so distracted and drained her. After a few years in a leadership position, however, Reham had managed to surround herself with a team of neurodivergent employees who, like her, communicated in their own unique ways. She'd also begun to practice unmasking in her friendships. Through the cultivation of a neurodivergent community and the self-love that came with it, Reham learned to stop policing herself and start shutting dismissive comments down.

"Another team lead asked me what my 'problem' was, because I was just sitting still and listening to him," Reham offers as an example. "I said, this is just my listening face. We all have one. I'm sure you want me to give your work the full attention it deserves.

"I don't even have to explain my 'flat' face anymore," she says. "The neurotypicals at work will even explain it to people *for* me. They'll be like, *Oh, that's just Reham, don't take it personally, she might look like she's staring into your soul but that's just how she is.*" Other people on Reham's team spin around in their office chairs, pace while thinking, or speak with stutters. Under her leadership, that too is accepted as just how some people are.

Here are a few questions to get you thinking about ableist stigmas you might be applying to yourself—and in your relationships.

Transgress Social Judgment
Rethinking Ableist Bias

Reflect on the following questions.

Write down some of the qualities that you associate with people who are stereotypically likable or "popular."

_____

_____

_____

Write down some of the qualities that you associate with people who are seen as unpopular, unlikable, or even as "losers."

_____

_____

_____

Do you agree with society's assessment of what makes a likable person? How do your own views align or diverge from that view?

_____

_____

_____

Here are some behaviors and personal qualities that tend to be looked down upon by people in mainstream neurotypical society. As you read through them, try to notice your initial, knee-jerk reaction to the thought of meeting someone with these qualities.

- Shifting, unpredictable movement
- An avoidance of eye contact

Friendship

Short, one-word replies to questions

Not speaking at all

Recreational drug use

Speaking in either a very loud or a very quiet voice

Ticking, twitching, or shouting that the person can't control

Having a noticeable body odor

Wearing clothing that is faded or frayed

Speaking about unexpected topics, or talking to oneself

Crying openly

Rocking or pacing

Showing up to a space or leaving it without advance notice

If you find yourself feeling judgmental or fearful toward a person with these qualities, or feeling shame about the qualities that you recognize in yourself, try telling your brain the following: "Thank you for trying to protect me from harm, but I am not in danger. There is nothing wrong with a person behaving in this way. We are okay."

Think for a moment about times when you have been criticized for behaving too "strangely" or "creepily," and then felt you had to alter your behavior. List a few examples below:

Hurtful criticism I received:

_____

Change I made to my behavior as a result:

_____

Hurtful criticism I received:

_____

Change I made to my behavior as a result:

_____

Hurtful criticism I received:

_____

Change I made to my behavior as a result:

_____

Think of how you might defend another disabled person against such criticism if you were to hear it today.

For example, if someone told you it was inappropriate to stare at others, you might reply, "You don't know how long another person needs to process information," or "There's nothing wrong with paying attention to things." When in doubt, a simple, "That's none of your business," can work wonders.

Write down the criticisms and your responses to them below.

Hurtful criticism:

_____

My response:

_____

Hurtful criticism:

_____

My response:

_____

Hurtful criticism:

_____

My response:

_____

Delilah looks back with embarrassment at the times she politely laughed along with co-workers when they mocked the unhoused people that wandered into her sandwich shop. "I've been fired for crying meltdowns. I can't hold down a job now. I'm not any better than people who are unhoused. That's why when we go into the city, I always have my boys give money to the people who are on the street and tell them to say hello and to wish them a good day." On the Discord servers she visits online, some of Delilah's most frequent contacts are people who are unemployed, depressed, and suicidal, as well as physically disabled and high-risk people who use the internet as their primary social outlet.

By warmly embracing people who understand her struggles, and who remind her of the sides of herself she once fought to suppress, Delilah is able to view the larger social world as less menacing. There is a place in the world for people like her, and she is helping to construct that place.

By being a little bit more openly freaky and nonconforming, we may discover that the right people actually like us *more*. Research by Noah Sasson and Kerrianne Morrison conducted in 2019, for example, found that most people's anti-Autistic bias dropped away once they knew that they were interacting with an Autistic person.[23] When non-Autistics could understand that a stranger's slow processing speed and carefully calculated expressions were caused by their being Autistic and not by their being "fake" or "manipulative," they showed a genuine interest in connecting with the Autistic person and learning more about Autism.

In fact, several studies published in the last few years reveal that when Autistic people disclose their disabilities and work on unmasking, non-Autistic people actually receive them better, and show less anti-Autistic bias.[24] Even more important, unmasking makes it possible for other neuro-nonconforming people to find us.

I have noticed over the course of my own unmasking journey that I actually don't need to fear unstructured, random encounters with other people the way I once thought that I did. When I was masking, I used to write entire conversations out in my mind and practice all my social gestures and mannerisms in advance. Everything I did and said was meticulously gamed out—and most people hated it because what they picked up on was the gaming. They got a premeditated, distant energy from me, and that made them wary. People could sense I was uncomfortable, and they didn't want to bother me or intrude, so they gave me a wide berth. Sometimes people forgot I existed because I'd made my personality so frictionless. Conversations with the masked me left absolutely no mark.

These days, I try to move forward with an open, authentic energy instead, and accept that I won't always know what to say or do. I made this change after encountering a post on the r/SocialSkills subreddit, in which a user reflected that most people don't care about the literal content of what you say—they care about the energy coming off you. And if you approach others with a receptive, playful energy that is open to unexpected turns of conversation and can roll with mistakes and flubs, people immediately feel more at ease, and want to "play" along with you, too.

Like so many Autistics, I used to believe the purpose of a conversation was to exchange information. I did not understand that many non-Autistic people talk simply to establish a rapport, show affiliation, or share their emotional energy. Chitchatting about the weather while waiting for the bus, I finally realized, was less like a news report and more like two birds chirping to each other across the trees. When a friend asked me how my day was going, I didn't need to compose a perfectly sensible answer. I could just be emotionally honest and present, and let the conversation flow from there. I stutter and begin sentences I don't know how to finish a lot more often these days, yet people actually find me more charming and better at communication.

As masked Autistics, many of us wish for our social interactions to be completely predictable, but part of the fun of getting to know other people is the act of discovery. We get to decide which conversational topics to pursue, which questions we want to ask, and the energy that we wish to bring to an interaction. If I'm walking down the street and I see a man with brilliantly dyed orange hair, I'm allowed to just call out to him and ask, "Hey, I like your hair! Do you have to dye it often to keep it from fading?" If my bank teller politely asks me if I've seen any good movies lately, I can honestly tell him that I just watched a four-hour-long YouTube review of Netflix's *One Piece* show, even though I've never watched an actual episode of *One Piece* itself. Then he can chuckle and tell me about whatever weird internet deep dives he's been on lately. Instead of working to seem normal, we get a genuine moment of human interaction. By asking questions I honestly want the answers to, showing enthusiasm, and letting my own freak flag fly, I've made countless friends and acquaintances as I move through my neighborhood. This isn't masking, it's finally letting myself *be* without a filter or assuming the worst of others. It's a form of engagement that makes me finally feel socially liberated.

Here are some affirming reminders if you're looking to overcome the pressure to be masked and want to engage with other people from a more honest place.

Engage Socially
Affirmations for Unmasking Your Interactions

You are allowed to ask questions you want the answers to.

You are allowed to show signs of the emotions you are feeling.

Your enthusiasm is a gift, and the right people will cherish it.

You are free to move toward things you're curious about.

You are free to step away when you feel uncomfortable or disrespected.

Of course, when we move through the world more openly as ourselves, we run the risk of sometimes being disliked. That is actually a good thing. If some people don't like us, that means we have a stable enough selfhood that people can form an opinion on it, instead of insecurely memory-foaming ourselves around everyone we meet. But being ourselves in the face of rejection and criticism can be very difficult, and we need to build up our distress tolerance and our boundary-setting abilities to be able to do it. In the next section, we will practice doing exactly that.

Identifying and Maintaining Boundaries

Unmasking ourselves socially doesn't just mean casting a wider net to increase the total number of friends we might make. It also means showing up more authentically within our existing friendships, and even paring down or altering the dynamics of friendships that don't feel good to us. Our goal is not to maximize how liked we are—that only leads down the path of people-pleasing and inauthenticity. Rather, when we unmask, we are seeking to improve the quality and intimacy of our friendships, and that means setting firmer boundaries and experiencing productive conflict.

Quiana is a young woman in her midtwenties who used to organize regular electronic music shows at warehouses in her community and throw big parties at her house. Her friends trashed her space regularly without helping clean up, and sometimes event co-organizers scammed Quiana by not sharing ticket sales with her or by stealing some of her equipment. Quiana didn't speak up about these problems early on because she was afraid of damaging her reputation for being easygoing and fun. She did a lot of drugs to cloud over her annoyance—and sleepwalked through her life.

"I figured there can't be anything wrong with me if I'm surrounded by hundreds of 'friends,'" she says, making quotes with her fingers. The people who drank all the liquor in her cabinets and scuffed up all her floors without apology weren't her friends, not really.

Because so many Autistic people struggle to find social acceptance when we are young, we tend to develop into adults who don't believe in our own right to have and enforce boundaries. We may be so accustomed to being mistreated and accepting whatever small scraps of positive social attention we do receive that we're not even sure when our boundaries have been crossed. Not only are Autistic people more vulnerable to interpersonal abuse than non-Autistic people,[25] we also face challenges in knowing the difference between casual acquaintances and true friends. We may find it unnatural to alter how much information or commitment we give others based on the depth of the relationship.[26] If our relationships are to become unmasked, we have to learn to voice our boundaries. But that begins with getting to know what our boundaries even are.

What does it mean to have a boundary? Broadly speaking, a boundary is an *expectation* you set for how others should treat you, combined with a *consequence* you will personally enact if someone's conduct does not meet it. Boundaries can be communicated to other people, but ultimately we are in charge of enforcing our boundaries. We cannot compel someone else to respect us, or to behave the way we wish them to behave. Telling another person what to do isn't setting a boundary, it is issuing a command; instead, we can honor our boundaries by asserting control over where we go, who we interact with, which kinds of treatment we tolerate, and when we choose to interject or step away.

The first step to setting better boundaries is articulating when we feel uncomfortable, intruded upon, or pressured, if only to ourselves. One relatively easy place to start is by looking for our no's—finding the many small moments throughout the day where something feels *wrong* to us, where we might wish to deny a request, leave a social setting, or ask that circumstances be changed. Here the challenge is to find as many small, fixable problems as you can, rather than ignoring them as you might usually do, and to bring them up early and often. It may sound like a small tweak, but for many unmasking Autistics, it is a major reorientation.

Accepting Change
Finding Your No's

Try spending an entire day noticing all the sources of discomfort in your environment. These might be physical problems with your surroundings, a lack of accessibility in public spaces, issues with how other people treat you, or anything else you don't want to put up with anymore. Write them down as you notice them over the course of your day.

Here are some example no's a person might encounter in their day. Read them over, and then add some of your own.

I hate that:

My desk is in a high-traffic area and the height of the keyboard hurts my wrists.

My roommate plays talk radio from her phone speakers while she's in the kitchen, and it hurts my ears.

There's a man on the train who is always hitting on me. I pretend to be polite, but I hate talking to him.

There's never any vegetarian food for me to eat at my work's team lunch.

My mom always calls me on the phone without a warning.

My girlfriend assumes she can sleep over every night without asking.

I hate that: _____

I hate that: _____

I hate that: _____

I hate that: _____

Now that you've named elements of your current life that are unacceptable to you, you get to *engage* with reality and other people to address them. Some of your sources of discomfort may be ones you can fix on your own: by rearranging your living space, for example, or buying noise-canceling earplugs. You may also wish to practice self-advocacy skills by involving other people in finding solutions. Instead of spending hundreds of dollars on a completely new desk setup, for instance, you can ask your friends for office furniture that they're getting rid of (or use a local Facebook Marketplace page, queer exchange group, Buy Nothing group,[27] or Craigslist page to request free or cheap items). Sometimes the best way to maintain our boundaries is to remove ourselves from an upsetting situation, or ask a trusted person to run interference to help keep someone intrusive from entering our space. Reinforce for yourself that your needs matter enough to address, and that it's okay to assert yourself within another person's life.

Due to masking and a lack of accessibility, it's often difficult for us to recognize when we are uncomfortable. When we were young, other people didn't seem to care that we were in constant sensory pain, or that we were confused and in need of clear explanations, and so we've learned to quiet that inner voice that signals there's something that we need. Finding our no's involves mindfully attending to our bodies and emotions, and sharing with other people the moment we feel even mild discomfort: "It's a bit stuffy in this car, could we crack a window?" for instance, or "I don't have the energy to hear about your problems with your boyfriend right now, can we continue this conversation later?" By starting with very small, relatively nonthreatening no's, we work against the instinct that tells us a problem must be sufficiently large and disruptive before we deserve to bring it up. We gain new practice in taking initiative in our lives and build up a greater tolerance for the initial distress we might feel when we worry about being a "bother" to others.

For Quiana, listening to her no's led to her confronting how much pain and stress she was coping with nearly all the time. "I love music, but I don't love my posters falling off the walls and having sticky floors [because other people made a mess]," she says. Quiana was filled to the brim with resentment—dozens upon dozens of no's screaming inside her every single day that she didn't dare voice, and drowned in ketamine and weed cartridges instead.

Quiana was able to address some of her problems on her own. She realized that she didn't like throwing huge, hundred-people parties anymore, so she simply stopped organizing them. But that didn't keep people in the music scene from harassing her for invitations, and it didn't undo the damage done to her house and finances. For those problems, Quiana needed to more actively assert her boundaries—by engaging in conflict in an open way.

When another person disrespects us, hurts us, takes things from us, or repeatedly triggers us without showing any concern, it's time for us to voice our boundaries. An effective act of boundary-setting happens in three parts.

Engage in Productive Conflict

Setting a Boundary

Problem: Describe the situation or behavior pattern that is a problem, and why it bothers you.

"I don't like when you invite other people to our hangouts without even warning me. When we make plans together, I want to be able to know what to expect."

Request a change to the behavior.

"From now on, if you want to include any additional people in

Friendship

our plans, I need you to ask me first. I won't always say yes, because sometimes I don't want to be around crowds and want to spend quality time with just you."

Consequence: Explain what you will do in response if this boundary is violated.

"If I show up to dinner with you and see that there's suddenly five other people there, I will turn around and leave. If you can't honor this request, I will stop making plans with you."

Quiana might request that some of her closer friends come over and help clean her house or replace some of her damaged household items, with the condition that they won't be welcomed back into her space if they don't. For her stolen music equipment, she can request restitution or warn others so they don't get taken advantage of. Quiana has already chosen to dramatically cut back on her drug and alcohol intake, and not being pressured to use substances is one of her firmest boundaries; she blocks people if they cross it. With all these steps, Quiana is not aiming to control other people or to avoid all conflict entirely—instead, she is fighting for respect and a solution.

Preserving our boundaries is hard, emotionally threatening work. Researchers have observed that numerous neurodivergent people experience rejection sensitive dysphoria (or RSD), which they describe as a profound state of panic and self-blame in response to any sign of criticism or potential abandonment. RSD has not been formally studied in the scientific literature very well, though it is an extremely popular term in both parenting and therapeutic circles. The coiner of the term RSD, ADHD researcher William Dodson, viewed his patients as "*overly* reactive" to negative social feedback that "objectively seem[ed] rather minor,"[28] and his impression really caught on among family members and care providers who tended to already view us as hypersensitive complainers. Anyone from an Autistic child who is picked last for the kickball team and cries about it to the ADHDer who tells their therapist there's no use in applying for jobs may be evaluated as having RSD.

What Dodson and many other professionals fail to understand in their writing about RSD, however, is that for numerous Autistics, ADHDers, and other neurodivergent people, to be rejected is to experience unemployment, houselessness, possible starvation, illness, and enduring loneliness without end. We're not irrational for fearing that others will dislike us; we are accurately perceiving a *pattern* of being held to higher standards than everyone else, and then being disposed of when we fail to meet those standards. This pattern has wreaked havoc within our lives. It makes sense that we perceive a flat-faced expression as a scowl of hatred, and repeatedly ask our friends for reassurance that they aren't mad at us,[29] given these traumas.

If we are to live comfortably as our unmasked selves, we have to be able to express our deep insecurities at times, as well as assert our boundaries, and learn through repeated positive experiences that there actually are people in the world who care how we feel and want us to be comfortable. Quiana partied hard because she feared fulfilling the stereotype of the boring, rigid Autistic person who didn't have friends. Once she started unmasking and living at a somewhat quieter pace, she needed loved ones to show that they still found her interesting. Her twin sister was a massive help, keeping her company with bad sci-fi movies and road trips. So were the handful of friends who did stick around, finding themselves inspired by Quiana to examine their own substance use. One of them has become a regular running partner that Quiana sees nearly every morning. It was only by embracing conflict that Quiana was able to forge these rawer, realer connections. Aiming to be adored by everyone never brought her the enduring friendships that she wanted—but being a little bit more open and difficult to deal with did.

Unmasking introduces new social threats into our lives. Some friends and family members will scoff at our boundaries or repeatedly cross them, forcing us to meet them with consequences. Our true opinions will offend some people, and our needs will be too large or unusual for others to meet. It may be hard to believe at first, but all of this is a good thing. By pruning away the relationships that are dysfunctional, we create room in our lives for healthier ones. Certain fights are worth having and will improve the relationship—and some opinions we can disregard entirely.

Tolerate Discomfort
Letting Other People Be Wrong About You

We can't always control what other people think about us. When we've spent many years masking, we may feel as if smoothing over all disagreements and managing other people's expectations is our life's purpose, but this doesn't allow us space to lead our own lives. This exercise is designed to help you disconnect from the judgments of people who you will never be able to please.

> Think of a person in your life who often leaves you feeling disapproved of or judged. Write down their name below.
>
> _____
>
> Jot down your impressions of how this person sees you. For example, they might think you are lazy or impractical, or they might think you value all the wrong things.
>
> _____
> _____
>
> Answer the following questions:
>
> Has this person ever been able to admit to me that they were wrong about anything?
>
> _____
>
> Does this person try to learn more about me?
>
> _____

Does this person respect my opinions?

Do I respect how this person thinks?

Does this person behave in a way I think it's acceptable to behave?

If your answer to most of these questions is "no," then this is a person whose opinion cannot be changed by your actions. Here are some affirmations to help you remember that.

I have no reason to take the advice of someone whose opinions I don't respect.

This person's input isn't helpful.

I don't need to worry about what this person thinks.

There's nothing I can do; they've made up their mind.

Their feelings can't hurt me.

When this person tries to tell you how to act or what to feel, here are some quick responses you can provide before moving on.

"That's one way to think about it, I guess."

"I have this figured out, thanks."

"I'm glad that works for you."

"I'm so bored with this conversation; have you seen any good movies lately?"

"..." (No response *is* a response.)

So far in this chapter, we've looked at meeting potential new friends, connecting with others from a more authentic position, and navigating competing needs and points of view assertively and with self-respect. Following these steps can help us get better at identifying what really matters to us, and who might be capable of accompanying us on some of life's harder journeys. Now we'll wrap up the chapter by considering how we might deepen our friendships with the people who really mean a lot to us, to make them more vibrant and secure—because having a robust, loving support system is essential to leading a fully unmasked life.

Deepening Relationships and Asking for Help

In her book *The Art of Showing Up,* author and lifestyle editor Rachel Wilkerson Miller discusses the many roles that friendships can play in our lives, and the deep ache many people feel for profounder connections with friends.

Miller suggests that in addition to forming new friendships, "it's worth considering whether you actually need more friends, or whether you need closer friends." And given the research literature showing that many Autistics lack close friends, and that many of us rely upon more superficial, incidental forms of contact in order to feel connected (for example, by chatting with store clerks, mail delivery people, or classmates and co-workers who don't know us particularly well), it may be the case that for some of us, a broader social circle isn't what's needed so much as a *deeper* one. That was certainly Quiana's experience when she moved away from party organizing and into more intimate one-on-one interactions.

If you've been following the advice from earlier in this chapter, then you've been able to put yourself out into the social world more frequently and with greater honesty, and by now you may have identified a few potential friends. You've probably also met a lot of people who you feel uncertain about and may not wish to pursue friendship with further. Remember that you get to play an active role in forming your own community, and that you don't have to get along with every person you meet. Even if another person is nice to you, you are not obligated to spend time with them.

You can identify potential close friends by asking yourself questions like these:

> Who am I intrigued to learn more about?
>
> Who makes me laugh or feel at ease?
>
> Who am I constantly learning new things from?
>
> Who shows, in their words and behavior, that they genuinely like who I am?
>
> How would I like to spend more of my time, and who do I want to join me?

By reflecting on questions like these, we can notice the ways in which our current social lives might be lacking, even if we are fortunate enough to have loving people already around us. For instance, as I moved into my midthirties, I noticed that many of my friends were becoming more retiring sorts who preferred to stay home watching movies or playing video games rather than venturing out. Most of them are Autistic people for whom unmasking has led to an embrace of life's quieter side. But my experience of unmasking has sometimes been the opposite—the more real I am around other people, the less drained I am by socializing, and the more I want to venture out of the house. I've become a lot more extroverted in recent years, and with that change has come a need for friends who like going to concerts, shows, conventions, and even sex parties.

It's a great comfort to me that I now have reliable people in my life that I can go dancing and cruising with, and share a heartfelt moment with on the sidewalk outside the bar. I also have friends that matter deeply to me but whom I see fairly casually, for the occasional game night or trip. The burden to keep the conversation going is low in these relationships; we can simply share activities together without pressure. Miller describes the importance of what she calls *deep shallow* friendships—but really, they're not shallow at all. They're not defined by turmoil and don't require intense emotional processing most of the time, but they hold a consistent place in our lives and allow us to enjoy shared experiences regularly. My hyper-analytical Autistic self used to think I could only be friends with someone who shared all my intellectual pursuits and emotional scars, and who wanted to talk about those weighty subjects all the time. Now I recognize that having friends who can help me lose my self-consciousness on the dance floor is equally important.

Intimacy and ease can both be very difficult qualities for Autistic people to cultivate in our friendships. For example, Itzel, an Autistic couples therapist, says they used to think of themself as a very candid person, but "every personal detail I shared with people was kind of sanitized and already processed. I was incredibly self-aware. I would joke about my trauma and not feel it, you know?" After they started unmasking, Itzel began fantasizing about having friends that would simply hold them as they cried. But most of their loved ones were like them, sarcastic types who were brutally honest but kept feelings at arm's length. Itzel decided they'd need to introduce more mushiness and emotional expression into their life. So they began going to cuddle parties and began pushing their existing close friends to get a bit more real with them.

If you have met people that you'd like to pursue a closer connection with, Miller recommends explicitly telling them that you are looking to make new friends. "So many people breathe a sigh of relief at that kind of statement and confess that they too want to make new friends and have been struggling with it," she writes.[30] This is an especially encouraging message given that Miller's book was written for a general audience, not just Autistics! Though the rules of neuroconformity dictate that we are never to embarrass ourselves by admitting we require social connection, the truth is that non-Autistic people also feel lonely and insecure and need reassurance that it's okay to make an approach. Though we have been conditioned to see ourselves as social incompetents, Autistic people can make the first move by telling another person explicitly if we'd like to be friends with them, and use our divergent, creative abilities to think up exciting new ways we can spend time together.

Conventional "adult" forms of socializing don't always hold much appeal for Autistics. Restaurants are expensive to visit, noisy, unpredictable, and frequently built upon a business model that mistreats cooks and service staff while perplexing neurodivergent people on either side of the labor equation with elaborate social rules.[31] Many of us pointedly do not want to sit perfectly still for an hour or two at a table, with a companion across from us, staring us in the face. Though some Autistics like me do crave intense sensory input in some forms, others loathe crowded rooms with echoey acoustics, and may not wish to visit sporting events, concerts, or popular bars. Since we tend to be poorer than our nondisabled peers, Autistics frequently lack the means to go on elaborate vacations, or to visit museums, spas, or art exhibits, and may be excluded due to the dress code and behavioral expectations of many such spaces. We have to get inventive about our social plans, navigating budget concerns, sensory complaints, and the unique nature of our interests, which aren't generally catered to.

This is where the powerful social skill of creativity comes in—alongside the one of transgression. Neurodivergent people are canny social engineers, though we often don't get credit for it; we have built collective movements for disabled liberation, organized all manner of conferences and conventions, and programmed open-source digital infrastructure that allows us to reach one another from afar. So if you are seeking to improve the quality and intensity of your friendships, or simply courting a new friend, you can think up alternative ways to bond that aren't what mainstream adult society often views as ideal.

In 2018, my friend Jess started holding regular "productivity circles" at their apartment in Chicago. Every Sunday afternoon, a rotating cast of friends gathered to draw comics, compose orchestral music, paint watercolors, write essays, do taxes, and complete other tasks we'd been struggling to find the motivation for. The rules of neurotypicality dictate that an adult person ought to be not only fully self-sufficient but fully self-motivated. Today, needing a friend around to get the dishes done or to complete one's homework is taken as a sign of weakness or diagnosed as "executive dysfunction."[32] But numerous neurodivergent thinkers such as Ayesha Khan, Jesse Meadows, and Marta Rose have critiqued the concept of executive dysfunction,[33] arguing that historically, humans have always needed to work together to complete difficult and boring tasks. Research into the *social facilitation effect* demonstrates that just about everyone's performance improves when we feel that our hard work is shared and the fruits of it recognized by other people.[34] Jess is an ADHDer, and nearly everyone who attended their productivity circles was neurodivergent. During a period when motivation was hard to find in many of our lives, we helped each other do work that was meaningful to us.

Neurodivergent people frequently make a social event out of trading support. Clutter-oblivious ADHDers invite their more tactile Autistic friends over to untangle bundles of electrical cords, and flavor-sensitive supertasters invite their anosmic (non-smelling) friends over for nutritious but bland home-cooked meals. That same non-smelling buddy can take out the garbage while an energetic friend self-stimulates by painting the living room a nice, muted color that will soothe their roommate's anxiety. Many Autistics take turns info dumping about our special interests, even organizing PowerPoint parties where we each get a time block to teach the crowd about midcentury modern furniture, Ming dynasty architecture, or fan fiction inspired by the show *Riverdale*. Inviting a friend over to simply sit on the couch together wordlessly playing video games or napping is a crucial stage of intimacy-building in many neurodivergent friendships. Taking day trips to visit hobby stores together can feel like embarking on a grand adventure.

There's truly no limit to the ways we can bond; all we need to do is identify a need or a source of pleasure in our life, and find a way to open that inner experience up to others. Below is an exercise to get you thinking creatively about how you might want to include new friends (or more deeply include your current friends) in your life.

Create Connection
Finding Neurodivergent-Friendly Ways to Interact

Parallel Play	Sitting near one another (or on a video call) to read books, play video games, enjoy hobbies, scroll through social media, or stim.

Create Connection
Finding Neurodivergent-Friendly Ways to Interact

Watch Parties	Gathering either online or in person to watch and react to movies, TV shows, a curated YouTube playlist, or a livestream.
Support Swapping	Trading responsibilities to tackle one another's household chores, paperwork, or errands, based on each person's strengths and sensitivities.
Productivity Accountability	Meeting regularly (online or in person) to work at the same time on necessary but boring tasks or creative projects.
Co-Napping	Coming together (either physically or online) to cuddle, meditate, or sleep, potentially with soothing music or background noise playing and dim lights.
Shared Wandering (or Elopement)[35]	Exploring a nature reserve, graveyard, public park, museum, or mall with one another, following your natural curiosity while sharing the responsibility of not getting lost.
No-Eye-Contact Conversation	Speaking to one another in a voice call, or while playing a competitive video game, driving in a vehicle, working in the garden, or completing any other stimulating task that removes the pressure to make eye contact.
No-Conversation Hangouts	Spending time together playing a sport or a game, watching a movie, or otherwise remaining occupied, but with zero expectation of verbal conversation. Any communication that does need to happen can occur via note or text.
Exchanging Messages and Gifts	Writing letters or lengthy emails, sending one another handmade crafts or home-cooked food, sharing artistic creations or therapy notes with one another.
Scripted, Structured Interactions	Performing in a play, learning dance choreography, playing a role in a tabletop role-playing game, participating in a conference, or some other form of interaction where the rules of social engagement are clear and explicit.
Think up your own:	

These are just a few examples of unconventional ways that Autistic people tend to socialize, and you can tailor them or invent your own to fit your particular needs. For example, because Itzel specifically knew that they needed greater emotional connection in their life, they asked a friend over to listen to sad music and cry.

"I took a risk, because I wasn't sure whether she'd think that idea was *insane*," Itzel says. But in this case, it worked. They both brought their favorite heartstring-pulling albums and lay down on blankets in the dark to listen to them and reflect about lost loves, dead relatives, and the passage of time. Afterward, Itzel says, "I was like, *Oof, I need a cigarette.*" They'd never really opened themself up to doing something so potentially embarrassing in front of another person before. It was a major step forward in their unmasking journey—enough to keep them working toward greater growth and openness even when some of their other friends turned down the "cry party" invites. "It's not for everyone," Itzel says, "and I really get that."

After indicating to someone that you'd like to spend some quality time with them and getting an encouraging response, you can take steps to build greater intimacy in your friendship as a whole. Diane Weston, an expert in conversation techniques and language, offers a three-step process to improve the closeness of your new relationships, represented with the acronym ARE:

> Anchor: Comment on your shared experience or surroundings.
>
> Reveal: Use the anchor to introduce something personal about yourself.
>
> Encourage: Invite the other person to respond or reveal something about themself.

For example, let's say that I have a friend with whom I play video games regularly but wish I knew a little better. I might anchor our interaction by making a comment about the game we're playing: "I love collaborative multiplayer games like this, there's something so clever about the puzzle design." Then I could use that observation to nudge our conversation into a more emotionally forthright place: "When I was a teen, my mom and I played this collaborative game for the PlayStation 2 called *The Adventures of Cookie & Cream*. She bought us the game during a really difficult time in my life, when I was getting in trouble at school a lot, and almost got arrested. It was a really meaningful gesture to show that while she was mad at me, she wanted to spend time with me, and we were still on the same team." Having made that vulnerable disclosure, I can now gently shift the attention to my conversation partner and encourage them to be as open with me as they like. "What about you? Have you ever bonded with someone over a game?" My friend is now free to share a special memory with me, but they get to choose how revealing of an answer they are comfortable giving.

In her writing on the art of small talk, Diane Weston recommends that people improve the depth of their conversations by bringing up the topics of family, work, recreation, and dreams[36]—but this is a place where advice that might make sense under neurotypical norms won't serve a neurodivergent audience. Few Autistic people have full-time jobs, let alone remotely fulfilling ones, and we tend to have tense relationships with our families, who might not understand us or who may project onto us any ashamed feelings they have about signs of neurodivergence in themselves. This means that asking our friends about their work or family lives directly may lead to the conversation veering into quite unhappy territory. If both parties feel comfortable delving into how hopeless they feel about the job market, or how abusive their fathers once were, then broaching these subjects may help develop closeness. But it's important to provide a respectful off-ramp from any conversation a person might not wish to participate in, or give them space for a break.

One excellent way to propose a new activity or line of discussion without pressuring another person is to ask either/or questions, rather than questions that must be answered with a yes or a no.[37] Many people find saying no difficult for fear of seeming negative; instead of asking "Do you mind talking about this serious subject?" you can ask "Do you want to continue talking about our childhoods, *or* do you want to get started making the cupcakes?"

Generally speaking, Autistic people prize honesty, and we may sometimes blurt out information we're not actually comfortable sharing or that might be risky to disclose. As we work on deepening our friendships and asking more directly for the help we need (and being asked in return), it's important to remind ourselves of this simple principle: we are always allowed to end a conversation, or to leave if it makes us uncomfortable. To that end, here are a couple of scripts you can practice when you find yourself feeling intruded upon, emotionally exhausted, or just uneasy.

Transgress Neurotypical Norms

You *always* have the right to end an interaction. Here are some statements you can use to protect that right.

> "I can't think about this subject anymore right now. Let's talk about something lighter."
>
> "The energy of this discussion has gotten too intense for me. I need a break."
>
> "I can give you an answer to that question, but I need [some time / to be able to write it down]."
>
> "This is a very personal subject for me, I hope you understand I'd prefer not to talk about it."
>
> "I really have to go, I'll talk to you tomorrow."

As an alternative to discussing heavier, more triggering topics, focusing a conversation on the subjects of recreation and dreams can foster warm feelings and trust without putting either yourself or your conversation partner in the emotional hot seat. It's rare that our society gives adults the room to be playful or to express longing, and so by asking another person about their most cherished hobbies or their greatest fantasies you may be able to unlock a youthful, unabashed side of them that rarely gets noticed. I love speaking to even my more neuroconforming friends about the communal farms they want to establish one day, or the boat trips they're aching to take all around the world. Many of them fear that their profoundest dreams are impractical or make them sound childish—but when we let go of our insecure adult filters and let ourselves truly imagine a rewarding life, we're doing a lot to unmask not just ourselves but our worlds. I've also learned a lot about whole realms of art and craft that I'd known nothing about simply by inquiring about a person's hobbies. Every single person on the planet is far more interesting than a few minutes of stilted, masked small talk might initially lead you to believe—and it's worth pushing past the superficial veneer to find the real them if you can.

I think masked Autistics might underestimate how unheard many nondisabled people feel. Many of them have also been abused or silenced and made to feel ashamed of their passions and true feelings. Together, we can overcome these insecurities, shift the social norms, deepen our conversations, and ultimately build better communities that support us all. Unmasking for life means unburdening ourselves of the pressure to constantly seem polite and normal. It also means making space in our lives for the fullness of others' messy, strange humanity, too.

In the next chapter, we will continue to apply the five core skills for unmasking to our relationships, focusing this time on the bonds that tend to be the most fraught with baggage and generational trauma: our families. So many neurodivergent people were raised by families that didn't know how to care for our unique needs or honor our gifts—even if some of our relatives were likely disabled in similar ways themselves. To continue to expand in our unmasking, we have to reset unproductive family dynamics, educate the loved ones who are open to learning more about neurodiversity, and reimagine what family even means.

Family

The diagnosis of one Autistic person within a family often unleashes a chain reaction throughout the entire family system, with some relatives embracing the new revelation, educating themselves eagerly on the topic, and perhaps even coming to apply the Autistic label to themselves, and others strongly rejecting the stigma that the Autism label carries and refusing to reexamine old family dynamics through a neurodivergent lens.

My own journey of Autistic self-discovery was set into motion when a cousin was first assessed, and numerous other Autistic adults that I have interviewed have similarly discovered their Autism following the diagnosis of a child, parent, sibling, or cousin. The revelation that many members of my family were likely Autistic came with considerable controversy: after I came out as Autistic and speculated in my writing that my grandfather George had been as well, an uncle reacted with embarrassment and asked my mother why I felt comfortable issuing such a judgment on the family publicly. He viewed my proudly brandishing the Autism label as something of an attack, and wondered if other relatives were angry at me speaking openly about our potentially shared disability, too. This was quickly shut down once my grandmother read a bit more about what Autism was and agreed that, yes, her late husband who spent hours looking at satellite photos of his own house on Google Maps, who monologued about sports facts and butterfly migratory patterns endlessly, and whose idea of "letting loose" had been drinking a single beer slowly and napping in his chair had indeed been Autistic as hell.

I have been relatively lucky; after my grandmother was on board with the idea of Autism running in our family, she and my mother were open to further self-educating on the topic and picked up my first book about Autism. On family trips, my mother started emphasizing to me that I could take time for myself to decompress whenever I needed and expressed regret about not having understood my needs when I was younger. I am completely at peace with the fact that my relatives couldn't have known much about Autism back in the 1990s, when I was a child, and that they've chosen to be accepting toward me now. Still, I remember being pushed to go outside and socialize with neighbor kids by parents who were concerned I was friendless, which left me feeling pitiful. I recall my sister being held down and forced to brush her teeth because she detested doing it so much, and developing insecurities around food because adults criticized a "pickiness" that meets all the criteria for Avoidant/Restrictive Food Intake Disorder (or ARFID, which is highly correlated with Autism).[1] There were times when my relatives didn't understand what a meltdown was and upbraided me for crying or mocked me for having childish interests, not realizing what they were doing. I had to go entirely no-contact with my father when I was eighteen because of issues with how he treated me, and he died shortly thereafter; the impact of that estrangement lingers to this day. Forgiveness and mourning do not eliminate the long-term effects these experiences had on me. But I try to relate to my relatives as they are in the present, rather than reacting from the trauma of my past. Of course, we always retain the option not to maintain relationships that hurt us at all.

Being one of the first-identified Autistic people within a family introduces all kinds of hard conversations about the flawed coping strategies we were taught as children, the sensory complaints we used to voice that long went ignored, the expectations our parents set for us that weren't realistic given our limitations and abilities, and what a truly meaningful familial relationship might look like, if we even want to have one. Once we have begun to unmask and gotten better acquainted with our needs, we may have fresh demands that family members who have known us for decades might resist. Or we may find that, despite all our best efforts to live in a more liberated, authentic way, within our families we are still discouraged from speaking up or diverging from societal norms due to issues within the family system as a whole.

If we have children, we also have to figure out how to parent and build family in ways that affirm neurodivergence and avoid causing future generations the shame and confusion we have endured. Our own past traumas and experiences of rejection may get dredged back up by the kids around us, or we may be horrified to discover that we still harbor some anti-Autistic attitudes that bleed into how we treat family during their toughest moments. Throughout our unmasking journeys, we may hold ourselves responsible for educating our relatives about Autism and helping them unpack their prejudices against disabled people—even though we've been on the receiving end of such prejudices from them in the past. It can be difficult to determine how much effort and compassion are worth extending to our families—where the line between patiently advocating for change ends, and enduring further abuse begins.

Genetics research shows that Autism runs in families, but it is not determined by any single gene.[2] Rather than having one straightforward biological "cause," Autism is in fact linked to a variety of different genetic pathways, as well as some differences in how the brain and synapses develop that genetics can't explain.[3] We do see in research, however, that Autism is highly heritable, as are Autism spectrum traits among the undiagnosed.[4] What this means in practice is that if we are Autistic, many of our biological relatives may share some of the markers and genetic factors that resulted in us being Autistic, but these might manifest in completely different ways for them, or they might share numerous traits with us without fully wanting to identify as Autistic. Our family members' personalities and struggles can mirror ours, but the reflection we see might seem somewhat distorted—either because they're more capable of neuroconforming than we are, or because they've been masking their disability for longer than we have and grew up in a time even more hostile to disability.

Of course, as we review such research, we should always remember that Autism is pervasively underdiagnosed in women, people of color, queer people, people in poverty, and older people—and that such groups are more likely to have been misdiagnosed with some other mental health label instead, or to be treated as if their needs do not matter. Our relatives with "subclinical" Autism spectrum traits may feel ashamed to see us openly stimming because they were beaten for far smaller acts of weirdness when they were kids, or they may find it "unfair" that we live on disability benefits because they were forced to work all their lives. Navigating these complex forces with grace while still maintaining our ability to unmask is tricky, and it requires the full marshaling of our five core skills of acceptance, engagement, transgression, tolerance, and creativity.

Aisha struggles to explain to her much older, deeply masked mother, Bettie, that she doesn't force her own neurodivergent children to smile, hug unfamiliar adults, or go to family events that make them uncomfortable. As an older Black woman who vividly remembers an era of even more overt systemic racism than the one we live in now, Bettie had raised Aisha to grin and bear every single one of these unpleasant experiences, and also forced her children to dress up in stiffly starched, presentable clothing so that they'd always be seen in the best possible light. Bettie had good reason to think that teaching her children to conform to high standards of respectability was keeping her children safe. But because Aisha doesn't do that, her mother sees her as a slob and screwup.

Being trained to be respectable hasn't served Aisha well. For many years she believed herself to be a straight woman—or rather, she thought she had no choice but to be one. She got married to a wealthy software developer, moved to the suburbs, and had kids. Bettie approved of her daughter's new life, thinking that at last her unpredictable Autistic child had succeeded in assimilating to mainstream society. Then Aisha's life disintegrated when she finally realized that she was attracted to women and couldn't handle living far away from the city. Her divorce was a protracted, gradual process, beginning with Aisha moving out and being demonized by her husband for "running away." She allowed her ex to blame her for the divorce so that she'd be able to leave with minimal conflict. Still, she was reprimanded by her mother and her sister for "breaking" her family, "ruining" her finances, and "dooming" herself to a lifetime alone.

"I leapt from security and plummeted into the abyss," Aisha says of her mother's impression of her. There is no script for what the rest of her life should look like.

Recently, Aisha's eldest daughter was also diagnosed with Autism and ADHD. Now Aisha is faced with the immense challenge of raising her daughter to have pride in her neurodivergence and to stand up for her autonomy, while Aisha also works on reparenting and unmasking herself from within a family where all signs of neurodivergence have only ever been punished.

This chapter will explore how unmasking Autistic people can manage their families: from transgressing the demands and expectations of parents, to honoring the needs of Autistic kids within the family structure, to tolerating the internalized stigma of our still-masked Autistic relatives, to finding space when our loved ones mistreat us. It will also provide tools for reimagining what family looks like for those of us who have experienced familial abuse, or have never been served by the nuclear family ideal. In addition, it will provide concrete strategies and skills for engaging with one's family as a realized and unmasked Autistic—not only to help soothe the wounds of the past but also to help our loved ones heal and prevent future generations from suffering in the ways that we did.

The Masked Autistic Family

Jared is pretty damn certain his eighty-year-old father is Autistic.

"When we were kids, we'd go to the grocery store with Dad, and sometimes he'd suddenly stop in the middle of the aisle and then just storm out the door and drive home, leaving us behind," he tells me. "He would be filled with rage after. Looking back at it now, I can see he was getting overwhelmed from all the sensory things going on."

When Jared was a kid in the 1970s, nobody knew about sensory issues and Autism. His only frame for understanding his father's actions back then was to be terrified of his unpredictable meltdowns. Today,

Jared and his sister can discuss their father's unusual quirks and explosions and make sense of them, which has helped them to feel more compassion. But their father has never had the chance to actually understand or to make amends for his own behavior, and he's largely "coped" with his likely neurodivergence by isolating himself.

Instead of hiring a home health aide to assist with overstimulating errands, Jared's dad subsists on cold sandwiches and beer from his favorite tiny, dimly lit corner store. Though they only live about fifteen miles apart, Jared's dad has never visited Jared's house. He says he doesn't like the "feel" of the highway that leads there, and that it's bad for his truck, which he adores and lavishes with more affection than he's ever given his kids. Jared does his best to love his father and understand him, while still engaging him in conversation and encouraging him to broaden his comfort zone where he can.

"But it's very heartbreaking!" Jared says emphatically. "I want to sit him down and make him see that he needs help."

Older generations of undiscovered Autistic people often cling to the masking strategies they believe helped them get by in the even more inhospitable world of the past, and they may harshly judge their children and grandchildren for embarking on the messy, revealing but ultimately worthwhile journey of unmasking themselves. They also may feel threatened by their unmasked children and grandchildren's attempts to get them to open up because they associate being hidden with maintaining safety.

In speaking to a variety of unmasking Autistics about their families, and from reviewing the literature, I have observed that masking among older generations of neurodivergent people tends to take on a couple of different forms. Autistics who have masked their disability for a half century or more have often had to develop themselves and their lives *around* the handful of coping strategies they had available to them, regardless of whether those strategies worked all that well, and may have clung to one particular external goal (such as making a lot of money or avoiding any vulnerability whatsoever) to make sense of their own motives and ignored needs. Accordingly, long-term masked Autism can often present in one of the following subtypes.

Long-Term Masked Autism
Common Subtypes

Mask Type	Example Behaviors	Primary Motivation
Withdrawn	• Closing themselves off in a bedroom or office during all their free time. • Not discussing their feelings or inquiring into others' feelings. • Pursuing one or two safe, solitary special interests. • Disinterest in maintaining their physical or mental health.	To prevent overwhelm and not risk emotional exposure.
Explosive	• Seemingly unpredictable mood swings and verbal or physical outbursts. • Binge drinking, gambling, or other risky forms of sensation-seeking. • Viewing any questions or concerns voiced by other people as a form of attack. • Seeming to provoke other people to dislike them as a way to claim personal space.	To unload dysregulated emotions and prevent others from controlling them.
Rigid and Controlling	• Demanding their children or partners meet their standards of behavior, cleanliness, and presentation. • Regarding alternative points of view as morally wrong or an attack. • Discomfort around, or outright hostility toward, people with competing value systems. • An interpersonal pattern of passive aggression and heavy criticism.	To rein in an unpredictable world and render it explicable and safe.

Long-Term Masked Autism
Common Subtypes

Mask Type	Example Behaviors	Primary Motivation
Codependent	• Moving from one long-term, serious relationship to another, without any significant breaks. • Altering their identity and lifestyle to accommodate their current partner, no matter how contradictory their various past selves might seem to be. • Attempting to manage the emotional reactions of others at all times, and not tolerating disagreement or unhappiness. • Confusion about who they are, how they feel, and what is important to them.	To meet the need for closeness and stability and not risk rejection.
Workaholic	• Identifying excessively with their professional identity, at the expense of the rest of their lives. • Working long hours without regard for familial obligations or health. • Expecting their children or other loved ones to be high-achieving according to their standards. • Viewing any illness or life challenge as an inexcusable attack on their productivity.	To justify their existence to others and ensure their financial security.
Addicted and Dissociated	• Reliance upon drugs, alcohol, or some other compulsive behavior in order to self-regulate. • Retreating from difficult emotions or experiences using escapism, denial, or their preferred substance. • Denial of reality or responsibility when something bad has happened or they have done something wrong. • Lacking any interest in regular life, and having no life pursuits they find fulfilling.	To avoid feeling pain or experiencing conflict.

You might notice that these profiles of long-term masked Autism reflect how a person's behavior might look to us from the outside, as their unmasking children or grandchildren. This comes with the same problems that occur when psychiatrists and psychologists judge us Autistics from the outside. What looks like an infuriating level of avoidance and social isolation to us might be, for our parents, the only viable way to narrow the world down to a manageable amount of stimuli. What we disparage as substance abuse may have been the least harmful way to reduce anxiety that a relative ever knew. In evaluating the behavior of other people and the impact it's had on your family, you will inevitably show bias. But remember that the goal here is not for us to heal our relatives (who may not even want healing) but to more effectively navigate our relationships.

If our primary goal is to unmask for life, then taking our own side does become necessary to a degree. Recognizing that our loved ones' behaviors have reasons behind them and occur within a broader social context can help us make peace with our pasts and allow us to behave more compassionately toward them. It can also aid us in setting appropriate expectations—because a parent who has never discussed any emotions with us will never become the affectionate mother or father of our dreams. Understanding another person's point of view does not justify any pain they may have caused us, particularly when we were young and dependent upon them, and it's not a violation of the relationship for us to have our own negative feelings about the past. We can take an interest in our relatives' well-being while still dwelling firmly within our own perspectives.

You can start to unmask family relationships by practicing the skill of acceptance and acknowledging that you are allowed to keep growing, even if that means growing away from where your family dwells. Improving your authenticity, self-awareness, and self-advocacy skills may necessarily drive you away from loved ones who are not so accepting of you or themselves, and while this is sad, it doesn't mean you have betrayed anybody or done anything wrong. It also offers them the possibility to examine their assumptions and find new ways of relating to others, too. Here are some affirmations to repeat to yourself, should you find yourself feeling guilty about any friction that your unmasking might introduce.

Accepting Change
Affirmations for Growing Away from Your Family

> I am allowed to have different values than my family has.
>
> My life is for me to live, not for my parents or grandparents.
>
> The people who raised me are not perfect, and it's not a betrayal for me to notice their flaws.
>
> I am an adult now, and I don't need the approval of my family to survive.
>
> I know better than my family about a lot of things.
>
> I am not controlled by my family member's disapproval.
>
> Though I might wish I had a closer relationship with my family, there are some factors I just can't control.
>
> I've never had the family I wanted, but I'll be okay even if I never do.

In her books on emotionally immature parents, therapist Lindsay Gibson speaks about encouraging her patients to differentiate their own points of view from those of the sometimes diminishing, invalidating people who raised them. Not all emotionally immature parents are neurodivergent, at least not as Gibson describes them, but like many deeply masked people, they avoid intimacy, struggle to accept responsibility for any harm that they've caused, and may mock their children for differences of opinion. Accordingly, many of the strategies Gibson outlines for dealing with emotionally immature parents also apply quite clearly to those of us on unmasking journeys with unaccepting relatives.

Gibson says that short visits with more challenging and critical loved ones can help ensure that everyone remains on their best behavior,[5] and prevent us from slipping into old patterns that we wish to leave behind. Taking adequate time and space away from our relatives can help us to develop our own value systems that aren't shaped by constant worries about what they might think of us, and can also help us feel less bitter.

"During contacts with emotionally immature parents, don't wait for them to show an interest in you," Gibson writes. "You'll feel less drained if you plan things to do that don't involve trying to have a conversation . . . [Meals, games, or puzzles] can lead to a sense of conviviality that may not be achieved through conversation attempts."[6]

Jared has already arrived at this insight in his dealings with his father. Once per week, Jared drives up to his father's house so they can watch golf and play cards. If his father complains about his loneliness or demands to know why Jared does not visit more often, Jared reminds him that he's welcome to visit as often as he likes. He also reminds his father that he and his sister have offered to hire a home health aide to assist him around the house. "But I can't make him accept help he doesn't want," Jared says with a sigh.

Unmasking has led Jared to become a more emotionally effusive and sensitive person than his father knows how to accept. Jared cries easily, and is sentimental and physically affectionate, and he knows that making these changes has vastly improved his own life. His mental health is better, his romantic relationships are more loving, and he can look ahead in his life with a spirit of hope rather than feeling depressed all the time, as he did back when he was masking as a taciturn, masculine sort of person. But his father doesn't have many nice things to say about touchy, feminine men, and the only way to preserve his newfound happiness is for Jared to create a loving distance between the both of them.

Gibson also stresses that as adults, we have the power to shape our relationships to our family members. We don't have to accept their lectures about how they think our lives should be, or endure political rants that go against our beliefs. Instead, we can engage on our own terms, taking charge of our interactions with agency and directness.

"You could start by asking if [your relative] would listen to you for just ten minutes, setting up a mini-foundation for a more meaningful interaction," Gibson writes.[7] "When your ten minutes is up, thank them for listening so well and tell them how much you enjoyed talking to them. Ask if they want to tell you anything, but if they don't, that can be the end of the interaction." She also suggests probing more deeply into offhand statements our loved ones make, for example by asking them what they enjoyed about a television show they just watched or inviting them to share stories from their youth. These gentle gestures toward depth can sometimes be mild enough that we get a bit of the authenticity we'd desperately like to see as unmaskers, while still granting them enough control to feel safe.

When I spoke with Jared about his father, I shared some of these strategies with him and asked his thoughts. His eyes lit up at the idea that he could take charge of how he and his father relate. "I can ask Dad to look at the photo album with me for a few minutes during our visits," he says. "I'm so aware that he won't be around forever, but what quality time can mean for us is so limited."

When we unmask our once-hidden disabilities, we choose approving of ourselves over being approved of by others. If our families have been discouraging toward our sensitivities, stimming, nonconforming behavior, or unusual lifestyles, then we may have to sacrifice elements of our relationships with them in order to be ourselves. With time, some family members may realize that they miss our close presence in their lives so much that they're willing to change their behavior and show us greater acceptance, but this outcome is never guaranteed. So, before we move forward into discussing what it will take to establish new relationship patterns with our relatives, let's briefly pause to accept the potential of loss.

Accepting Loss
When Unmasking Changes the Relationship Dynamic

By unmasking yourself, you may lose some or all of the following from your family relationship.

- Time together
- Feelings of emotional closeness
- Frequency of contact
- Approval
- Praise
- Financial support
- Housing
- Childcare support
- The ability to share in memories together
- Inclusion in family traditions
- Inheritance of family wealth and possessions
- Inclusion in family burial plots or generational records

As you review this list, contemplate which losses you find acceptable, which you will need to build an alternative to, and which you find so unacceptable that you'll endure some discomfort to maintain. It's okay if you can't stand firm in your boundaries in all ways, at all times, particularly if you are currently financially dependent upon your family. You are in charge of your priorities, and we each have to juggle practical concerns alongside emotional truths as we work on building lives that allow us to live comfortably with our disabilities. Once you know the changes you are interested in making within your family dynamic, and the losses that you are comfortable incurring, it's time to engage with your family in a completely new way, enforcing some of your newfound boundaries.

Establishing New Familial Patterns as an Autistic Adult

Discovering one's disability status usually comes with the revelation of previously ignored needs and boundaries. Many newly self-realized Autistics figure out that they've always needed far more time alone than they've ever been allowed by their families, for example, or that decades of both full-time work and raising a child simply are not in the cards for them. If an unmasking Autistic person does decide that they want to have children or build a family, they're likely to need additional accommodations that the average parent doesn't receive, and might want to request financial support or childcare from their relatives. Making the necessary changes in one's life to accommodate neurodivergence almost always requires resetting the expectations of family members who have known and judged us by the standards of a neurotypical.

If we wish to change how our family members relate to us (and if we have reason to believe they are *open* to change), we should begin by engaging in education. Providing our loved ones with books, articles, and videos about Autism that are created by Autistic people (or books about ADHD written by ADHDers, and so on) can slowly expand their understanding of disability and help them see us as members of a diverse group that is deserving of support, rather than sick people in need of a cure.

In my earlier professional life, my primary research specialty was intellectual humility and the changing of other people's attitudes. I found this work to be incredibly discouraging because, as it turns out, we cannot force other people to alter their attitudes, and most people are frustratingly closed off to change.[8] Psychological research consistently shows that attitude change is a very slow process, when it happens at all; people must consume a lot of information that runs counter to their existing views and think on it carefully, in a receptive and nonbiased fashion, before they will arrive at a new position.[9] Most people also require some emotional or social motivation for changing their perspective. Logical arguments don't generally work, and most people are not swayed by facts alone.[10]

I share all of this to help you manage your expectations, and to encourage you to approach educating your relatives with patient detachment. If your grandmother believes that kids today are self-diagnosing with Autism because they want to feel "special" and spend too much time on TikTok, a single conversation will not convince her to honor your self-identification. You still get to live proudly as a self-realized Autistic. If stoicism and self-denial have been the guiding principles of your father's life, he will have a difficult time respecting that your Autistic children eat dinner alone in their rooms with the TV on. Your kids still have the right to do what they need. Your life remains yours to live, even if your relatives are skeptical or say cruel things about it. When they complain, remind them that you have offered them resources to help them understand, and that you would be so grateful if they would read or listen.

Try to present these efforts as a way to make your relatives' lives easier, rather than treating it like homework for them, and don't bombard them with too much information at once, which might cause overwhelm. You can also express gratitude if they do show interest, even if it's not to the degree you might want. Once they have self-educated a bit, ask for their thoughts and questions.

Introducing family members to actually Autistic (or otherwise neurodivergent) people in real life can further deepen their learning. By bringing an Autistic friend around for Christmas or your birthday party, you're also giving yourself some emotional backup if anyone in your family gives you grief for wearing headphones or needing to take a walk. More open-minded relatives can also be invited to attend an Autistic Self Advocacy Network (ASAN) chapter meeting or similar group, or even a protest against more stigmatizing organizations like Autism Speaks. Think of your loved ones as slowly being moved down a funnel toward greater Autism acceptance; wherever they are currently located, do what feels manageable to encourage them along.

Here is a general list of tips for educating your loved ones about Autism, and some suggested resources you can use.

Engage in Education
Helping Your Loved Ones "Get" Autism

1. Give your loved ones materials on Autism that have been created by actually Autistic voices. Try not to overload them with too many at once. One book and one video at a time is a good place to start.

2. Explain why it matters to you that they educate themselves. For example, you might say, "This book really helped me to take better care of myself. I think you'd understand what I've been going through better if you read it."

3. Give your loved one some time to learn at their own pace. When you can feel a fight beginning, try telling them that you hope they will learn more on the subject, and that you can wait to have a conversation until they have.

4. Ask your relative questions about what they have learned. Share your favorite part of the book or video, and ask them to do the same. Explain how a particular resource changed your own viewpoints, without pushing them to agree with you.

Do not: Tell a relative what to think or believe, criticize them for not learning "quickly enough," assume that they share all the same knowledge and vocabulary that you do, or take their resistance as a reason to doubt your own experience.

Suggested Resources

Books

Strong Female Character by Fern Brady

Uncomfortable Labels: My Life as a Gay Autistic Trans Woman by Laura Kate Dale

We're Not Broken: Changing the Autism Conversation by Eric Garcia

Ido in Autismland by Ido Kedar

I Overcame My Autism and All I Got Was This Lousy Anxiety Disorder: A Memoir by Sarah Kurchak

The Secret Life of a Black Aspie by Anand Prahlad

YouTube Videos

TikTok Gave Me Autism: The Politics of Self Diagnosis by Alexander Avila

Stop Gatekeeping Mental Disorders by Elliot Sang

Unmasking After Late Autism Diagnosis—Embracing Authenticity by Orion Kelly

Ask an Autistic series by Amythest Schaber

Websites, Podcasts, and Blogs

Sluggish by Jesse Meadows, Sluggish.substack.com

Divergent Design Studios by Marta Rose, Divergentdesign.substack.com

Today's Autistic Moment by Philip King-Lowe, Todaysautisticmoment.com

Deconstructing Neuro by T Jamaica Pogue, Tjamaicapogue.com

Real Social Skills by Rabbi Ruti Regan, Realsocialskills.org

Mental Hellth by P. E. Moskowitz, Mentalhellth.substack.com

The strategies listed here can also work when we suspect a loved one has some hidden neurodivergence themself, and we want to shepherd them into greater self-understanding and acceptance. Most people don't want to be diagnosed with a condition they barely understand by somebody else, as my own experiences with my family attest. Though you might be excitedly noticing signs of Autism all throughout your family and want to share your discoveries, you should allow other people to make their own meaning out of their experience. People feel defensive against insinuations that somebody else knows them better than they know themself, so try to let them develop their own relationship to the material you have shared.

"I picked up books about Autism to learn more about my grandson," shares Ana, a retiree in her late sixties. "But when I read about it, I was like, *Wait. This is a bit uncomfortably familiar...*" It wasn't long before she started joining neurodiversity-focused discussion groups online for her own benefit as well.

The next step after education is to engage in more direct *communication* about your particular needs. If your self-conception has dramatically changed following an Autism diagnosis or self-realization, it may feel frustrating to get your entire family to catch up. Here's an example of how you might signal to your family that many things in your life are about to change: "I recently found out that I am Autistic, and this has really helped me better understand many things in my life that I previously found difficult. Finding out that there is a reason I've been struggling all along and there are ways for me to get help have been very good news. I hope you will support me in making the changes I need to manage my mental and physical health. I'll do my best to tell you how you might help."

There are a couple of elements of this announcement worth noticing. First, you might have caught that this statement does not specify whether you were diagnosed as Autistic or have self-realized that identity. Accessing a fair and affordable Autism diagnosis can be extremely difficult in most parts of the world, particularly if you are a person of color, an LGBTQ person, or a woman; beyond that, a person's private medical information is no one's business but their own. You do not owe anyone in your personal life details about your diagnostic status, and if you are a self-realized Autistic, your status within our community is no less than that of a person who has been diagnosed. If your family is receptive to new information that challenges their viewpoints, you can explain to them how difficult it is for adults to access an Autism diagnosis, and perhaps even point them to personal narratives from Autistic women, people of color, and other groups that have long been ignored and misdiagnosed. Some of the reading materials above are a great way to do this.

If your family tends to be dismissive and poke holes in your arguments no matter what you do, you can simply state you are Autistic as a fact, with no further elaboration. Statements like "I found out officially last month" (if last month was when *you* finally arrived at the decision) or "I had my suspicions and my therapist agreed" (even if your therapist is not a psychiatric assessor) can help lend your statement authority while shutting further conversation down. Rather than trying to justify yourself to an argumentative relative, respond to the emotional truth of what they are saying: "I understand this information might be hard for you to hear because it's not how you see me. But it's the truth, and there's a lot more to Autism than what most people think. Here's [a book/a video/etc.] to help you understand." Repeat statements like these as often as you need to and remember that no one can take your belonging to the community away from you.

You'll notice that the statements I've provided ask your family member to take an active role in helping you manage your health. Many relatives will respond better to a request for aid than to a long list of new expectations and rules. In preparation for this chapter, I interviewed Sarah Casper, a consent educator, the founder of the Brooklyn-based organization Comprehensive Consent and the author of the book *The Kids & Consent Curriculum*. She told me that when we're establishing new boundaries with our families, we can get them on board with the idea by assigning them a task that they can feel good about, rather than instructing them in what they can and cannot do.

"People don't like being told what to do," Sarah says. "Me too! But you can include them and ask them for help. For example, *I'm trying to get better at setting boundaries. Will you please help by double-checking that my yes is really a yes, or by asking my permission before doing something that affects me?*"

Sarah also suggests using this method to introduce the concept of bodily boundaries and consent to older relatives, who may not have been given any control over their own bodies when they were young.

"You can tell a grandparent, for example, *We need your help to teach our child that their body belongs to them. Will you help us? Will you ask them their permission before giving them a hug?* Employing someone to be helpful works so much better than telling them what to do."

You can also use this method to enlist your relatives' help in avoiding unfriendly sensory stimuli for yourself, such as bright lights or overly spicy food. Instead of your aunt feeling rejected because you won't touch her three-pepper chili, you can let her know in advance that you have new dietary requirements and ask her to help you keep an eye out for foods with certain ingredients. Some relatives will really latch on to the role of the helper, bustling around the house dimming the lights or scoping out the department store for comfortable fabric textures you might like. Among many masked Autistic relatives in particular, the desire to scrutinize the environment and to people-please can be turned on its head and used as a way to connect. Specific expectations can soothe their anxiety, too.

This method will not always work, however. A family member has to trust your competence and care about your comfort in order for your requests to influence their behavior. Don't beat yourself up too much if your uncle seems to "forget" that you can't drive every time he suggests you apply for a job in the remote suburbs, for example, or if your sister keeps insisting that you're overreacting and couldn't possibly be afraid of her new, ferocious dog. It doesn't mean that you've failed to stand up for yourself, or that you've communicated poorly. As Lindsay Gibson writes, "If a person doesn't want to understand you, it doesn't matter how you say it. The most skilled communicator in the world fails in the presence of a closed mind."[11]

Sometimes, the best way that we can both establish and maintain our new boundaries with our loved ones is by introducing some space. Recall from the previous chapter that every boundary assertion consists of a request, followed by a potential consequence if the boundary is violated. If you've given your relatives a chance to learn a bit more about you and told them what you need and they still disregard it, a common consequence for crossing that boundary is to remove yourself from the situation. Stepping away from the dinner table, hanging up the phone, going outside for a walk, or getting your own ride home are common strategies for establishing space.

Another way to increase the space between yourself and your relatives is giving them less information about your personal life. Most Autistic people default to being open books, especially if we're still driven by the instinct to seek others' approval: when asked about being unemployed we may explain very thoroughly every single thing we are doing to try to find a job, as well as how we're reducing our expenses, learning new skills, and researching disability benefits. But every detail we provide can be torn apart by those looking to criticize us, and unfortunately, that's frequently what family members do when they don't approve of our life paths. They may think they're saving us from making a terrible mistake, but really they're just feeding into our already debilitating self-doubt, making the urge to mask reemerge. You can end this cycle by telling your relatives that you just don't want to talk about how job applications are going, or say that things are going fine and change the subject.

When a family relationship needs to change significantly, it can also be beneficial to create a hard reset by taking a break from contact for a while, or by eliminating some forms of contact from your life for good. A close friend of mine only talks with his parents over the phone; he hasn't seen them in person for years, and when they ask if he's coming to visit for the holidays, he tells them honestly that he can't afford it (though he means this in terms of both finances *and* mental health).

Similarly, after Aisha came out as gay, she switched from calling her mom almost every day to chatting with her far more sporadically. She truly mourned the loss of their closeness, but she lost her fear of maternal rejection in the process, too. Aisha's silence conveyed to her mom that she could remove herself from situations where she wasn't respected, and in the years since taking this step, her mother learned to stop saying overtly homophobic things that would get her hung up on.

Boundary violations are distressing. They teach us that our bodies are not our own and that our perceptions do not matter. But as unmasking Autistic adults, we can learn to keep a clear head through that distress by planning the consequences we will enact in advance. In the exercise below, try thinking of at least one boundary that you want to set with a family member, and the consequence that you'll follow through with if they violate the boundary.

Tolerate Distress

Maintaining a Boundary

Describe a boundary that you'd like to set with a family member.

> For example, *"I will not debate my choice to be child-free with my mother."*
>
> Or, *"I will not visit if the cousin who used to bully me is around."*

What are some strategies you will use to enforce this boundary?

> For example, *"I will keep repeating that* this is not open to debate, *until my mom stops talking about wanting grandchildren."*
>
> Or, *"I will get up and leave the wedding venue if I see my cousin is there."*

Over time, as unmasking Autistic people get more accustomed to telling our family members no and stepping away when we feel uncomfortable, we may naturally start feeling more detached from the family unit as a whole. We may stop judging our sexualities through the lens of our parents' religious beliefs, for instance, or stop worrying about how our personal styling choices might look to them—or we may just notice one day that a critical voice that used to constantly drone in the back of our heads is a lot quieter. But it takes a lot of daily battles resisting the pressure to fold and mask before we can get there. Even after we've created completely free, proudly neurodivergent lives for ourselves, some of that external pressure may mount again if we have kids. In the next section, we'll take a look at the many emotional and practical challenges of trying to parent self-accepting neurodiverse children—especially within a family that still wears the mask.

Parenting for Neurodiversity

Norah used to find it disturbing that her son, Miles, doesn't verbally speak, and the fact that he won't hug her or show her visible gratitude absolutely broke her heart. She poured thousands of dollars and countless hours into therapeutic treatments, books, language learning videos, interactive toys, and social skills groups in an attempt to make her son more "open" to her.

"I heard that Autistic children were 'locked inside' themselves, so I would have to treat him to bring him out," she explains.

In reality, nonverbal Autistics are not "locked away" behind their disability; they are fully formed people who are typically capable of communicating with the help of assistive devices, letter boards, sign language, texting, or through their behavior. Roughly 25 percent of diagnosed Autistic individuals have either limited or no speech, and being nonverbal can be caused by motor control differences that make forming words in the mouth difficult,[12] as well as divergences in brain functioning,[13] which seems to result in some of us not processing the world in words at all. Though some nonspeaking Autistic people do develop speech or other communication abilities later in life, forcing a nonspeaking Autistic person to speak does not work, and decades of research as well as the traumatized reactions of Autistic people who have been forced through such "treatments" can attest to that fact. In all likelihood, Miles was striving to communicate with his mom all his life—she just couldn't hear it.

Conversely, when nonspeaking or minimally verbal Autistic people are accommodated and listened to in whatever form their communication might take, they exhibit fewer "behavior problems," meaning they experience less distress. From a neurodiversity perspective, the reasons for this are obvious. If you're being treated like a caged parrot and asked to repeat phrases, of course your only way of exercising autonomy will be to lash out.

Miles angrily resisted all his mother's attempted "fixes," his rising stress levels causing him to self-harm and tear up the house. At her wit's end, and having exhausted all the treatment programs supplied by her son's school and her family's health insurance, Norah finally hopped onto a Facebook group for local parents of Autistic children. It was there that another mom recommended Norah work *with* her son's communication style. It turned out that all Norah had to do was provide Miles with an iPad loaded up with an augmentative and alternative communication (AAC) app, help him figure out how to use it, listen to the messages he selected, and accept her son as the person he was meant to be.

While I'm on the Zoom call with Norah, her son spams the button on his AAC device for juice. When she doesn't immediately answer, he adds the word *please,* and then *now.* Norah gets up and runs to the kitchen to pierce a straw through a juice box, laughing. "Sorry, I'm being commanded!" she says. "A moment like this? This? This would have been an hour of him crying and me losing my wits, before we got the AAC."

Now Miles has the power to express himself, so he's far less frustrated and anxious. And Norah has noticed that her own tendency to talk a mile a minute about everything and nothing serves as a mask for how socially anxious she can be, and how afraid she feels of being abandoned. It also triggered Miles's meltdowns. "I don't know if Autistic is the word for me . . . but I sure don't feel normal. Maybe none of us do," she says. After Norah finally started accepting and listening to her son, they got closer. Now they can enjoy hours together in silence.

Even after a parent warmly accepts that their child is neurodivergent (or that they are neurodivergent themself), schools may remain unaccommodating, peers and fellow parents might keep being judgy, and the world mostly persists in its hostility to difference. Unmasking parents face a litany of challenges and tough questions: How do you parent a proud Autistic child when you're not sure how they'll survive in a world that demands independence? How do you unlearn your own internalized mental health stigma and end the cycles of masking and abuse? What does setting your kid up for a successful future look like when you've abandoned conventional benchmarks of success like graduation or getting a job? Thankfully, we can leverage the five core skills of unmasking to form our own answers to these quandaries.

I hear from the parents of neurodivergent kids a lot, and one of the most common questions I get asked is whether a parent should tell their child that they are Autistic, and when they ought to do so. Learning that a child is Autistic typically causes parents feelings of anxiety and grief because the disability is so unfairly stigmatized and fearmongered about in society.[14] Advertisements from organizations like Autism Speaks have trained them to see Autism as a dark force that steals their children away from them. It's understandable that many parents assume their children will also perceive the Autism label in a negative light. Even many well-intentioned parents who are accepting of neurodiversity fear that by telling their children they have a disability, they will be giving their child a reason to feel limited, or ashamed of who they are.

But disabled children are *already* marked as different in the eyes of their peers and the public, whether they're given insight into why they're being singled out or not. Avoiding applying the Autism label to a child does not spare them the pain of exclusion. In fact, it only makes it more difficult for them to understand who they are, what they are experiencing, and that others go through it, too. So by all means, tell your child about any disabilities that they have early on, and speak with them about what it means. Autistic children deserve to know who they are, and to find their place within a much wider community that understands their challenges. They will feel far less defective and self-doubting if they know they're not alone.

If you want your child to grow up truly accepting their neurodivergence, you should take early steps to surround them with a variety of other neurodivergent people of all ages. Like Norah, you may want to hop onto local Facebook groups or Meetup groups for the parents of Autistic children, and organize playdates (or *parallel playdates*, as is often the case for us). Speak with other parents, but also seek out Autistic adults, who can help you understand your child's needs better and expose them to a vision of how their future might look. You'll also want to seek out neurodiversity-focused groups that cater to Autistics of all ages, such as the Autistic Self Advocacy Network, the Neurodiversity Network, or the Society for Neurodiversity, so that both you and your child get to see numerous diverse examples of what Autistic life can be like.

Accepting a child's neurodiversity is inherently transgressive. There are numerous adjustments to regular life that you will have to make, expectations you'll need to loosen, and even social insecurities that you'll have to get over if you want your family to be as fully unmasked as possible. On YouTube, Autistic mother Lizzy Taylor shows how she cuts apart her young son's books page by page using an X-Acto knife, because he likes to stack the pages to the side while he sits on the floor and reads.[15] It's a simple hack to accommodate her son's motor abilities—but she received intense criticism for it because a vocal subset of viewers disapproved of books being destroyed.

"My son is expressing his needs when he's struggling to tear the pages out," Lizzy explains. "And I'm just helping him . . . He's in his safe zone, and he loves his books."

Josie, the mother of an Autistic daughter, told me that she fully accepts her daughter's hatred of all things elastic, and has replaced the elastic with drawstrings in all her daughter's pants. Josie's daughter hates wearing underwear, so she goes without it, too—but the one place where Josie's had to enforce the rules is by making her daughter wear socks.

"She's learned from experience that if she doesn't wear socks it causes problems for her, and problems for other people," Josie explains. When I asked her to clarify, Josie said that she meant smells—as well as sweat, and blood from small blisters her daughter gets on her feet. Josie has found some 100 percent cotton socks on the internet that don't bother her daughter too much, though she still strips her feet bare the moment she gets indoors. Balancing her daughter's sensory comfort with her physical safety is an ongoing process, but Josie tells me that it deeply matters to her because she wants her daughter to grow into a woman who believes she has the right to inconvenience other people and say no to things.

Consent educator Sarah Casper suggested that parents keep their personal values in mind as they navigate decision-making on behalf of their child. Honoring your child's control over their own body is one important value, as is regulating their sensory sensitivities—but you probably also value their physical well-being and the ability to leave them with a babysitter so that you can take care of yourself, and sometimes these competing values will force parents to make imperfect decisions.

"If someone's falling into a street, and the car is coming, I'm gonna pull them to the side of the road and touch them without their permission," Sarah explains. "Am I violating their bodily autonomy? One hundred percent. I don't know if I have permission to touch, but right now I'm choosing saving their life over that." She emphasizes that we all are forced to make trade-offs between our competing values, and so it's important to be up-front with ourselves about what truly matters, and how those values contrast with society's dominant ones. Sometimes we choose bodily consent over pleasing a grandparent who wants a hug, as Aisha does with her kids. Other times, we must choose the physical protection of a vaccine over a child's discomfort with painful injections, but we can still do so in a respectful, communicative way.

In the table on the next page is a list of some values that are commonly upheld in society—some of which you may feel are important to impart to your kid, and some of which might not matter to you at all. You can take this space to reflect on how you might respond when two or more of your values are in conflict with one another in your parenting.

Transgress Norms
What Do You Value?

In the columns below are some values that families may use to guide their parenting. As you read through the list, notice which values catch your attention in either a positive or negative way.

Body autonomy	Helpfulness	Dignity
Freedom	Patience	Cleanliness
Self-reliance	Connection	Conformity
Tradition	Generosity	Strength
Faith	Curiosity	Safety
Creativity	Resilience	Reliability
Expression	Perceptiveness	Stability
Honesty	Sensitivity	Equality
Justice	Modesty	Diversity

Growing up, which values did your family prioritize?

_____

_____

Which values are most important to you? (You can choose values from the list or invent your own.)

_____

_____

Family

When two of your values are in conflict (for example, when stability is threatened by honesty), how will you decide what to do?

There are no simple answers to questions of values. What a parent determines is the best choice for their family may not be what their child would ultimately prefer. Responsible caregivers will take accountability for the decisions they made when their children were small, accepting that one day their kids will have their own perspectives. Standing by our beliefs may sometimes require violating society's most deeply ingrained laws—as is the case for parents in states with homophobic and transphobic laws, who bravely keep educating their kids about queer topics anyway. Realizing that no value system is universal and that living by our own ethical codes will invariably alienate other people can be freeing—if we're never going to please everyone or meet every societal standard, then there's far less reason to mask. People will disapprove of us, and we will make mistakes—and instead of trying to prevent that, we can tolerate it instead.

Aisha values her children's freedom and self-esteem, and so she doesn't want to expose them to the harsh judgments and strict rules of her mother, Bettie. At the same time, she also deeply values her kids having positive memories of their grandmother. Bettie isn't a horrible person; she's only ever wanted Aisha to lead a successful life. The two women just have wildly deviating ideas of what a successful life for a Black neurodivergent woman ought to be. To reconcile these hard realities, Aisha sets limits on how often Bettie gets to see her grandkids, and which activities they get to share in together as a family.

"My kids get to have lunch with Grandma every couple of weeks and go to the park or the zoo, and they're always left wanting more time with her," she explains. "Everyone sees me as at fault for not letting them all hang out together more, and I'm fine with that, if it means my kids don't get dragged to a church that's homophobic and don't get pressured to throw their depression medication in the trash."

In other words, Aisha has decided to place family connection, fond memories, and her kids' autonomy over winning her mother's approval. Her kids get to wear pajamas around the house and fall behind on homework when life gets too stressful, and Aisha has the privacy to heal from her own life traumas without her mother tut-tutting at the moldy dishes in the sink. She can tolerate the judgmental remarks she gets, and even the emotional distance between them, knowing that she's made a conscious choice to endure it in order to prevent far greater forms of distress for everyone involved. Things are not perfect—and that's where unmasking in our families leads. To conscious imperfection, rather than a façade of no flaws.

Unfortunately, shrewd boundary-setting and self-advocacy is not always enough to reorient dysfunctional family dynamics. Sometimes we have no choice but to pull away from our loved ones in a more dramatic way if we are to protect ourselves. And so, in this next section, we will discuss the harrowing process of navigating abuse and familial estrangement.

Navigating Abuse and Estrangement

In 2019, author and Dear Prudence advice columnist Danny Lavery suddenly estranged himself from his entire family of origin. One moment Danny and his immediate family were in a warm and comfortable relationship, and in regular contact, then the next Danny vowed never to speak to them again. Their estrangement occurred because Danny was outraged at what to him was a clear act of moral indifference from loved ones who had often presented themselves as kindly Christian people; it recontextualized his entire life within the church up to that point, and cast many of his memories of his family in a completely new light.

"Two weeks ago I learned something I could not live with," Danny wrote back then. "... Estrangement from my family of origin, which had the day before been the furthest thing from my mind, became a matter of the keenest urgency."[16] In the years that followed, Danny would contemplate the various ways in which he felt his family hadn't been supportive of him, and all the ways in which, throughout his life, he felt they hadn't taken him seriously.[17]

I followed Danny's writing about these events closely for several reasons. His stint as *Slate* magazine's Dear Prudence advice columnist was deeply helpful to me during the mid-2010s, while I was coping with an Autistic identity and trying to figure out how to better relate to people. Danny's a transgender man and he has ADHD, and so as a fellow neurodivergent transmasculine person, I could see some of my life journey paralleled by his. But most of all, I knew what it was like to have to create a permanent rift between oneself and a family member, having done so myself, and Danny's writing gave me a place to siphon off some of my complex, festering grief.

My own abuse is hard to untangle from my neurodiversity. As a lonely kid who got made fun of for expressing myself in movie quotes and sitting in unusual positions, I frequently sought the approval of adults. My dad, for his part, had no friends or close relationships, and extracted a lot of age-inappropriate emotional support from me, until I believed that it was my job to apologize for the insults he hurled at other people and to soothe his frequently frayed nerves. Once I entered puberty, my father's emotional inappropriateness became sexual impropriety, too; he made repeated lurid comments about my body and attractiveness that made me feel pawed over and used, though he never touched me. By the time I was sixteen, I had resolved to stop speaking to him, and at eighteen changed my last name to cement this estrangement; he died within months, and for years I blamed myself for having left him so miserably alone that he'd had no choice but to kill himself. All these experiences were informed by my masking and the profound need I felt to placate other people and make myself useful to them. It also deepened my reflex to mask because my dad's death taught me that other people desperately needed me, and that to let them down was tantamount to leaving them to die.

Numerous Autistic people report having endured domestic violence, neglect, or emotional abuse from a young age. A study in *Disability Studies Quarterly* reports that we are singled out by abusers because we're especially vulnerable, and because our signs of having been abused don't register to neuroconforming people.[18] A recent study in *Nature* similarly found that Autistic people face an elevated risk of physical and emotional abuse (so do our peers with ADHD, Schizophrenia, and Bipolar Disorder).[19] In recent years, clinicians have started to grapple with the fact that they systematically overlook the problem of abuse among neurodiverse people, and tend to mistakenly identify our signs of trauma as "symptoms" of our disability itself, even in situations where doing so doesn't make sense.[20] For example, an Autistic teen's sudden refusal to use the toilet or bathe may be attributed to stubbornness or pathological demand avoidance, rather than to them no longer feeling safe getting undressed.

For a long time, psychiatrists have taken it as a given that Autistics suffer from *alexithymia* (the inability to recognize emotions and body feelings) because of our disability. Many of us are detached from our inner feelings, and it's been widely assumed (without testing) that this is caused by some neurological disconnect. However, emerging research suggests instead that our detachment from our bodies is a learned trauma response, not an innate disability.[21]

Trauma tends to cause survivors to dissociate from their bodies, both as a means of escape from the pain we're in and because we've learned that how we feel doesn't matter to others and won't be taken seriously. Childhood survivors of abuse and neglect have been observed by clinicians to develop alexithymia,[22] as have transgender people who were forced to present as the wrong gender.[23] Trauma conditions members of these groups to attend to their inner feelings less often, until they lose the instinct to take care of their bodies or honor their emotions. It stands to reason that many Autistics are similarly unable to tell when we're hungry, sad, or happy because we grew up constantly being told our feelings were wrong.[24] As we unmask, we may come to feel resentful toward parents who told us we were overreacting to sensory pain all our childhoods, or who insulted us for not sitting or moving correctly. Telling ourselves that our families didn't know better than to treat us this way may not always be enough to bridge the emotional rift.

As visibly disabled kids, many of us were also placed on ineffective medications designed to "cure" us, pushed into therapeutic treatments that only trained us to neuroconform, or forced through institutions (such as school or church) that shamed us and singled us out. We may hold our family members responsible for these traumas—and feel completely alienated from the institutions we grew up with. We also may be utterly terrified of any change, uncertainty, or conflict within our own lives because trauma has rendered us so hypervigilant. Whenever I stood up to my father, he would berate me and threaten to die. These intense, manipulative overreactions were probably related to his own mental health struggles, but that didn't lessen their damage—I needed to get as far away from him as possible so that my own unmasking could begin.

When self-advocacy is not enough to change how a dysfunctional family system operates, or in cases of ongoing abuse, estrangement is a tool Autistic people can use to protect ourselves. Having to end a familial relationship is an incredibly painful decision, and it can come with financial and practical challenges on top of emotional turmoil. In order to move through an estrangement assertively, with your own long-term well-being in mind, you can proceed through the following four steps:

1. Affirm your choice to end the relationship.

2. Create a plan for handling practical concerns such as childcare, housing, and finances.

3. Find support to help you uphold your decision, even when facing pressure or guilt.

4. Grieve the loss.

Many people contemplating a family estrangement are stuck on step number one for a very long time. We know that we dread every conversation that we have with our family member, and we can admit to close friends that their past behavior sure *sounds* like abuse, but we don't have the confidence to name the dynamic for what it is, or don't believe that we deserve our independence.

To this, therapist Lindsay Gibson says, "You have the right to stay away from them—period. It doesn't have to be the 'right' reason, just your reason."[25] Your life is lived only by you, and so you should make it one that you can stand.

I will add a piece of advice that my therapist Jason gave me when I was debating whether I'd endured true abuse. He told me that he couldn't travel back into the past and prove that anything I'd endured was abuse, but he could see that my behavior patterns were those commonly found in a person who had been repeatedly treated like their emotions didn't matter. Just as a surgeon can recognize a fracture that is consistent with a physical struggle, Jason could look at my behavior and fears and recognize the lingering effects of being emotionally invalidated, neglected, and used by adults for comfort.

If you feel, think, and behave like a person who has been sorely mistreated, consider that you have been. If you don't trust your family with intimate truths and feel terrible after spending time around them, that alone is a sufficient reason to limit how much access they get to you. As Sarah Casper further stressed to me, many survivors believe that they have to categorize their past experiences as a clear-cut violation in order to receive care—but you need care regardless. We perish when we don't have sufficient support. And so you get to pursue the relationships that provide loving care to you, and end the ones that threaten your ability to be cared for.

Danny Lavery says that far from being a rash decision, "Estrangement is acknowledging what's been true for a pretty long time."[26] He suggests that you consider writing a letter to your relatives, explaining to them that you don't appreciate the way that you've been treated and that they should not expect to hear from you anymore, but cautions that even the most carefully worded message will not convince someone to honor your request for distance if they do not respect you. Estrangement is a boundary you must maintain for yourself and does not require anyone else's agreement.

If you've decided you wish to pursue an estrangement, you should plan to deal with some of the following practical concerns.

Creating a Plan for Estrangement

- Finances: Which kinds of financial support do you currently receive from your family? How can you reduce expenses, pool resources with others, and seek out alternative aid to fill that gap?

- Childcare: Do your family members help you take care of your kids? Do you want them to still be able to see your kids? If so, how will you maintain your distance? If not, where will you turn for childcare support?

- Housing: Will you move farther away from your family to minimize contact? Do you need help keeping your new location a secret? Do you need roommates or a friend to stay with to lessen expenses?

- Holidays and traditions: Do you wish to leave behind your family's religious or cultural traditions? If not, how will you make them your own? How do you plan on handling the pressures of relatives sending holiday gifts, telling you that they are praying for you, inviting you to weddings and funerals, and so on?

- Accessibility needs: What role did your family play in addressing the needs that come with your disability? Are there any forms of support you will need to find somewhere else? How will you adjust to the dramatic change in routine that this estrangement will create?

You may also find that at the present moment, it is not safe or feasible for you to become estranged. If you're a minor, you may have few legal avenues at your disposal to help you become emancipated, for example, or you might fear that contending with the foster system or poverty would be far worse. If you're physically disabled or have high support needs, an abusive relative may be your only current source of caregiving. Perhaps you need to bide your time while building an alternative support network, or you want to finish college on your parents' dime before cutting them off for good. In these situations, you need a plan for survival and minimizing conflict while maintaining your sanity, so consider the following strategies:

- Grey rocking:[27] This time-tested approach to emotional abuse involves giving your abuser(s) as little information, attention, and emotional responsiveness as possible. Become a "grey rock" whenever your family is around by saying very little, agreeing noncommittally to their statements, initiating nothing, and saying the minimum required, ideally in a bored, passive-seeming way.

    Abusive people often wish to distress you and subdue you at the same time, but by subduing *yourself* before they can, you provide them with very little excuse to be angry and thus de-escalate them. Try using very repetitive statements to questions and pretending to have less mental and emotional depth than you actually do to help make your abuser incurious and find mistreating you less fun.

- Specific compliance: When your abuser becomes emotionally explosive or criticizes your behavior, ask them exactly what it is that they would like you to do. If they are just looking for a way to off-load their own unregulated emotions, this question may defuse them because they won't have an answer. If they're seeking to control you and make you miserable, this tactic still de-escalates the problem because it provides you a single, specific action you can take at that moment, broadcasting to them that you are not trying to be "difficult" or make them unhappy.

    This tactic will help protect you by making you look obedient and helpful without forcing you to guess at your abuser's every need or perform as much emotional caretaking for them. The book *How to Deal with Emotionally Explosive People* by Albert J. Bernstein is especially helpful in dealing with this.

- Look busy: Find ways to occupy your time and attention that keep your abuser from singling you out, and that also provide you with a mental escape. If you are a student, join lots of clubs that your parent might approve of. Even if you're not actually passionate about band or Science Olympiad, it can buy you time away from them. If you work, take on extra shifts; if you work from home, find more freelance work (or say that you did) so you can spend more time on the computer. Find ways to occupy your attention that they generally approve of, like fixing things around the house, reading, or volunteer work that can earn you "points" in their mind and lessen the need for manufactured drama.

- Practice strong information security (InfoSec): Be aware of the data that gets stored on your computer, web browser, and phone, and limit your digital footprint. Use encrypted chatting apps such as Signal or Telegram to coordinate with friends; delete your browser history, search history, and deleted files; and search your devices for spyware and trackers. Don't keep a diary that can be accessed in your home. Be careful about hiding burner phones or using encrypted apps on your devices, as getting caught can escalate abuse and control.

- Bide your time: It is often easier to escape an abusive dynamic (or even just to live within it) if your abuser believes that you are under their control and share their values. Try to passively agree with assumptions your abuser makes about your future life, or lie if you need to drop your guard. For example, if a parent is insistent that you go to college and study pre-medicine, pretend to actually share this goal, and consider leaving home for their preferred school as a potential way out. If they claim you do not need support from disability services, pretend that you also do not want it, but that your school is forcing the issue and your hands are tied.

As best you can, avoid making a legal or financial commitment that will be difficult for you to extricate yourself from, such as taking on a loan in your abuser's name or marrying someone that they want you to. Beyond that, you'll generally be afforded more social privileges, greater access to technology, and more freedom of movement if your abuser thinks you mirror their own values.

- Cultivate allies wisely: Locate friends and potential support network members who know how to be discreet. Ideally, you should find classmates, family friends, or community members whom your abuser approves of, or who know how to tell flattering lies that placate them. Be careful about sharing your true feelings or desires with someone who might rat you out. Start with small requests for help that seem relatively innocent; for example, ask them to supervise you for an errand so that your abuser doesn't have to. Anything that buys you more time away from your abuser without severe consequences is a net gain for your mental health and future safety.

- Research available resources: When you can do so safely (practicing strong information security!), look up local domestic violence shelters, transitional living facilities, youth programs, independent living supports, and other resources for disabled people and victims of abuse. Learn what you can about their policies and reputations: Are they inclusive toward trans people? Do they involuntarily commit individuals who are having psychiatric crises? Do they expect clients to attend church or be abstinent from sex or drugs? Unfortunately, some shelters and service providers do not treat neurodivergent or marginalized people with respect, nor do they afford them much autonomy. Knowing which resources you can safely access should you choose to leave your abuser(s) will be very important. If you're not sure of where to start, try calling 211 (in the United States) or RAINN (the Rape, Abuse, and Incest National Network) at

800-656-4673. For those who can't use the phone, chat-based resources are available at www.rainn.org/resources.

Thinking through these questions and time-biding tactics in advance will help you when it comes to the third stage of the estrangement process, which involves finding ways to uphold your decision even when faced with pressure or guilt. An estrangement is rarely a single step; instead, it's a series of firm refusals to repeated phone calls, letters, unwanted visits, and manufactured crises, which sometimes occur over the course of numerous years. Even when we are stuck living with an abuser, we can begin a kind of mental and emotional estrangement by detaching our sense of self from our abuser's evaluations of us and granting them less access to our inner worlds.

A year after we last spoke, my dad tried baiting me back into acknowledging him with a heartrending handwritten letter; he also worked as a landscaper at the same pool where I was a lifeguard, and so I had to prepare myself for the possibility of seeing him regularly. It helped that my mom and sister supported me in breaking contact with him and were able to shut down his advances. If you can, try asking safe loved ones, a partner, or a friend to pass along any necessary messages to your estranged family member on your behalf so that you don't get pulled back into their web.

The anonymous blogger Issendai has performed a breathtakingly in-depth analysis of the contents of estranged parents' forums, places on the internet where mothers and fathers whose children no longer speak to them attempt to justify their own past abuse and continued boundary-crossing. It's a lengthy read, and can be quite triggering, but if you have decided to stop speaking to a manipulative or invalidating family member, or simply want to stop justifying their way of thinking to yourself all the time, I highly recommend it. With incredible precision, Issendai breaks down how unrepentant estranged parents on these forums tend to think: they see their children as setting out to personally *wound* them with their assertions of boundaries, and frequently describe their grown children as entitled crybabies and fakers who weren't really abused but simply have convinced themselves they were (for some reason). When an adult child does explain to their parents their reasons for estrangement, these parents attempt to disprove them, as if matters of autonomy and consent were subject to debate; they also tend to claim they "don't understand" their child's choice to go no-contact no matter how many times they have been told. In resisting their children's requests to be left alone, these parents sometimes plan to stage fake health crises or deaths, or hatch plots to temporarily kidnap their grandkids—all in hopes of forcing their children into their lives.

If you have trouble wrapping your mind around the shallowness and disrespect of an abusive parent's thinking, and you keep finding yourself wishing you could find the right words to make them respect you, paging through this blog can be quite helpful. Much as Lindsay Gibson frequently stresses in her work, we can find peace when we acknowledge our family's limitations. Those who have never been gentle or kind with us are unlikely to ever be. People who have never shown signs of listening to us likely never will. If we have chosen estrangement, it's probably because we've accurately recognized there is little hope of changing how our families treat us. Therefore, we should feel no pressure to try to change their minds about that estrangement, either.

If you are interested in reading Issendai's thorough account of what typically gets posted on estranged parents' forums, you can visit www.issendai.com/psychology/estrangement/.

Maintaining an estrangement in the face of pressure, confusion, and guilt will demand the full power of your distress regulation skills. So here are a few tips to help you stand firm.

Tolerate Distress

Maintaining No-Contact with Estranged Relatives

Digital boundaries: Block your relatives on all social media and in your phone contacts, and consider setting your digital profiles to private. Turn off notifications from people you do not already follow, and use filters to send their emails and messages straight to the trash. Change all your passwords and usernames to prevent hacking.

Physical boundaries: Get your phone number and address unlisted (you can work with your phone's service provider as well as services like DeleteMe). Throw away any unexpected packages and pieces of mail. Check your vehicles and devices for signs of trackers.

Social boundaries: Appoint a trusted friend to be the enforcer of your estrangement if you can. Have them communicate to other people that you are no longer speaking to your family, and have them tackle the practicalities of ensuring this with your friend group, church, or with any relatives you are still on good terms with. This person can also be on the lookout for signs that your family has figured out your contact information or is planning any action against you.

Emotional boundaries: Use journaling, support groups, therapy, physical activity, stimming, or art to get your bad feelings about your family out. Anticipate how you will cope with guilting emails or letters, and events like family illnesses or deaths.

Do not be ashamed of how messy your feelings can be—Danny Lavery says he fantasized about beating his relatives with baseball bats every night for a *year*. Find ways to honor your feelings of loss as well—share fond memories with a friend, ask your trusted social circle for a reminder of why you chose estrangement. Read sites like Issendai's blog or your own old emails and journals to affirm your choice.

The final and ongoing stage of managing an estrangement is finding safe ways to experience grief and mourn what you have lost. Much of what we lose when we detach from our families is any hope of them giving us the love that we deserve—no matter how unrealistic that hope may be. But few abusers are horrible all the time, and we may harbor fond memories of special times that we spent with them, or feel profound sorrow that they weren't able to unmask themselves and grow into more fully developed people in the ways we were. You may want to create your own versions of beloved holiday traditions or visit familiar places from your childhood with people who truly love you in an active way, to help honor the past while also rewriting it with a healthier present. It's also completely fine to write letters to your family members that you'll never send, hold conversations in your mind with them that you won't ever be able to have, and cry over what your life is missing as often as you want.

"The three-year mark seems to me to mark a shift from the acute to the chronic—my estrangement is no longer recent," Danny Lavery wrote in 2022.[28] "It feels more settled, less surprising than it once did, and a new life has grown up around it." I have to say it took over a decade for me to reach that point of settlement. From the time I was eighteen until I was well into my early thirties, I believed that my father had died because I had not loved him enough. And then finally, one day, I no longer believed that. Instead, I was thankful he was dead, and that I would never have to hear any new bizarre, intrusive statement from him ever again. By then I was surrounded by a loving community of neurodivergent people who understood me as I really was, and who would have never dreamed of taking advantage of me in those ways. I was only able to forgive myself for ending my relationship with my dad thanks to their support.

In the final section of this chapter, we'll examine and celebrate the many beautiful ways that unmasking neurodivergent people can reinvent and create truly supportive families for ourselves.

Creating Family

In the spring of 2023, a viral *New Yorker* profile introduced the world to Agnes Callard, a philosophy professor at the University of Chicago who divorced her husband, married a former graduate student, and then continued to live with both men while raising children with each of them under the same roof.²⁹ Agnes's life became something of a scandal, but she remained incredibly candid about it all, sharing how she negotiated such a complex relationship structure and explaining the many steps she took to ensure she didn't wield institutional authority over her more junior academic spouse.³⁰

Agnes is Autistic, and it's clear from how she philosophizes about love and relationships that her hyper-analytical neurodivergent brain informs her unique worldview.³¹ Everything about Agnes absolutely screams *Autistic*, from her brightly patterned, cozy tights and dresses, to her bold assertion in *The New Yorker* that travel is pointless because it is unfamiliar and doesn't last long.³² Agnes even held a late-night discussion on her university campus about the philosophical nature of marriage—alongside her ex-husband. Agnes's lifelong devotion to studying the works of Socrates resembles many Autistics' special interests, and part of what drew her to her current husband was the way he speaks about Aristotle. She has shaped her life around her passions, surrounded herself with people who view love as an exercise in intellectual and spiritual "aspiration," as she puts it, and though the world may judge her for it, she's created family in a very unmasked way.

Autistic people can be incredible nonconformists. We are far more likely than other groups of people to be open about being gay, bisexual, or trans, to practice kink or express unique sexualities, and to form relationship structures that flout the nuclear norm. And because many conventional full-time jobs do not accommodate Autistic people, circumstances cause us to become even more creative in how we structure our lives, form families, and build supportive communities that can carry us through tough times. We have the power within ourselves to build lives that serve our needs. We just need a little help leveraging the skills to make that life possible. From massive, thirteen-person polyamorous polycules, to interdependent families that all live under the same roof, to spouses that maintain separate residences, to best friends that get married, Autistic people break the relational mold and openly come into conflict with the rules that dictate how love and mutual support ought to function. And that's a beautiful thing.

If you've been working to unmask yourself from within a family unit that is not always supportive or understanding, and particularly if you've considered creating greater distance or an estrangement, then now is the time to truly ponder what family means to you. In the queer world, we speak often about the importance of "found family," but we aren't always precise enough about what that means. A found family is more than just a fleeting social clique, or a group that brands itself a community but lacks any enduring commitments. If we are to really make up for what our families of origin have failed to give us, we ought to be clear with ourselves about what our lives are missing and what we have to give.

Within the traditional family structure, a number of roles and relationship norms are essentially taken as a given. Typically, parents or grandparents call the shots when it comes to holidays and annual traditions for their kids, and one's closest relatives are assumed to carry the responsibility of providing emotional support, financial support, practical daily life assistance, and to serve as a sounding board throughout life's regular struggles. Families also provide a sense of continuity across the generations, and many people derive immense life meaning from the fact that they are part of a family. But if your family is unsupportive of your Autistic traits and mannerisms, has abused you, or simply lacks the emotional tools to really show up for you in these ways, it's worth thinking intentionally about who will step in to fulfill each of these roles, and how you might use your Autistic powers of transgression and creativity to make and maintain family in your own way.

On the next page is a sidebar summarizing some of the many reasons that we lean on our families—gaps in your life that you may wish to fill with other relationships and alternative arrangements. Go through each item on this list and consider whether it represents a genuine need in your life, and if so, how you might satisfy it if your family of origin cannot meet it.

Creating Family
What Is Family For?

Tradition: Maintenance of religious practices; serving as a "living memory" of how past events were done; a reminder to honor those who are dead, and the past.

Alternative sources of tradition: Membership in a religious or cultural organization, researching your ancestry or local history, creating new practices with your chosen loved ones.

Multigenerational contact: A sense of connectedness across long periods of time; an enduring legacy as a source of life meaning and purpose; a sense of perspective that comes from seeing others at different life stages.

Alternative sources of multigenerational contact: Volunteering at youth centers or senior homes; researching the history of groups you belong to (Black history, queer history); visiting museums, libraries, book clubs, and other mixed-generation spaces; getting to know your neighbors.

Holidays: Having predetermined plans for important days on the calendar; a sense of bonding from the exchanging of gifts and sharing of meals; a relatively affordable way to take time off and relax.

Alternative ways to mark holidays: Create new holiday traditions with your friends and neighbors; host holiday parties or dinners in your home; spend special days in contemplation or out in your community.

Financial support: A roof to live under; assistance in paying the bills; a family home to visit for free meals; access to tools, cars, and appliances to borrow.

Alternative sources of financial support: Friends and fellow community members; mutual aid groups; food kitchens; places of worship; social service organizations; pooling resources with roommates and chosen family; tool libraries.

Positive connection: Someone to share good news with; people to give gifts to and do favors for; relationships where you can be expressive and affectionate.

Alternative sources of positive connection: Selecting a group of close friends to be told first about any personal news; group chats or messaging threads for spreading support; being generous with loved ones and community members; cultivating relationships where cuddling, words of affirmation, and loving expressions are welcome.

Shared experiences: People to accompany you on road trips, vacations, museum visits, or shopping trips; people who have been by your side through illness, big home repairs and moves, graduations, breakups, and other important life moments.

Alternative sources of shared experiences: Taking intentional steps to remain connected with classmates, former co-workers, former neighbors, or childhood friends; including loved ones in your support circle when you are struggling, and showing up when others are having a difficult time, too; forming regular vacation plans or day trips with loved friends.

Sources of wisdom and advice: Experienced elders to call when faced with a new problem; a sounding board for life's quandaries; a reminder of your values.

Alternative sources of wisdom and advice: Seeking out people with expertise relevant to your problem; developing your own power of discernment and judgment; joining organizations that reflect your principles; volunteering with elders; cultivating a circle of friends that you can trust as advisors, and who help you maintain faith in yourself.

Commitment: Legal bonds such as marriage, parenthood, or an inheritance; a sense of rootedness in a location where your family dwells; the comfort of knowing certain people will always be there for you.

Alternative sources of commitment: Queerplatonic and committed roommate relationships, domestic partnerships, membership to a committed polyamorous relationship structure (a polycule); belongingness in our friendships; listing trusted friends on your will or deed; offering to be a trusted loved one's cosigner on a lease or for a loan; developing strong community ties.

Since establishing firmer boundaries with her family of origin as part of her unmasking process, Aisha has started to find sources of family connection in unexpected places. First, she's actively involved in her kids' lives, and has taken on the role of a queer mother figure for numerous kids at her children's school. "None of the parents at my kids' school knows that I'm gay, so I can provide these kids a place to be away from judgment and ask questions without anybody suspecting they're queer," she explains. She's also befriended an elderly neighbor, a retired disabled man who is going blind and often needs Aisha's eyes in navigating his apartment. She brings him meals, and he lends her tools and lets her wash her laundry in his apartment. They talk about politics and queer issues, and though he was once a deeply conservative Christian Republican, friendship with Aisha has opened up his perspective.

Aisha's also started venturing back into dating, though so far the best connection she's been able to form is a friendship with an older lesbian who lives down the street. Neither of them felt a romantic spark, but they're passionate about the same TV shows, like *Severance* and *Mr. Robot*, and take Aisha's kids out together for superhero movies and ice cream. When Aisha has a depressive episode and can't bear to leave the house, her newfound loved ones visit with her, or leave groceries on her doorstep, never calling her an embarrassment or accusing her of weakness the way her mother would.

In many ways, Aisha is still piecing together a life that can accommodate her neurodiversity. Trying to live as a straight, neurotypical woman under the watchful eye of an overly critical parent and a manipulative spouse cost her a lot, and she wishes she could experience love and romance as a lesbian finally. But she's on the right path—and feels less defective and alone with each step. And she still prays that one day, her mother will pick up a book or two about Autism and begin to heal herself.

One common reason that masked Autistics become so heavily reliant upon our families is that we're incredibly financially vulnerable and need somewhere to live and someone to help us pay the bills when we're unable to work. When we do seek employment, the societal pressure to mask becomes only more intense, with our every mannerism and thought process being strictly scrutinized for deviance, and our ability to feed and house ourselves being constantly put on the line. For many of us, to remain gainfully employed necessarily means to remain masked, and to unmask means to put our employability and financial futures forever at risk. That's why the next chapter is devoted to the question of work—whether to pursue it, how to endure it, and more broadly, what it means to survive under capitalism as your neurodivergent self.

Work

Work is the bane of most Autistic people's existence. We enter the job market at a sharp disadvantage compared to non-Autistic people because we're less likely to have succeeded in school or to have built up a professional network.[1] We're more likely to leave a career path early due to burnout, social rejection, bullying, and Autism stigma.[2] As disabled people who typically require longer rest periods following strenuous tasks, who struggle to self-motivate when required to follow rules or execute orders that we don't see the purpose of, and who are especially drained by social demands, many of us are largely viewed as unemployable[3] by hiring agents and managers alike.

Television shows like *The Good Doctor*, *Criminal Minds*, and *Bones* advance the myth of the hardworking Autistic savant who is brusque and challenging to be around, but obsessively devoted to their field; in reality many of us are far less career-driven and far more terrified of alienating other people than any of these depictions would suggest. Our difficulty in making a living means we suffer from a heightened risk of poverty, depression, and a reduced quality of life.[4] Rather than being well-compensated surgeons or genius criminal investigators who've received massive accolades, we're far more likely to be on unemployment or disability benefits, and leaning upon family members or roommates to help cover costs and solve the endless logistical puzzles of staying fed, clothed, washed, housed, and relatively healthy. Just staying alive can demand so much of us that making time for work seems like a cruel joke to consider: if it takes an hour to psych oneself into taking a shower, three hours to complete a grocery store trip, and another five hours afterward to recover from the incredible stress of the errand, then looking for a job or regularly reporting to one remains out of the question.

Even if we are lucky enough to be genuinely passionate about a field of employment that could theoretically sustain us, the actual day-to-day requirements of getting and holding down a job may prove so vexing and exhausting that we can't succeed. Professional norms are a haze of unspoken expectations and superficial snap judgments, job interviews are high-performance situations that require face-saving lies, and the majority of workplaces bring us turmoil on both a social and sensory level. It's small wonder, then, that the majority of Autistic adults are either unemployed or underemployed worldwide,[5] and that the roughly 16 percent of us who do manage to hold down a job often do so at the expense of our social lives and emotional well-being.[6]

I have been one of those rare Autistics to "successfully" hold a full-time job for a number of years, and the process has not been pretty—and even then, it was only possible thanks to a high degree of privilege and good luck. In my early twenties, I enrolled in graduate school because I was quite skilled in navigating an academic environment, which cared only about my output, not how I looked or how much time I put in. I moved to the city where my graduate program was, and managed to live on the $14,000 per year I was paid because I had an active eating disorder, no hobbies, and few friends. Devotion to my studies left me with a PhD at the age of twenty-five, little debt, and a debilitating case of burnout that made it impossible for me to really work for the next several years. I taught online classes and did freelance data analysis work from a spot on the floor of my apartment, feeling miserable and depleted most days, until eventually one of my online teaching positions became full-time. With the stability of a salary and health insurance, my yearslong case of burnout finally began to ebb, and I started writing books. A fog of depression had parted at last, and I found a true calling that spoke to my passions as a psychologist and my life experiences as an Autistic person who'd frequently been misunderstood.

Though I've been immensely fortunate to find a job that I can do well, and I'm thankful for it, I still dart between panicked overwork and despondent listlessness month by month. I work myself to the bone when I can, anticipating that I won't always be able to. Each time Autistic burnout visits me, it takes away some of my capabilities seemingly forever, and I am left a weaker, needier, and yet more self-accepting person when the exhaustion finally recedes. I'm saving for an early retirement, taking on every well-compensated gig that I can handle, gambling each time that it won't be the obligation that finally makes me crash for good. It seems I have to earn my keep on this planet while I still can.

This is an outlook I share with many Autistic people in the workforce, one of them being the Scottish actor and comedian Fern Brady. Fern writes in her memoir *Strong Female Character* that she accepts nearly every performance gig that comes her way, even when the stress leaves her melting down and smashing up furniture inside her house, because she can't trust that she'll continue being able to make money in the future.

"I figured if I could make enough money before I was 40 and had the career-ending nervous breakdown I seemed to be hurtling towards, I could retire and go live as a hermit back in Scotland," she writes.[7] But this decision meant subjecting herself to endless auditions and potential project meetings with entertainment professionals who treated her like a dear friend before ghosting her, or who took advantage of their influence by calling her up late at night to flirt. She has figured, quite understandably, that she has no choice but to play along with these games and boundary violations. "Masking was surely better than being poor?"

The data shows that masking isn't always better than being poor. Though being systematically excluded from the job market does leave Autistics with poorer health, less integration into society, and a higher likelihood of being abused,[8] the evidence is clear that masking in order to maintain a job is psychologically perilous, too. A majority of employers asked in surveys will outwardly admit they discriminate against Autistic job applicants.[9] Even those that don't openly discriminate are likely to view an Autistic employee through an ableist lens, thinking they speak too candidly, ask too many questions, take too much time meticulously fulfilling their duties, and do not participate enough in team icebreakers and office parties. In recent years, some large corporations have launched diversity and inclusion initiatives for neurodiverse people and expressed an interest in recruiting Autistic employees; however, employers mostly seek out neurodivergent workers because they believe we'll be more productive and loyal than nondisabled ones at a cheaper price. During times of increased labor strikes and unionization pushes, companies often seek us out, believing that because we are desperate for work, we will demand less respect.[10] When we actually behave as disabled people do, with our own needs and problems, we are typically the first ones to be fired.

Masking to fit within such an environment takes more than just a ton of our energy, it also drains our sense of integrity and self-respect.[11] A recent article in the journal *Issues in Mental Health Nursing* rightly calls the need for Autistics to mask in order to get along in public a "recipe for trauma," and a 2021 article in the journal *Autism in Adulthood* found that, while all employees are expected to mask their true emotions and wear a false face of professionalism to an extent, for Autistics doing so is both far more pervasive of an effort and a significant predictor of suicide.[12] Masking is also a leading contributor to Autistic burnout, which further limits our ability to earn a living.[13] Smiling at every customer and carefully editing our ideas into corporate-friendly speak may be necessary for us to keep our jobs, but no longer putting on such performances may be required in order to preserve our sanity. Accordingly, many of us ultimately have to choose to abandon the professional world for the sake of staying alive, even if it means never knowing independence or stability.

Coping under capitalism as an Autistic person is tough, even now that our disability is better understood than ever before and corporations are investing heavily in neurodiversity initiatives. This chapter will explore from a highly pragmatic perspective the countless challenges Autistic people face in making a living and navigating the professional realm, and offer tips and tricks for deciding whether to pursue a job, securing disability accommodations, and surviving the world of professional euphemisms and small talk when we have to. As always, our work in this chapter will rely upon the self-advocacy skills of acceptance, engagement, transgression, tolerance, and creativity. It takes a whole lot of careful planning, shrewd outside-the-box thinking, and courage in order to get by in a world obsessed with work that was not built for you. But as the profiles of Autistic people in the coming pages will attest, it is possible to survive while remaining true to ourselves.

Surviving Under Capitalism as an Autistic Person

Because the majority of Autistic individuals do not hold full-time employment, and because the ability to participate in the labor market in no way determines a person's worthiness, I will not assume that securing a stable job is either a realistic or desirable goal for the majority of people reading this book. This chapter is really about how Autistics can unmask while identifying our best means of survival—and for many neurodivergent people, that may exist beyond the realm of employment.

Autistic people get by on food stamps, disability benefits, mutual aid funds, rent support, and through crowdfunding; we live in vans, campers, tents, squatters' communes, or on boats instead of paying rent. Autistic parents elect to stay at home and raise their children, as well as community members' children, being compensated for that labor rather than entering the workforce. Some of us are lifelong students, getting by on one student loan package after another, or we run up significant credit card debt to pay our therapy and medical bills, navigating the financial and legal systems as cannily as we can so that collections don't come after us. We perform sex work, sleep on friends' couches, sew our own clothing, and spread what little money we have around. These solutions aren't ideal, and all come with genuine costs—but the same can be said for donning a cashier's uniform and a neuroconforming mask and toiling away until the (often premature) end of our days.

Every Autistic adult who is contemplating how to survive under capitalism has to contend with a series of tough decisions about what we value and where we can find safety, and our answers and preferences may shift over time as our abilities fluctuate. The following flowchart summarizes just some of the many choices that we must weigh.

Accepting Uncertainty
Tough Choices Facing Autistics Who Are Fighting to Survive

Later in this chapter, we'll look at some potential solutions for unmasked Autistic people who decide they do want to try to work some kind of job. But before we contemplate any of that, let's consider the alternatives to employment—so that any decision to pursue employment is a genuine choice, one made in awareness of other possible solutions. If you're not certain that you can or would ever want to have a paying job, then you should review what alternate forms of support exist in your area. This may include disability benefits, social welfare benefits, charity, support from religious groups and nonprofits, familial support, government aid, and community mutual aid.

Here in the United States (and in Canada as well), a person facing homelessness, hunger, or a number of other vulnerabilities can immediately get plugged into local resources by dialing 211. Dialing 211 connects the caller to a 24-hour hotline where they can learn about all manner of health and social service offerings, and numerous neurodivergent people have told me they wished they'd been made aware of the service far sooner. You do not need to be facing immediate eviction or starvation to access 211 services—many people qualify for aid in paying their bills, free food, immigration services, reduced rent expenses, therapy, healthcare coverage, or other benefits even if they can't document their need. Particularly in large cities, there are a variety of types of support that the average person simply is not aware of, and calling 211 just to ask questions can grant you peace of mind and make you aware of options should you or anyone you love suddenly experience crisis. In other countries, similar resources exist: there's Citizens Advice in the UK, Moneysmart in Australia, the National Social Assistance Programme in India, the National Social Investment Programme in Nigeria, public assistance programs in Japan, and many more. For those of us who cannot use the phone to access such services (due to language processing disabilities, hearing disabilities, or anxiety) free captioned telephone services do also exist—the Telecommunications Relay Service is the most popular option in the United States. In the United States we also have DIAL, the Disability Information and Access Line, which matches disabled people with necessary resources; it can be accessed at dial.acl.gov.

Many Autistic people who can't work have to apply formally for social welfare benefits of some kind: unemployment, Medicare or Medicaid, food stamps, Social Security benefits, or rental assistance being some of the most common. The bureaucratic systems that distribute these forms of aid make themselves quite challenging and confusing to navigate, and this is very much by design: the more forms to complete and hearings to attend, the fewer people will be able to demonstrate they have a genuine enough need, and the less financial assistance will be given out as a result. At the heart of most social welfare systems is a core skepticism of disabled people, reflecting the widespread cultural belief that poor people aren't working hard enough, and that most disabled folks are just fakers gaming the system. Unfortunately, investigating welfare applications thoroughly to root out any sign of a manipulative "faker" costs agencies so much that many researchers have concluded it would be cheaper to just give money to anyone who asked, regardless of need.[14] In the long term, a solution such as universal basic income and universal healthcare would probably do a lot to keep disabled, elderly, and impoverished people safe, at a lower cost than the systems we already have.[15] For now, though, it's useful to recognize that the social welfare system often feels like an inscrutable maze because it was intended to be one, not because you are foolish, lazy, lying, or undeserving.

Most Autistic people will need assistance in accessing these resources. If you can, try engaging a friend or two for help reading through unemployment or food stamp application requirements, and to hold you accountable for submitting them on time. You can ask for help from your local librarians too, or visit your local welfare office or Department of Health and Human Services. These government offices may feel quite unpleasant to navigate as a disabled person, sadly. They tend to be placed in bright, echoey old buildings filled with people and the smells of dusty furniture and harsh cleaning products. Tired, overworked government employees with limited training on neurodiversity may be impatient with you and ask you questions you can't understand in a rapid-fire way.

Bring a friend or loved one to serve as your advocate in these moments; even just having someone by your side to slowly repeat questions and be baffled by all the application requirements right alongside you can do a lot to help manage distress. Here in Chicago, organizations like Thresholds assign social workers and other aides to neurodivergent people to help them make their way through the social programs available to them. Similarly, the Transformative Justice Law Project of Illinois provides support to queer people who need help moving through the legal system. Your area probably has organizations devoted to supporting people in need as they interface with large bureaucratic systems, so make sure to seek them out (or ask for a loved one or librarian to look them up for you).

Another way that many Autistic people attempt to make ends meet is by applying for their country's version of disability benefits. In many countries including the United States, if you have a diagnosed disability, you are entitled to regular payments as well as health insurance. People who know very little about what it's like to be disabled and oppose government benefits programs tend to portray disability payments as a lavish affordance that people take "advantage" of easily, but in reality applying for benefits is a highly involved and thoroughly gatekept process in which an applicant must secure a diagnosis of a qualifying medical condition, collect documentation from medical providers attesting to the fact that they cannot work, have their case reviewed by a disability examiner, and in many cases appeal an initial rejection of their application by requesting a formal disability hearing.

It's an open secret among disabled people that first-time disability benefit applications are highly likely to be rejected; according to the organization Ascend Disability, the initial rejection rate is about 40 percent.[16] And though the Social Security Administration states that they aim to review applications within two to four months and begin issuing payments approximately five months after that, their own data as well as external surveys reveal that the average wait time is far longer: 38 percent of applicants have to wait longer than six months, as of 2023, and for an applicant who must request a hearing, the average wait time to receive benefits is a staggering twenty-seven months.[17]

Very little high-quality data exists regarding the outcomes of Autistic people applying for disability benefits. We do know, however, that since Autism remains wildly underdiagnosed among people of color, women, transgender people, people in poverty, and older adults, these groups are far less likely to receive benefits. Recent research has shown that systemic racial bias leads to Autistic people of color receiving fewer

Medicaid and Medicare benefits,[18] and it's likely that these groups are being excluded from disability payments as well, as they have been historically.[19]

Once an Autistic person has found a competent assessor and attained a diagnosis, their disability application will be more harshly scrutinized if they mask, are a member of a marginalized group, or have been able to work or attend school in the past. Long-term disability benefits in the United States are only provided if a condition will last more than one year or result in the applicant's death; if an Autistic person's functioning has fluctuated over the years, or if they're newly incapacitated due to trauma or burnout, it can be hard to prove that complete disability will last the rest of their life.

Once a person has received disability benefits or other government assistance, the fight to survive is sadly not over. Applicants may be required to have their disabled status reexamined regularly, anywhere from every seven years to every six months.[20] Additionally, a person's ability to receive benefits will also depend on several legal and financial conditions. For example, recipients of Supplemental Security Income (SSI) in the United States must not accrue more than $2,000 in wealth of any kind (including bank accounts and possessions), and their benefits can be reduced or terminated should they get married.[21] Social Security Disability Insurance (SSDI), in contrast, comes with no asset limit but does place restrictions on how much other income a recipient can receive month to month, forcing many disabled people into lifelong unemployment. Disability justice groups vocally oppose these policies, as well as the inaccessibility of the benefits approval process. Unfortunately, at the time of this writing, policymakers have not taken these concerns seriously enough to pass new legislation that could streamline applications or make living on disability payments more financially viable.[22]

I share all these worrying statistics not to demotivate you but to help you make an informed decision about the path you will pursue and what it will take to proceed. When you find yourself feeling stuck and demoralized by the length and complexity of the process, remind yourself that this is exactly how gatekeeping policymakers would like you to feel. They want you to give up, but by using the skill of engagement, you can remain involved in this lengthy process and access some of the practical assistance and moral support needed to stay in the fight. Below is a table listing some of the ways that you might need to engage for help as you seek financial aid.

Engage with Others
Help to Request as You Apply for Aid

Help researching options online	An advocate at the social services office	Assistance filling out forms and organizing documents
Crowdsourcing resources and information	Help finding a competent Autism assessor	Emotional support at your benefits hearing
Companionship at a library or coffee shop while you work on applications	Regular reminders about filing deadlines	Encouragement that you deserve this kind of aid
Connections to existing disability resource groups	A place to sit comfortably to work on applications	Validation that this process is unreasonably hard

Throughout this process, take the time to remind yourself that you deserve financial support, and that being unable to work is not shameful. Research shows that the stigma associated with needing financial assistance is so extreme that many vulnerable people do not choose to seek it out at all, no matter how desperate their circumstances.[23] But if we truly believe in the projects of disability justice and neurodiversity, we have to treat every life as valuable and all persons as deserving of comfort and dignity, regardless of their ability to work or produce. As the writer Susan Sontag once wrote, all people who hold a passport to the kingdom of the well also hold a passport to the kingdom of the sick,[24] and each one of us will enter that second kingdom eventually—and so life must be for something other than being abled and earning our keep.

The book reviewer, podcaster, and BookTok influencer Nathan

Shuherk (also known as @schizophrenicreads) lived on government disability benefits for several years. In his videos, he states that federal disability payments made his life as an avid reader and BookToker possible. As a writer I'm staggered by the sheer number and breadth of books that Nathan manages to review, and the critical depth of his analysis: he devours books on ecological justice, abolitionism, history, linguistics, queer issues, racial justice, decolonization, mental health, disability justice, and more, as well as the occasional work of fiction; distills his perspective beautifully in clips that help viewers determine if a book is right for them; and places those books within a wider literature. I encountered Shuherk when he reviewed my first book, and his feedback was refreshing: he really understood what I meant when I said *Laziness Does Not Exist*. As a disabled leftist with a voracious aptitude for reading, he resonated with the book's radical message in a way other reviewers couldn't. That he's able to focus on his passion for reading and reviewing books is a wonderful outcome of our country's disability benefits system. I only wish that the monthly payments he received were larger, that he was legally permitted to accrue savings while on them, and that other disabled people could similarly be free to pursue their passions instead of breaking down their bodies and minds with day jobs.

Numerous Autistic people that I have interviewed over the years have elected to live in modified vans in order to keep their living expenses minimal; some have built kitchens and work-from-home office setups into their vans, or travel with their service animals to perform gig work or visit a rotating cast of friends and relatives. One English Autistic person that I spoke to lives on a modified narrowboat. On subreddits for tiny-home dwellers and people who live in vans, it's common to encounter Autistic people who have chosen to live in an unconventional way to either limit expenses, reduce exposure to sensory and social stimuli, or both.

Other Autistic people get by through providing childcare or eldercare around the house for loved ones who support them financially, or by negotiating some alternate arrangement where they provide a needed service to their friends.

"I've successfully escaped the capitalist grind for now and am working as a live-in maid and chef for some rich tech bro friends of mine," says L, an Autistic friend that I first met online. In addition, L runs a virtual book club for disabled people; members are currently reading Naomi Klein's *The Shock Doctrine* and discussing neoliberal economic policies. Many members of the group are ADHDers, Autistics, and traumatized people who typically find it difficult to sit down and read a longer work, but with L's guidance and the structure the club provides, they're getting to learn about political issues they've always wanted to understand better.

Similarly, my close friend Madeline has been unable to work for a while due to a mix of neurodivergence and exhaustion, and while her chemist spouse pays the bills, Maddie serves as a pillar of her community, hosting visitors who are struggling with their own chronic illnesses or personal crises, supplying N95 masks to protestors, helping members of her family, and organizing weekly streaming events that are well-attended by disabled people from all across the globe. Maddie also edits videos and produces music and digital art; like so many disabled people who are not seeking employment, her vitality and originality give the lie to the idea that human beings are fundamentally selfish or slothful and do not want to work. Every human being has a creative drive and wants to feel that their life matters, whether that is made manifest in their work or in their relationships. When we stop having to mask as neurotypical in order to hold down a job, we are finally free to chase the pursuits that do make life worthwhile.

It takes a lot of bravery for Autistic people to accept our limitations without moralizing them and dive headfirst into unfamiliar modes of living like these. You can use the table on the next page to brainstorm a bit about what living solutions beyond the demands of capitalism might work best for you.

Transgress Expectations, Create New Solutions
Alternate Sources of Stability for Disabled People

Housing	Co-operative housing, shelters, tiny homes, van life, camping, multifamily housing, having roommates. *Housing options that might work for me:*
Financial assistance	Disability benefits, welfare, food stamps, support from friends and family, nonprofit support, government grants, government loans, aid from religious and cultural institutions. *Financial assistance options that might work for me:*
Alternate income and housing sources	Freelance work, skills sharing or trading, nannying, tutoring, sex work, digital content creation, crowdfunding, aid work around the home, caring for one's family's or friends' home or children *Income sources that might work for me:*

I want to acknowledge that none of these solutions is foolproof or entirely pleasant, and that in a truly just world, a person in need would not have to choose any of them. As much as L enjoys working as a maid and chef, for example, relying upon wealthy friends for housing and an income makes them vulnerable, in many of the same ways that a stay-at-home parent depends upon the continued employment and good graces of their spouse. Freelance work is unpredictable, sex work can be dangerous or traumatizing (as most other jobs can be), and social welfare benefits can be unceremoniously cut off. You know your own situation best and you should only pursue the means of survival that you can truly live with. Regardless of the path you take, you will need additional social and emotional support.

Because so many of these fallback options are unreliable and can be confusing to navigate, many Autistic people do desire the income and autonomy employment can provide. In the next few sections, we'll take a look at how to make work more workable for the unmasked Autistic.

Finding and Interviewing for Jobs

After an Autistic person decides that they would like to try pursuing employment, the next step is *career discernment:* taking an honest stock of the options that are available, as well as one's skills and limitations, in order to identify the positions that could be a reasonable fit. Career discernment can help us to narrow the field of potential job opportunities, and keep us from wasting time and energy applying to positions that we won't find accessible in the long term. The next section suggests some questions that every Autistic person can ask themselves prior to selecting a job position to apply for.

Transgress Capitalist Norms

Finding Work that Actually Works for You

- Can I comfortably manage a position that involves regularly interacting with the public?

- Can I comfortably manage being in a workplace that requires frequent meetings or socializing?

- Can I stand on my feet for multiple hours per day without exhaustion or discomfort?

- How long of a commute can I tolerate without becoming tired or overstimulated?

- What are some workplace-relevant skills that I enjoy using? (For example, data analytic skills or organizational skills)

- What are some workplace-related tasks that I can do with effort but can't make a regular part of my everyday? (For example, writing lengthy reports or giving presentations)

- Can I comfortably work as a member of a team, or do I require a job that allows me to work solo?

Career discernment is an inherently transgressive skill. Mainstream capitalist conditioning would have us believe that we don't have the right to be selective in our workplaces and should be grateful to accept any position we are given. These norms work in employers' favor, and their influence is powerful: just look at how many news articles have claimed that a return to the office is necessary in the years following COVID lockdowns, despite the empirical evidence showing that work-from-home teams are happier and more productive than people forced into a physical workspace.[25] I'm a Millennial who entered the job market during the Great Recession of 2008–09, and people of my generation vividly remember the onslaught of news articles, opinion columns, and books admonishing us to "lean in" to our careers and withstand endless professional abuse for the sake of getting a leg up. The rewards for all that effort and endurance never materialized; we earned less than older generations and received fewer benefits, despite working longer hours and remaining perpetually connected to our employers by cellphones and Slack.[26] Thankfully, the power dynamic has shifted in recent years, with many employers struggling to find qualified workers and having no choice but to renegotiate contract terms and reduce expectations.[27] Neurodivergent people who require flexibility and gentleness from their employers have the collective power to claim what we deserve, and career discernment can help us remember that fact.

An Autistic tech support worker named Obinna tells me that when his company pivoted from remote work to mandatory in-person shifts, he immediately announced his resignation to call their bluff. "I knew that they'd been searching for a manager of my department for numerous months," he says. Ultimately, Obinna's employer granted him a temporary exemption of the return-to-office policy of six months; by then, he'd secured another job at an all-remote company.

Another important way to practice career discernment is to speak to people who have left a field or quit working at a company. Professional norms dictate that a person never speak badly of their current employer, so it is impossible to get a straight answer from someone who is at a company about what the organization is truly like. Many people feel a strong pressure to justify their own past decisions or to rationalize away any mistreatment they've received, so even in fields where burnout is incredibly common such as teaching, counseling, medical care, or academic research, you're likely to hear frustrating platitudes about the importance of dedication and the weakness of people who quit, rather than earnest observations about how long the hours are and how little support management gives.

When I was in graduate school and thought I wanted to be a tenure-track professor, I surrounded myself with tenured professors and students who wanted to be tenured professors. All they ever talked about were the career milestones I'd need to hit if I wanted to get a tenure-track job. It wasn't until I read the book *The Professor Is In* by Karen Kelsky (a neurodivergent scholar who has left academia) that I learned a majority of graduate students wind up working outside the academy. The people who'd won under the current system seemed to assume success was both easier and more controllable than the data actually said it was. But the number of tenured professor positions was on a steady decline and had been since the Reagan administration,[28] all while the number of people with PhDs continued to rise. When I completed my dissertation, I entered the worst job market PhD holders had ever known—and it's gotten worse *every year* after that.[29] If I were to follow the scripts for my life others had laid out for me, I'd likely still be applying for more than a hundred tenure-track jobs per year (as many of my peers do), and consider myself lucky if I received even one interview. I'd also be expected to take any job I was offered in any corner of the country, no matter how transphobic, remote, or inaccessible the location might be.

I wish I'd spent more time during graduate school speaking to the people my department considered "failures" who "lacked the drive to succeed," because they actually represent the statistical norm for my field. They were the single parents, people from lower income backgrounds, and folks with mental illnesses and disabilities, like me; people who could not afford to spend fifty hours per week conducting research while also trying to pay the bills. I witnessed people like them being discouraged from continued study; advisors told them they weren't "graduate school material" if they found any readings confusing or lacked the time and money to visit conferences regularly and host on-campus brown-bag events every week. They could see academia's flaws and oppressions clearly because they'd lived them—and many of them ended up becoming part-time instructors, consultants, or government employees instead of pursuing the tenured professorship path.

Before you enter a career path, talk to some people who pursued it and hated it. Find the art school dropouts, the jaded K–12 teachers, the burned-out ex-bartenders, or the social workers who have become horrified by the number of patients they've had to lock away. You can find the former employees of an organization on sites like LinkedIn and Glassdoor, or sometimes at professional networking events. To engage with others and seek out discouraging information is inherently transgressive, and you'll be better positioned to survive in your chosen line of work if you recognize its flaws. Realistic expectations help us to plan for the insulting bosses, gossiping co-workers, unfair institutional policies, and discrimination in promotion or hiring we might face. We shouldn't have to expect these outcomes, but it's sensible and protective to do so.

Career discernment isn't only about identifying potential issues with a line of work, of course—it involves locating opportunities that suit your neurotype, too. I know many unmasked neurodivergent people who have found comfortable and rewarding positions as technical writers and content writers, for instance. These positions frequently pay better than other writing jobs, so long as you find a position within an industry that's well-funded, such as technology or contracting work. Because they require both precise communication skills and an ability to specialize in niche topic areas, a lot of masked Autistics and other neurodivergent people perform them really well, and they're typically remote and allow for flexible time. Bill tells me that when he switched from writing grants for arts organizations to writing grants for a biomedical company, his income nearly doubled while his work hours actually went down.

"A lot of these companies want someone who can understand the full complexities of their work, but write it up in a way that's approachable to the public," he says. Because he can't read between the lines of unspoken meaning, Bill asks a lot of questions that help clarify things. And because he devoted the first thirty years of his life to masking and imitating non-Autistic conversation patterns, he knows how to translate complicated ideas into normal-seeming speech once he gets them. It's as if his entire life path as a nerdy, undiagnosed Autistic who tried to seem fun and approachable has led him to his current position. "I'm the *normal* guy at work, compared to all the biomed nerds I work for," he says with a laugh. "Now I'm getting all this dental work done, seeing a masseuse, getting everything fixed that broke down when I was making $20,000 a year [writing grants] for a music school."

We don't have good data on the careers that Autistic people successfully pursue—particularly not for masked Autistics, who tend to be less interested in science, technology, engineering, and math than people with our disability are stereotyped to be. Some masked Autistics and ADHDers thrive in high-activity positions where socializing is mandatory, such as food service or sales (particularly those of us who are on the more sensory-seeking end of the spectrum). One Autistic woman that I spoke to told me that she's found success working in trendy coffee shops and record stores, where managers sometimes find it desirable to have staff who seem aloof rather than overly friendly. Numerous Autistic workers have told me they've enjoyed bartending or barista-ing far more than they ever liked working in stuffy office environments because every interaction followed a predictable script. Corporate jobs can be especially taxing for Autistics because everyone is expected to dress meticulously and to converse in highly formalized corporate-speak. Fields that demand a lot of emotional labor (such as healthcare and social work) tend to be exhausting, though they can also be deeply meaningful and appeal to our desires to help people or uphold our visions of justice.

After determining the types of positions that might be a good fit for your unique neurotype, applying and interviewing for jobs is the next step. Unfortunately, interviewing for a job is a highly inaccessible, confusing process for many Autistics, and can be uniquely triggering for those of us trying to unmask. Job descriptions don't typically provide enough information to determine what kind of work managers will really expect, or whether the work environment will be comfortable. The actual questions asked during interviews usually are not provided in advance, and may have little direct bearing on the actual work tasks you'll be engaging in. There is often a huge gap between how capable we are of actually performing the duties of any given position, and how we present ourselves socially during an interview.

Research published in the *Journal of Autism and Developmental Disorders* in 2023 demonstrates that neurotypical interviewers have an almost instinctual prejudice against Autistic job applicants. We struggle in video interviews consistently, even though we outperform neurotypical applicants when completing written interviews for the exact same position.[30] We may also be perplexed by the phrasing of many common interview questions. For example, when an Autistic applicant is asked what sets them apart from all the other applicants for a position, they may reply (quite honestly, and literally) that they have no idea, as they do not know who the other applicants are.[31]

In a series of simulated job interviews, psychologist Rebecca Flower and colleagues found that non-Autistic applicants made a better first impression than Autistics did, were rated as more employable, and were more likely to be offered a position.[32] However, when raters were told that a job interviewee was Autistic, they did report liking the applicant better and evaluated them as a job candidate more favorably than when they were not told the Autistic person had a disability. This parallels some of the earlier research cited in chapter two of this book, which also showed that non-Autistic people are less biased against us when they realize they're interacting with a disabled person because it offers a justification for why we seem unusual to them.

The cards are clearly stacked against Autistic job applicants. We should not have to compensate for society's pervasive biases against us, but given the reality that we are disadvantaged, we can better prepare for job interviews while remaining unmasked by using every single one of our core unmasking skills in some of the following ways.

Unmasking for Job Interviews

Using the Five Core Skills

- **Accept uncertainty:** Prepare for your interview by researching common interview questions online (try searching for ones specific to your field or the company in question). Conduct a mock interview where a friend asks you these questions but also throws you some unexpected follow-ups and icebreaker-type questions that you haven't scripted a response for. Do this many times until the initial anxiety of the unexpected becomes more manageable for you.

- **Engage other people:** Contact people in your desired field to ask for their mentorship, or to take part in an informational interview where you can learn more about what to expect. Attend networking or career development events offered by your college, library, queer community center, or parks system, and try speaking to people about opportunities. Participate in discussion boards, subreddits, Discord servers, or listserves for your profession online.

- **Transgress ableist norms:** Ask to see interview questions in advance to be able to write down your responses before speaking, or for other accommodations that you might need in order to perform your best. Weigh the benefits and risks of disclosing your disability in this way and consider asking forthright questions to determine whether the workplace will be right for you.

- **Tolerate being disliked:** Notice any pressure you feel to fawn or people-please at your interviewer and make an intentional decision about how much masking (and which forms of masking) are acceptable for you. Try not to mind-read your interviewer, and mentally detach from their reactions of you. Be your own best advocate and try to focus on figuring out how *you* feel about the workplace rather than managing what they think of you.

- **Create effective answers:** When asked about your past work experience, think expansively and creatively, and make sure to give yourself credit for volunteer positions, educational experiences, personal projects, and other accomplishments that might be overlooked. Challenge yourself to think up a narrative that paints your skills and experiences as the ideal fit for this specific job. Leave out information that doesn't benefit you, and emphasize your knowledge and capability as persuasively as you can. Non-Autistics "round up" their experience and competence in a job interview, so remind yourself that it's only fair for you to do so, too.

Despite adopting all the strategies outlined above, you may still find that you face a sharp disadvantage on the job market as an Autistic person. To an extent, this is a logical consequence of being unmasked: you are choosing to prioritize your authentic feelings and accessibility needs over hiding yourself away and being widely palatable, and so you can pat yourself on the back for alienating some of the right people. Early in my own career, I was turned down from jobs for which I was overqualified because I showed up unshaven, dressed too casually, or answered questions about myself too honestly by, for example, telling a school psychologist colleague that I'd been in special education myself. A neighbor of mine who worked in Human Resources once told me that I should only ever wear gray suits to job interviews, with no facial piercings or heavy makeup, saying that he expected everyone he interviewed to look as clean and neutral as possible. I consciously didn't take his advice, wearing bright purple jackets to interviews with a Monroe piercing sticking out of my face. I wasn't able to get a full-time position for years, and I knowingly didn't change my behavior despite this. My noncompliance was a test of potential employers' open-mindedness, and I am thankful I never contorted myself into a shape that would have hurt me.

Honoring ourselves while navigating the job market will almost always mean incurring some costs. We may be passed over for positions, receive odd looks and comments, or develop a professional reputation for going against the grain. Anticipating these potential consequences and determining which among them we can tolerate can help keep us confident that we're remaining aligned with our values. Here's a brief exercise to get you thinking about which losses and uncomfortable moments you can tolerate for the sake of preserving your well-being:

Tolerate Discomfort

When Being True to Yourself Comes at a Cost

In the professional world, maintaining your personal values and authenticity will sometimes mean coming into conflict with an employer or with professional norms. How will you navigate these tensions? Consider your answers to the following questions:

- **Values alignment:** In your chosen line of work, are there specific companies you would never consider working for? What are some reasons you might refuse to work for a company? (For example, discriminatory policies or involvement in warfare.)

- **Institutional injustice:** Many organizations suffer from a culture of overwork, unclear distribution of duties, and unfair promotion and compensation structures. How will you know when a company has gone "too far" for you to continue to put up with mistreatment? What will you do when a company has demanded too much of you in return for too little?

- **Quality of life:** What do you require from a work facility in terms of physical comfort, safety, and accessibility? What is an absolute dealbreaker for you in terms of maintaining your physical well-being in the workplace, and what will you do if an employer violates it?

- **Interpersonal difficulties:** Do you need to be on friendly terms with all of your co-workers, or do you prefer your colleagues to mostly leave you alone? Can you live with some co-workers or even a manager disliking you or excluding you from social events? Determine how much social awkwardness you can live with in your workplace, if any, and what you will do if you experience bullying, ostracism, or the pressure to socially perform.

For unmasking Autistics who struggle to advocate for themselves within the job interview environment, Obinna offers this advice: "Remember that you have all the knowledge about who you are and all the amazing things that you have done. Mostly you are a mystery to the interviewer, until you tell them a fabulous story about what a genius you are and how ideal you are for the role. When I got my first tech support position, all I had been doing was fixing the computers at my church and helping my aunts and uncles with their devices. I said I was a technology support specialist at a not-for-profit organization specializing in demystifying digital tools for elder populations, or something like that, which was true enough, and it worked."

At multiple points in this chapter, we've briefly looked at research regarding the impact of Autistic disclosure. We've seen that when polled, hiring managers say they see Autistic employees as less capable, but we've also seen that Autistic people are more fairly evaluated in interviews when an interviewer is aware of their disability. Both on the job market and once you have secured a position, you will be faced with the tricky decision of whether or not to disclose your neurodivergence. Should you take the risk? The next section will explore the various pros and cons, and ways to work around some of the negative consequences.

Self-Disclosure: When to Be "Out"

Three years ago, Sandra was hired as a designer at a company on the West Coast. A year and a half later, following the diagnosis of her son, Sandra figured out she was an Autistic ADHDer (or AuDHDer) herself. This explained why Sandra always felt most inspired late at night (as many ADHDers have sleep-wake cycles that favor nighttime activity)[33] and thrived in the chaos of an approaching deadline. She celebrated the good news, took on a role within her company's neurodiverse employee resource group, and asked to be transferred to one of the organization's most competitive and high-pressure teams.

She was proud to know herself. But Sandra's boss wasn't so enthused to get to know the real her.

"He believed I was being 'impulsive' and said my goals had to be more realistic," Sandra says. It's hard for her not to see ableism as a factor in these judgments. Sandra's transfer request was denied, then she was passed over for a promotion, then demoted to a project with less impact. "I was amped and doing well, and taking on new responsibilities. Why was I being punished?"

As she grew continually more frustrated and pushed to be included in new programs, eventually leadership stopped responding to Sandra's emails or including her in meetings for product launches she was involved in. "I was doing nothing all day, going crazy in the office," she says. "I had to quit."

Sandra was a victim of *constructive dismissal*, a labor practice in which an employer sidelines an employee, excludes them from work processes, or hinders their work to such a degree that they almost have no choice but to quit. According to the Great Lakes ADA Center, constructive dismissal is a common way that employers retaliate against disabled employees for either requesting accommodations that they don't want to provide, or for pursuing a legal discrimination case.[34] In my own work, I have heard numerous stories that echo Sandra's, wherein neurodivergent employees speak out about injustice they have encountered at work or simply name their needs openly as disabled people, and then find themselves fired for being a "bad fit with the culture" of the company or suddenly treated as if they were incompetent. Most countries' labor departments view constructive dismissal as a violation of employees' rights,[35] but in practice it's quite hard to legally prove—and unfortunately, the same thing can be said for any disability discrimination in the workplace.

Discrimination against disabled people is illegal under the Americans with Disabilities Act (ADA) and many similar statutes in other countries, and this includes obvious prejudice in the hiring, promotion, and termination processes. However, the reality is that disabled employees lose over 90 percent of discrimination lawsuits against their employers.[36] Since the early 1990s when the ADA was first passed, employers have openly celebrated that the law has proven difficult to uphold in court.[37] Very few disabled workers can afford to sue their employers for discrimination, and even if they can, they may not be able to find documentation that proves they were fired because of disability. Managers rarely admit outright that they fired or demoted a worker because of any diagnosed condition. Instead, they point to the behavioral quirks or signs of principled resistance that distinguish Autistic people from many other groups: we get axed for throwing away expired food that the head chef instructed us to cook with, for example, or for speaking up when we notice an obvious pay disparity between men and women.

Much of a workplace's ableism can be easily shrouded behind concerns for company culture or "fit"; an employee who cannot smile on demand can be criticized for lacking openness, and one who keeps a set schedule may be fired for not being "agile" enough in an office dominated by chaos. I know an ADHDer who was pushed to quit their position as a programmer because they wrote emails that were "too long"; their colleagues mistook the detail and care in their messages as a sign of anger. In the era of artificially intelligent language learning models, some Autistic workers are even accused of being "robots" because we draft emails that supposedly "lack warmth," as happened recently to one Autistic professor.[38]

The ADA allows discrimination against disabled people when their disability hinders their ability to perform work duties, and states we are only entitled to "reasonable accommodations" in order to make our jobs possible. But judgments of what's reasonable are highly subjective. Sandra wanted more flexibility and a greater challenge level as an accommodation for her AuDHD; other neurodivergent people get fired for needing time off for therapy appointments, skipping office Christmas parties, or for continuing to wear N95 masks as COVID numbers spike.

In many cases, outing ourselves as disabled leads to us being more heavily scrutinized and our bosses regarding us as potential problems in the making. When a close friend of mine was slow to jump into a "fun" icebreaker exercise at her work, her boss yelled in front of everyone that he'd fire her if she kept acting so "Autistically." She was let go from the company not long after, her employers chiding her for no longer being the chipper, agreeable person that she had been when she used to mask. It's rare for anti-Autistic bias to be quite so explicit, but reactions like these constantly simmer beneath the surface in a neuroconformist world. Yet some data does suggest that when we disclose our Autism, other people generally like us better because they finally have an explanation for what about us seems so odd to them, which puts them at ease. So what's an unmasking Autistic in the workplace to do?

The research literature on Autistic self-disclosure is mixed: while "coming out" as Autistic tends to improve the quality of a person's private relationships, in the workplace it can result in being more heavily scrutinized, othered, or infantilized.[39] Experimental research has found that non-Autistic employees find it very difficult to understand the motivations of their Autistic colleagues, assuming, for example, that an Autistic worker who spends a lot of time alone in the breakroom is doing so because they're antisocial, rather than because they're coping with sensory overstimulation,[40] or presuming that we dress in less formal clothing because we care less about the job, rather than because the uniform causes us intolerable pain and being comfortable helps us focus.

Autistic gender minorities and people of color are especially unlikely to feel belonging at work, probably because our populations tend to wear a mask heavily, which makes us seem hard to know,[41] and because we don't fit the portrait of stereotypical cis male Autism that people are most sympathetic with.[42] If Sandra were a man, her request for more challenging work would have likely been rewarded, perhaps even if she were openly disabled; but when her managers saw a capable, accomplished professional woman with a fresh diagnosis asking to have the bar raised, they saw her as unreliable and incapable of knowing herself.

It bears mentioning that approximately one-third of Autistic people who come out at work do have positive experiences, either because their managers implement changes that improve workplace accessibility, or because the disclosure inspires a culture shift within the organization.[43] One of those people is Shuài, the graduate student we heard from in the introduction of this book. Though Shuài's still terrified of how coming out as Autistic might make him look within his competitive graduate program, he has told his boss at the university library.

"I was given permission to work in the back, and not have to deal with students so much," he says. Now he gets to sort and catalog returned books and process the library's new acquisition requests rather than expending all his social energy on the customer service element of the job. "Before sharing that I am Autistic, my boss gave me those duties because he believed I would need help practicing my English," Shuài says. He was already quite confident in his English, though, and found it more important to get a job where he wasn't constantly dealing with random strangers. Once his manager understood, Shuài's working conditions improved. He says he finds the quiet, streamlined work restorative.

If you do choose to explain your disability to your colleagues, here is some sample language you might use.

Engaging with Co-workers
Seeking Understanding in the Workplace

The intentions of Autistic employees are often misconstrued. If you have chosen to disclose your disability to your colleagues, here is some sample language you can use to explain some of your preferences and needs.

> "Before we move on, can we take a pause to reflect on all this information?"
>
> "I might have a question or comment, but I need to gather my thoughts first."
>
> "I have trouble shifting attention to my work duties when I'm in and out of meetings all day. Can you send me an email about this instead?"
>
> "Don't mind me, doodling just makes it easier for me to listen to you."
>
> "I'm taking notes, so don't worry if I seem to be looking away."
>
> "I really get into the zone when I'm focused on something. You might need to [tap me on the shoulder/say my name multiple times/check in later] if I don't seem to hear you."
>
> "It's great spending time with you all, but I'm so done with people-ing today. I'll be [in the storeroom/in a private corner/etc.] introverting."
>
> "That [light/noise] is making it hard for me to get things done, can you turn that down? If not, I'll need to move to another area."
>
> "I'm Autistic, so if it seems like I'm missing something here, it's because I am."

"Could you give me a specific example of what you're looking for? I don't want to guess and get it wrong."

"I'm Autistic, so how I show excitement might not register to you, but I think this is a really great idea."

"I know my voice sounds [sarcastic/dry/singsong] to some people, but that's just how it naturally is. You can trust me when I tell you how I feel."

"My work process looks a little different from most people's because of my disabilities, but this helps me get the most done."

"I [dress this way/sit this way/etc.] so that I can put as much attention as possible into my job. If my sensory issues were getting set off all the time, I wouldn't perform as well."

Using self-disclosure to secure disability accommodations is certainly a mixed bag. In the next section, we'll examine several ways that Autistic people can advocate for the workplace adjustments we need, whether or not we choose to come out.

Securing Accommodations

There are several different strategies an Autistic person can use to advocate for accommodations, with varying risks of exposure—and some of them can even potentially work for the self-realized and undiagnosed. But first, let's review some of the common workplace accommodations that Autistic people and other neurodivergent folks might want to ask for.

I think many of us fail to realize just how dramatically organizations could be changed for the sake of our inclusion. It's not just our physical workspaces that could be made more comfortable; professional communication norms, evaluation and promotion processes, and new employee onboarding could all be dramatically improved, too. As you read through this list, think creatively and really dream of what an encouraging, supportive work environment would be like for you.

Creating an Accommodating Workplace

Common Accessibility Features Neurodivergent Employees Need

- A private workspace
- Work-from-home options
- Flexible scheduling (flex-time)
- Employee evaluation based on project completion, not hours spent in the workplace
- Communication via email or private message, rather than verbal instructions
- A warning before being called on the phone or called into a meeting
- Not having to interact with customers
- Control over the lighting and temperature of the workspace
- Limits on the number of meetings or calls held per day
- Fragrance-free policies
- A full agenda and all materials given out well in advance of a meeting
- Extra time to respond to proposals or questions
- The ability to submit feedback in writing after a meeting has ended
- No expectation of participating in workplace social functions
- Waived uniform or dress code policies
- Modified workplace furniture: a chair at the cash register, a standing desk, a chair that can hold a full body in a curled-up posture
- A mentor or support person to approach with any questions

The ability to shadow an employee before taking on their role	An explanation of social expectations before entering work events
Space to pace around or access to outdoor areas	Regular check-ins for feedback and reassurance
More frequent breaks	Documentation of all instructions and workplace communications
Fidget toys or other sensory items available at desks and during meetings	
Reduced travel expectations	Clear separation of job tasks to minimize competing demands
A private room or sensory-friendly space at conferences or retreats	Strong organizational systems with clearly labeled materials
Examples or templates of successfully completed work when taking on a new task	Noise-canceling sound panels, access to headphones and earplugs
Well-moderated meetings that make it clear when each person is invited to speak	Walls, doors, or cubicles that block out visual distractions, or privacy signs
	A hierarchy of job priorities to make decision-making easier

---

The potential for accommodation is truly limitless, and what you'll personally need will depend largely on how your disability manifests and the distinct ways in which your current job setting disables you.[44] A researcher and instructional designer that I know has persuaded the organization where they work to expect less socializing and fewer days in the office from them as a form of disability accommodation. They've also convinced their manager to message them with questions, rather than provoking anxiety with unexpected phone calls. They don't feel safe unmasking around their co-workers; their manager knows they are Autistic, and the workplace professes to be tolerant of neurodiversity, but they know that every professional environment has unspoken social lines that employees might get punished for crossing. And so, rather than unmasking completely, they choose to minimize their time around others. They've been willing to transgress social expectations and tolerate the mixed feelings that being so private elicits from their co-workers, and this has allowed them to actively create a work-life balance that is feasible.

When Autistic people draw attention to the fact that meetings and socialization are tiring activities and forms of labor, it can shift the workplace culture dramatically for everyone. After Evan, a data scientist, convinced his workplace to cut down on mandatory meetings, other employees who are not disabled began replacing brainstorming sessions with emails and interactive Slack threads, too. Small assertions of our perspective can illustrate to everyone that the rules of professionalism are not set in stone, and that many of the unwritten expectations we are held to at work should be subject to change.

If you determine you do need disability accommodations at work, there are a few tactics you can consider using:

- Approaching Human Resources with your diagnosis, your accommodation requests, and a doctor's letter explaining why they're necessary.

- Coming out as Autistic to everyone on your team and explaining your needs.

- Privately disclosing your disability to a boss, but not telling anyone else.

- Requesting accommodations but citing a reason that's less stigmatized than Autism (for example, migraines, anxiety, or allergies).

- Not disclosing your disability at all, but meeting your accessibility needs in more covert ways.

- Volunteering for work duties that are less stressful for you and withdrawing from ones you dislike, presenting this as you "doing a favor" for others.

- Organizing with your colleagues to advocate for changes to be made on an institutional scale.

Each of these tactics has its potential use cases. For example, if you've had positive experiences with your HR representative but not with your boss, you may choose to trust HR with your diagnosis and have them negotiate on your behalf for the accommodations you need (but remember, HR works for your employer first and foremost, so there is always a risk in giving them vulnerable information about yourself). On the flip side, if your current manager is approachable and nonjudgmental and the company itself is slow to change, it may be easier to ask them informally for permission to modify your uniform or workspace rather than engaging in a formal process.

If you're afraid of facing disability stigma, you may want to request changes to the lighting or air-conditioning by citing frequent headaches rather than Autism. If your request is denied (and many migraine sufferers are *also* mistreated and denied accommodations), that is a surefire sign that disclosing an Autism diagnosis would not have worked out well for you anyway. In particularly hostile or conformist work environments it's often best not to state one's needs overtly at all; you may prefer to simply volunteer for back-of-house duties every single day at your food service job and present it as doing your co-workers a favor, rather than framing it as a desired adjustment.

It is the first instinct of many Autistic people to be as candid and dedicated in our professional lives as humanly possible, and it's often this very impulse that leads to us facing years of unfair scrutiny and burnout. Make sure to think carefully about the potential consequences of exposure and frame your accessibility requests in terms of adjustments that will help you succeed and that will benefit the company. Avoid giving your employer any information that might unfairly lead them to see you as needy or overly sensitive. The writer and disability advocate Emma Barnes suggests flipping the typical disability request on its head by explaining how your *environment* has disabled *you*: instead of saying "I am sensitive to strong smells," for example, say that "The heavy use of perfume in this department disables me from focusing on my work tasks."[45] Locating the problem within the inaccessible environment instead of within yourself can encourage non-Autistic people to understand that disability has a social and structural component. It's not that you are bad at reading subtext; your workplace has a culture of not conveying information clearly. This culture will exclude other employees, such as immigrants and non-native English speakers, too. If company leadership could lay out specific, measurable expectations and an ordered list of priorities instead of vaguely articulating goals, it would benefit everyone.

One of the final ways that an increasing number of neurodivergent people seek workplace accommodations is through their company's disability-focused Employee Resource Groups (also known as ERGs). While the popularity of these groups certainly illustrates a growing public awareness of neurodiversity, the unfortunate reality is that they usually lack the institutional power necessary to have a big impact, and investing energy into them can sometimes do us more harm than good. At the same time, they can be a fruitful space for meeting other disabled people at your workplace and developing a sense of camaraderie. Let's take a look at the role of disabled employee ERGs, and consider some alternative ways we might push for needed changes more collectively.

Neurodiversity Initiatives and Labor Organizing at Work

In the past five years, organizations have gotten wise to the value of neurodiverse workers on a level they never have before. The tech industry in particular has come to embrace the *idea* of Autistic employees, if not the reality of us, and neurodiverse employee groups have emerged everywhere from Salesforce to Etsy to Nike.

I've delivered workshops at these and many other organizations, and the experience has left me cynical about the future of Autism inclusion at work. Frequently, the large corporations that hire me are uninterested in parting with the sixty-hour workweeks, keylogging software programs, and mandatory office hours that pervasively exclude so many of us. One neurodivergent ERG leader who invited me to speak at her company was fired less than two months after I'd visited her workplace. She went from being the head of the organization's disabled employee group to being on unemployment with a noncompete agreement, simply because she'd continued wearing an N95 mask to work, worked from home when she felt ill, and wouldn't shake potential clients' hands at conferences. Her manager told her that she was being "weird" and "making everyone feel guilty" about not adhering to COVID protocols, though this was never her intention. She was simply doing what she believed to be right, and what all the quality public health data recommended. Another Autistic person that I know was forced to leave his job after divulging to his boss that he was feeling suicidal; his manager threatened to call the police to his house every single time he was late to a meeting, and my friend, fearing he'd be forcibly institutionalized or attacked by the police, had no choice but to quit.

Employee Resource Groups are something of an emergent trend in the professional diversity and inclusion realm.[46] Though the very first ERG was formed by Black employees at Xerox back in 1970, the ERG as we know it today has really only become widespread in the past five years. Today, approximately 40 percent of companies have Employee Resource Groups, increasing at a rate of about 9 percent per year.[47] In 2021, 70 percent of companies with ERGs rolled out new diversity and inclusion initiatives of some kind—neurodiversity efforts being among the most popular emerging trend.

In numerous cases, the leaders of ERGs do their work on an entirely volunteer basis, without any additional compensation. Furthermore, ERGs are company-funded, so they can't push for programming management does not approve of. If an ERG (or a diversity and inclusion office) were to push for any change that leadership deemed too radical, or that really threatened the current distribution of power, it would then cease to exist—or the hardworking, predominantly Black, brown, female, disabled, and queer employees who lent their energy to such efforts would be summarily removed.

Once, when I was speaking to a large Fortune 500 company's disability ERG, I began explaining how the use of employee monitoring software on company computers creates problems for workers with disabilities like Autism, anxiety, ADHD, or OCD. Having one's every move carefully watched and micromanaged provokes extreme stress for many of us and distracts us from performing our duties. The stress of surveillance harms just about every worker, leading them to feel infantilized and mistrusted. For disabled employees this is doubly true because we have a slower processing speed and our ways of completing tasks might not look like everyone else's.

As I said this, employees shared in the virtual meeting's chat box that their company did in fact monitor all employees' computer use and that it was distracting. An event moderator from HR deleted all these messages instantly, hoping I wouldn't see them. When I realized this was happening and said explicitly that such surveillance programs ought to be removed, my talk was ended early, and the Q&A portion of the talk was cut. I've heard from many Autistic and ADHDer workers at other companies that their employers have denied their ERG's requests to purchase more comfortable furniture or noise-blocking wall panels, or eliminated resource groups entirely when workers began openly discussing compensation and benefits inequalities.

In theory, gathering alongside fellow disabled employees to air common grievances, build community, and collectively voice complaints to management ought to be useful. Many of the workplace adjustments that Autistic employees need would benefit *everyone* (no one likes harsh fluorescent overhead lights, for instance). When accommodations are made across the board to the workplace rather than having to be formally requested by an individual, the company becomes more accessible to the self-realized and undiagnosed. So there is good reason to bring together a large coalition of employees to push for institutional change—but that should be done by collectively bargaining and working toward a union, not by joining an employee-sponsored ERG.

"ERGs are a scam," a disabled union organizer told me. "It's employer-driven at the end of the day. There is no meaningful transfer of power [from the company to the workers]." Another organizer told me that

ERGs are often used to monitor dissent at the company—by creating a space where employees are encouraged to out themselves as marginalized and express their dissatisfaction, companies can collect data on who might present problems.

"ERGs are no replacement for a union," another seasoned labor representative said. "But they can be helpful to identify folks who could be agitated." Meaning that by attending ERG meetings, you can take note of who else at your company is dissatisfied with how disabled employees are treated, and from there you can follow up with more serious, private conversations that could one day lead to strikes, walkouts, or a union vote.[48]

A report by the IZA Institute of Labor Economics found that disabled workers at unionized companies were less likely to be fired, and experienced a 29.8 percent wage premium, compared to disabled workers at companies without unions.[49] The institute also found that unionized companies were more adept at responding to accessibility requests. The Center for Economic and Policy Research similarly finds that unionized workplaces are better at identifying and addressing pay gaps faced by disabled employees.[50] No such benefits have been found for ERGs.

Engaging in labor organizing at work is a challenging, lengthy process, and it's one that many companies actively punish. Many Autistic people fear we lack the social skills necessary to organize our workplaces. But the truth is, bringing people together over a common cause doesn't require incredible persuasive abilities or charm. Each and every one of us can take positive steps toward building community at work by participating in some of the following actions:

> Accept change by approaching co-workers you don't know well and asking them about their lives.
>
> Engage other employees more deeply by privately sharing your concerns about the workplace, and asking to hear theirs.
>
> Transgress unhelpful social norms by discussing your salary, benefits, and promotion experiences openly, and challenging

co-workers to imagine solutions they'd like to see to common problems.

Tolerate the discomfort of not being the best-behaved, most devoted worker in the world. Meet expectations, but do not exceed them, to help lower the pressure being put on your colleagues.

Create opportunities for community to form among employees. Hold cookouts or parties away from the work site, invite colleagues out for drinks, and show up for your co-workers in times of need.

We can also further educate ourselves about the process of labor organizing, and share some of our learning with interested colleagues. I recommend the books *Red State Revolt* by Eric Blanc; *How to Jump-Start Your Union* by Alexandra Bradbury, Mark Brenner, Jane Slaughter, Jenny Brown, and Samantha Winslow; and *Work Won't Love You Back* by Sarah Jaffe. For those in the nonprofit sector, *The Revolution Will Not Be Funded,* published by the Incite! Women of Color Against Violence collective, is especially helpful.

When we mask as neurotypical in the workplace, we aspire to make ourselves as useful and exploitable to others as possible and hide our genuine needs away. It's a fundamentally isolating impulse. To work and survive as an unmasked Autistic we must oppose this instinct, making ourselves louder, larger, slower, more demanding, and crucially, more connected to other people than we have been before. The modern workplace is not only inaccessible to Autistic people; with its long hours, low pay, ever-dwindling benefits, and reduced employee freedoms, the professional landscape has disabled a great many other people as well.

When people who are not formally disabled recognize themselves as exploited and silenced, just as we are, we have the power to accomplish great things together. Just look at how many workers have outright refused to be pressured back into the office, a half decade after the first appearance of COVID. The principled mass movement of the labor force has the ability to change our workplaces and to create means of survival that don't leave us all tired, faking a smile through our pain, and miserably sick.

Disabled people have every right to find survival on our own terms, and to do so without shame or apology. We are not lazy for relying upon government benefits, needy for being pained by tight hairnets, or shameful troublemakers for speaking up when our companies behave in unethical ways. We should be able to live in comfort and dignity no matter how our bodies and brains function.

You as the reader are the expert on what you are capable of; you will be able to determine what the best route to finding a survivable life is for you. Know that doing so is a responsible, brave thing to do, and that you deserve to use every single one of your self-advocacy skills to find the financial support, housing, and accommodations that will suit you. A world that overlooks and stigmatizes Autistic people has disabled you, and in response you get to create the conditions where you can feel more whole and capable.

Life as an Autistic person shouldn't have to be all about survival, of course. We deserve to luxuriate in pleasure and chase after the experiences that fulfill us as well. Just as Autistic people can harness the skills of acceptance, engagement, transgression, tolerance, and creation in order to eke out a living under capitalism, we also can harness our skills to build a life we genuinely enjoy. In the final two sections of this book, we will take a look at how unmasking Autistics can move beyond simple survival and start living our lives to the fullest—starting with the pursuit of romance, companionship, and sex.

Love and Sex

For the same reasons that Autistic people struggle to find fulfilling friendships, we also have a hard time exploring the realms of dating, romance, and sex. A profound yearning for a truly accepting connection to other people lingers deeply inside many of us, but because our wants are wonderfully unique and our ways of chasing after those wants don't always line up with the socially approved script, we're often left unfulfilled or believing that we're broken.

A 2021 literature review conducted by psychologist Rui Ying Yew and colleagues found that Autistic people expressed an interest in romantic relationships at approximately the same rate as non-Autistic people, in sharp contrast to the stereotypes of us as socially disconnected and incapable of loving others.[1] However, the researchers found that we struggle initiating and maintaining close relationships. In a 2020 survey of over 450 Autistic people, Grace Hancock and colleagues found that we encounter fewer opportunities to begin a romantic relationship than non-Autistic people do (perhaps due to our social isolation and exclusion), and that our relationships tend to have a short duration and be more marred by feelings of insecurity.[2] However, the study authors also found that Autistic people who were more socially engaged with others were less likely to experience relationship difficulties. These findings are a testament to the fact that when Autistic people stop shutting ourselves away from society and begin engaging with others from a genuine and unmasked place, we can find belonging. Of course, we have to be in a safe environment and surrounded by people who respect us to be able to do so.

Some promising research by psychiatrist Sandra Strunz and colleagues found that Autistic people's romantic relationship satisfaction had nothing to do with their degree of disability, their empathy skills, or the degree of social support they needed from others.[3] What did positively predict relationship satisfaction was being in a relationship with a fellow Autistic person. A study comparing the relationship needs of Autistics and non-Autistics found that both groups built intimacy with their partners by communicating openly, sharing their interests, showing respect for each other, making each other feel safe, and by actively working on the relationship as problems came up.[4] Romantic relationships that included Autistic people were no less intimate than those only including allistic people, though Autistics did experience unique struggles related to feeling uncertain and confused by some forms of communication.

All of this is yet further evidence that we can find and build love, no matter how divergent from the norm our disabilities might make us. It's entirely possible for us to forge lasting, fulfilling bonds to another person—even if we can't "feel their feelings," pick up on their subtext, buy them expensive romantic dinners, keep the house clean, or tolerate a public wedding ceremony. Furthermore, the data is clear that when we unmask by expressing ourselves openly or normalize our neurotype by dating other people like us, our relationship outcomes are better than when we conceal our real feelings to try to fit in. Unmasking our relationships is essential to fully unmasking our lives. And when we use all our self-advocacy skills to unmask our relationships, we can approach other people with a level of pride and self-knowledge that is infectious, and helps to liberate the ones we love, too.

The conventional rule book for dating is all about concealing one's actual personality and projecting an enviable yet unremarkable appearance to the world. But for Autistic people, those rules will never quite work. We need to create our own ways of building sexual and romantic connection, and nurturing our relationships into something resilient, unique, and capable of evolving with change. And since so many of us are kinky, polyamorous, asexual, or aromantic to some degree, it's important to consider the lives of those who don't want sex or romance, or who have it in ways society would never expect.

Flirting and Dating

Rose is an Autistic lesbian in her early twenties, and she's frustrated by the lack of sexual and romantic activity in her life. "I'm almost done with college, and I have good friends, but to my knowledge no one has ever had a crush on me. I've never kissed anyone, and no one has ever asked me out, not even as a kid at recess or whatever. I've tried to talk on dating apps, but I just have zero confidence, because nobody has expressed interest in me."

Rose worries that she's doomed to be loveless and unkissed for the rest of her life. She's also taken on a noticeably passive view of her own dating prospects. Like many masked Autistics and queer women, she has been repeatedly conditioned to view herself as a *recipient* of attraction, rather than as a person with agency who can act on her desires and approach people.

Yulia is a straight woman living in eastern Europe, half a world away from Rose's home in North America. Despite their differences in sexual orientation and geography, many of her romantic struggles sound quite the same.

"I have no idea how to flirt," she says. "Most of the things that people say you should do, like pretending not to understand something so a guy can explain it to you, just feel so cringey and fake." She also shares that in her culture, it's expected that a man will always be the one to ask a woman on a date, and that he should select the restaurant they will visit and the meal the woman should order. To be a successful woman in the dating market, then, is to inspire a man's interest enough that he will take the lead. But Yulia has no idea how to do it. The other women around her seem to entice men into dating them without ever making an overt move.

A lot of the typical dating "rules" teach us to act like a person with fewer wants and unique qualities than we actually have. *Don't text back too quickly. Laugh at your date's jokes even if they aren't funny. Don't let your date know if he's offended you. Open doors for her without asking if she likes it. Pretend you know less about a subject than your date does, so they don't get intimidated. Pretend you don't have goals for the future that will rule out many potential dating partners.*

It ruins many neuroconforming people's dating lives to enter intimate relationships based on this much inauthenticity. It makes communication impossible and sets people up for false expectations and resentment. A person can play by all the rules of the dating game, and "win" themselves a long-term partner or a spouse—only to find out years later that the person they're attached to has incompatible views on marriage, finances, or child-rearing, or doesn't even enjoy the activities they pretended to like while on dates. For a neurodivergent person, following such rules is even more destructive. We can waste years stuffing down our stims and unusual habits, for fear they'll make us "unattractive," and even send ourselves into Autistic burnout by pretending to agree with everything a potential partner says.

We cannot successfully identify if someone will make a good partner if we have to wait months (or even years) to find out who they really are. In fact, we can't truly trust anyone when every romantic prospect we meet is expected to lie and conceal themself in order to be liked. If we wish to build genuinely accepting relationships as unmasked Autistic people, we have to unmask ourselves first, and communicate openly with potential dates about our interests, limits, habits, and even long-term plans. Candid assertions of desire will scare off many neuroconforming people who believe that dating should follow a prewritten yet undiscussed script, and our specific preferences will eliminate many romantic partners from the dating pool. But this will spare us the time and turmoil of being expected to be a person that we are not, making it easier for us to focus on genuinely compatible prospects.

Both Rose and Yulia have taken on a view of themselves as a romantic *object*, a thing to be desired by others. But what about what each of these women wants for herself? To move forward in their romantic unmasking journey, they must think of themselves instead as *agents*, people who can initiate the dates and the life that they want. For many disabled people, especially women who have been conditioned to be passive and agreeable, this can be quite the dramatic reframe. Admitting that one experiences romantic longing or sexual attraction can feel guilty, creepy, or selfish. But asserting oneself isn't a bother, it's essential to building a life that is fully one's own. Here are a few questions to get you thinking about yourself as a fully realized person with sexual and romantic agency.

Accepting Change
Pondering What You Want in a Relationship

1. What kinds of people are you interested in dating? If you're uncertain, try browsing dating apps and wandering through public spaces, and observe the types of people who catch your eye.

    Describe any trends or patterns that you notice in the people you are interested in.

    ---

2. How do you know when you are attracted to another person? Do you fantasize about having sex with them, or do they appear in your dreams? Do friends tell you that you can't take your eyes off people you're crushing on? Do you laugh and smile at them a lot, or do you avoid their gaze?

    Every person shows attraction a little bit differently. Write down some of the signs of attraction you've noticed in yourself here.

    _____

    _____

    _____

    _____

3. What do you want out of a relationship right now? Would you like someone to have casual sex with, or do you want someone to take you on dinner and movie dates? Would you like to spend time with someone as a friend first before dating them? Which kinds of activities are comfortable dating outings for you?

    Jot down what you are currently looking for in your dating life.

    _____

    _____

    _____

    _____

    _____

4. Name a few absolute deal-breakers in a potential relationship partner, even a short-term one.

For example, you might only be willing to date someone of the same faith community as you, or if you're child-free, you may not wish to date anyone aiming to one day have children. Keep your personal boundaries in mind as well, and exclude anyone who treats you in ways you find disrespectful.

Some dating deal-breakers for you are:

_____

_____

_____

After we have a reasonably good sense of what we want in a relationship and find desirable in a partner, our next task is to engage with others to express those feelings. Though some Autistics will always have a hard time starting a conversation with a stranger out of the blue, each and every one of us can find our own ways of conveying interest. Messaging a prospect on a dating app, asking a close friend to set us up with someone they know, and sliding a cute stranger a note from across the bar are all completely acceptable strategies for engaging with our romantic interests. The people who will make good partners for us will not judge the modes of communication we find natural or the help we need to find our courage.

It does not matter that most neuroconforming people flirt with light touches on the arm, shy glances, and playful insults that a majority of Autistic people cannot process. We can just tell people explicitly that we are into them or not into them. And we can ask other people directly whether they are flirting with us. Forcing a covert, hard-to-read message into overt communication is a considerate, responsible thing to do, even if the other person finds it jarring. Our ability to participate in conversation is just as important as somebody else's, and there is a power to throwing back the curtain of avoidance and subtle manipulation that is conventional dating and shedding a little Autistic light on it.

Here are some potential scripts for how you might convey romantic or sexual interest.

Engaging Other People
Scripts for Expressing Romantic or Sexual Interest

> "I hope I'm not bothering you, but I love your whole look and the energy you're giving off. Can I buy you a drink?"

> "I don't know many people at this party, but as soon as I saw you, I wanted to get to know you better. Would you like to chat for a bit?"

> "I really enjoyed speaking to you tonight. Here's my Discord handle, I'd love it if you would message me with the link to that video you told me about!"

> "I've always enjoyed being your friend, and I'm wondering if you'd be interested in pursuing something deeper, too. Would you ever want to go on a date with me? If not, I will be happy to continue being good friends."

> "Your dating profile says you're into bondage. I am too, and I think you're super cute. Would you like to get a coffee with me and see if we have some chemistry?"

> "I really like you, and I'd like to see you more often."

> "Seeing movies with you these past few months has been so much fun, and I'd like to make it into a more regular thing. Would you be open to having a regular standing date on Saturdays?"

"Do you ever imagine us living together one day? When do you think you'd be ready for something like that?"

"In the long term, I need to be in a relationship that is [sexually exclusive/polyamorous/kinky/committed/etc.] in order to feel fulfilled. What about you?"

Jasmin is a bisexual woman who left a long-term relationship after she started unmasking and discovered she wanted greater independence and more sex out of her life. She picks up potential sexual partners exactly the way she's seen her gay male friends do it: by hopping on dating applications like OkCupid and Tinder, identifying the people that she finds the most attractive, and asking them directly if they want to have sex. It rattles a fair number of them, but Jasmin doesn't care. If a partner can't talk about sex openly, and doesn't enjoy casual hookups, they will never be a match. She has a lot more sex that she enjoys now that she plays the leading role in her own dating life.

On the opposite end of the spectrum, Norman is a shy Autistic man who's long feared romantic partners viewing him as creepy or intrusive. He is seeking significant social and emotional support in a long-term romantic partner—a person he can lean on for help conversing with strangers and exploring the world. He mostly sticks to the Autistic-centered dating application Hiki, and lets potential partners make the first move. After a romantic interest has made it clear that they'd like to get to know Norman, he outlines his specific needs in a partner and requests their consent to start flirting with them.

"I don't trust myself to know when another person is uncomfortable or not, so I leave nothing ambiguous," he explains. More neuroconforming women used to find his carefulness to be a turnoff because they believed men were "supposed" to be brazenly confident. But plenty of Autistic women like Norman's straightforward yet cautious approach. Though his self-advocacy might not look quite as bold as Jasmin's, he's still engaging with other people honestly, and transgressing social rules about what it means to be sexual as a man. He's found ways to accommodate his insecurities, showing himself care while also teaching potential partners how to care for him. Unmasking doesn't have to mean never experiencing anxiety or shyness. It can mean honoring and crafting a supportive life around such feelings.

Because we face so much invalidation and shame, a great many Autistic people have trouble articulating what we want sexually, even to ourselves. This is especially true for those among us who have fetishes or kinks, or who are within the LGBTQ community. Thankfully, we can build greater awareness of what gives us pleasure by using our core unmasking skills.

Autistic Pleasure

In 2023, my producer and co-host, Madeline, and I hosted a livestream event in which we asked neurodivergent people to share their most unusual sexual fetishes.[5] The event was a true celebration of unlikely sources of Autistic pleasure, and we were absolutely delighted at the sheer variety of interests that got shared. One neurodivergent person was turned on by a highly specific shade of dusty pink, another was aroused by the tendons on the feet of certain metal statues, and multiple people expressed a deep, sensual admiration for enormous pieces of strip-mining equipment. My entire adult life, I'd known Autistic people who wore fursuits in a sexual context, engaged in BDSM, dabbled in diaper fetishes, or wrote erotic stories about transforming into dragons and having carnivorous sex, but the sheer breadth of fetishes on display during this stream blew even me away. Everything from sock garters to anti-nausea wristbands to rubbing one's nude body against tree bark was eroticized. Dozens of viewers told me afterward that simply learning about other people's freakiest desires helped them experience less shame about their own.

More than most other groups of people, Autistic people report an interest in fetishes and kinks. We experience desire and love differently than most, and when we are passionate about something, we tend to love it *hard*, whether it's studying the history of sewage systems for hours late into the night, or devotedly mastering our rope-tying skills until we can safely suspend our lovers from a four-point wooden frame. In some ways, the Autistic tendency to develop fetishes mimics our tendency to form intense special interests; in both cases, we may find much of the drudgery of regular life unappealing, and take solace in the pursuit of a narrow range of deeply cherished activities that hold powerful meaning for us. Some of those hobbies are sexual and some are not, but both get stigmatized for seeming excessive or perverse according to polite neuroconformist society. But so long as the intimacy we enjoy occurs between consenting parties who know what they're in for, there's nothing perverse about feeling pleasure in our own freaky ways. Whether we're in love with trains for purely intellectual reasons or actively dream about having sex with Thomas the Tank Engine, Autistic people have every right to chase our bliss.

For all our brilliant nonconformity, most of us carry the heavy baggage of shame, particularly if we're used to masking as neurotypical in day-to-day life. This means that before we find out we are Autistic, many of us aren't even quite sure what our sexualities or romantic preferences are. Consent educator Sarah Casper says that one way that she gets clients better in touch with their true interests is by asking them to practice the skill of noticing.

"One activity that I do with kids is I read a list of words to them, like *chocolate, puppies, urine, roller coaster, hiking*," she says. "I pause between each one, and I ask them to notice how they feel, because our bodies do indicate to us in some way what our associations are with the activity. When I think about puppies, I smile, and when I hear urine, I might laugh or make a grossed-out face." The goal of this exercise is to help children better honor their own consent by realizing that their bodies do tell them what is pleasurable or not.

Many Autistic adults can also benefit from an exercise like this because we've been trained to tune out our own bodily signals. We've learned that other people don't like to see us scowling when we're confused, or consider it rude for us to huff and puff with frustration when plans are suddenly delayed. Through these experiences we learn to self-censor, and eventually, we stop noticing how we feel. Within the sexual and romantic worlds, we also pressure ourselves to want the things that "normal" people want so that we can better assimilate.

I used to force myself to accept oral sex from partners and would lie perfectly still, suppressing my disgust until I'd break down crying, and then I'd beat myself up for having "ruined" the moment with my emotional outburst. Everybody always said that receiving oral was the most pleasurable activity in the world, and that a partner wanting to give it to you was a good sign, so I vigorously willed myself to want it, and be normal. But I didn't want it. I never had. And if I'd sat down with a list of activities, as in Sarah Casper's exercise, and really listened to my body when I read the word *cunnilingus*, I would have realized that.

Our sources of pleasure, as Autistic people, will often be transgressive. We may not enjoy penetrative sex, cuddling, kissing, being naked, sleeping next to a partner, sweating during sex, or any number of other common sexual activities due to our sensory profiles and self-regulation needs. Conversely, we may find immense enjoyment in voyeurism, mutual masturbation, erotic fantasies, role-playing, pain, compression, restriction of movement, consensual non-consent, or any number of other strange or taboo activities. What's most erotic or sensual for us might not strike other people as sexual at all. As we unmask, we have to learn to dismiss other people's points of view, detaching from their judgments so we can experience reality as ourselves.

In the table below is a list of sexual activities a person might or might not enjoy. Read each one slowly, practicing transgression by noticing how you really feel, as opposed to how you might *wish* you felt if you wanted to be normal.

Transgress Normative Sexual Expectations
Noticing How You Feel

Read through each item on this list, pausing after each word to notice how your body responds. You can draw smiling or frowning faces or other symbols next to each word to convey how you feel.

Love and Sex

- Kissing
- Making out
- Sleeping next to someone
- Hugging
- Holding hands
- Showering together
- Dancing with a partner
- Dry humping
- Neck kisses
- Tickling
- Giving a massage
- Getting a massage
- Sexting
- Eye contact
- Playful teasing
- Penetrative sex (penis-in-vagina)
- Penetrative sex (dildo-in-vagina)
- Anal sex with a penis
- Anal sex with a dildo
- Vaginal fingering
- Anal fingering
- Hand jobs
- Blow jobs
- Eating pussy
- Eating ass
- Strap-ons
- Handcuffs
- Feet
- Cages
- Collars
- Spanking
- Slapping
- Dominance
- Submission
- Bondage
- Rope
- Punishment
- Transformation
- Training
- Exhibitionism
- Voyeurism
- Three-ways
- Vibrators
- Orgies
- Age play
- Piss play
- Blindfolds
- Bimbo play
- Pet play
- Food play
- Gags

Humiliation	Wax
Masochism	Needles
Latex	Body hair
Leather	Nipple clamps
Underwear	

It is impossible to fully encapsulate the diversity of human beings' sexual interests with one short list, particularly when we consider just how varied Autistic people's fetishes can be, and the physical sensations that might viscerally turn us off. I've taken care with this list to include activities that range from the relatively mundane to the extreme, so that most readers can identify at least one activity they feel neutrally or positively about on the list, and one activity they dislike. Seeing your exact sexual interests reflected here is not important, what matters instead is noticing what positive and negative reactions feel like in your body.

You can continue to practice the skill of noticing by exploring dating apps and kink-oriented websites like FetLife; when you encounter a term or an activity that you haven't ever thought much about, pause to check in with yourself, and notice the important signals your body is giving off. Also notice whether you are beating yourself up for not wanting something, not being certain, or for not being "open-minded" enough to see a person or an activity's appeal. Masked Autistics question our reactions so heavily that we are easily guilted into sexual activities we do not enjoy, in hopes of pleasing others or making ourselves seem more normal. If this is a problem for you, consider following self-help guru Mark Manson's advice: if it's not a "Fuck yes!," it's a no.[6]

If every sexual activity you consider makes you feel uncomfortable, or you're plainly uninterested in every person that you see, that too is beneficial information. Recognizing what we don't want is a necessary precondition to sorting out what we do. I had to say no to receiving oral numerous times before I truly felt empowered enough to state what I really desired—erotic hypnosis, not sex. At first, I hated myself for lacking all interest in the sexual activities most other people enjoyed. I thought I'd never stand a chance of finding sexual satisfaction or love if I didn't mold myself into a more conventional shape. But eventually, I came to accept that pretending to be a person I could never be would not make me lovable. I could only choose to hide myself or to be myself. Being normal wasn't an option.

"You don't get to choose what you find enjoyable," Sarah Casper affirms. "You just notice it, and then you can decide whether to act on it."

A number of Autistic people are asexual, which means they do not experience sexual attraction to any gender or to people in general. Being asexual is not the same thing as having no libido: some asexual people have a high sex drive, or enjoy the stimulation or endorphin rush of sex, whereas others might be sex-repulsed or simply feel indifferent to it. What distinguishes asexual people from non-asexuals (also known as *allosexuals*) is how they experience desire.[7] Most allosexual people are drawn to other human beings on the basis of their physical presence, their charisma, or their bodies; there's some kind of magnetic pull allosexuals feel toward the persons they are attracted to. Attraction happens on a very intuitive level: even just being around the right person can arouse some allosexuals. Asexuals, in contrast, don't really harbor sexual feelings for the way people move or look. They might recognize aesthetically that a person has a pleasing face, but there is no sexual twinge to their feelings, or any desire to act on them.

Research conducted by Elizabeth Weir in 2021 found that Autistic people were eight times more likely than non-Autistic people to identify as asexual.[8] Studies on asexual populations find that they are also more likely than average to identify as Autistic.[9] It's clear that these two populations overlap considerably, and various study authors have posited that the reasons for this might include sensory issues that make sexual acts less appealing, differences in how Autistic brains process people's body language and faces, and a tendency among Autistics to feel more closely connected to objects than people. I would argue that Autistics are probably more likely to be asexual for the same reasons we're more likely to be gay, bisexual, transgender, or otherwise queer (with more than 69 percent of us being non-straight, according to some studies):[10] we're so acquainted with social rejection and so consistently honest about our beliefs that we're more likely to be *out* about everything that makes us different. Through this lens, we can only ponder how many non-Autistic people actually harbor queer feelings, or asexual feelings in particular, but are simply too afraid of social rejection to ever voice it. This is the cost of neuroconformity: it demands that everyone feel, think, dream, and desire in exactly the same way.

Autistic desire comes in all forms, and many asexuals experience powerful sensuality. Asexual, neurodivergent writer Ana Valens puts it this way: "For an ace *[short for asexual]* person such as myself, all those emotional needs for connection exist, but not the attraction to a specific person for sex. We therefore seek out intense intimacy in unique ways. That's where *ace erotics* come in." For Ana, ace erotics can mean participating in a sexual power dynamic, providing service to a dominant figure, or simply enjoying an emotionally intense work of porn. But actually having sex with another person isn't required for her because she doesn't experience conventional sexual attraction.[11]

One Autistic ADHDer that I spoke to, Rayan, told me that in order to appreciate sex with a partner, he needs for it to incorporate elements of his special interest, anime. "My jackrabbit ADHDer brain is bored by sex just as an activity, I'm definitely somewhere on the asexual spectrum, it just doesn't do anything for me. But if we are role-playing characters from *Promare* or *Yuri on Ice,* now I'm interested." But, he clarifies, "It's really stepping into these characters that makes it all exciting for me. I could do with or without the sex."

Some Autistic fetishists and asexuals have sex by rubbing themselves against stuffed animals, or by clenching and unclenching their bodies while they ride roller coasters. Others among us find the physical sensation of arousal to be painfully unpleasant, so we avoid it as much as possible, or we can't handle the huge volume of nonverbal data that comes flying at us during sex with another person. We may partner with people who meet their own sexual needs outside the relationship while enjoying ace erotics privately on our own. We're wonderfully inventive in building ways of life and forms of sexual expression that work with our own distinctive wiring instead of warring against it. In this next section, we'll take a look at the creative and liberatory ways that Autistics experiment with love and relationships.

Autistic Love and Relationships

Brett and Avery first became acquainted as roommates when they were in their late teens. They got along well together, and for Avery, who had just escaped an unstable and abusive family, living with Brett was one of the first times he ever felt safe. Avery had been neglected during childhood, and he hadn't learned many important life skills, such as cooking or cleaning, but Brett walked him through it all without any judgment.

"He never yelled at me, he just explained why dish soap didn't go in the washing machine, and why you have to wash a knife after cutting chicken," Avery says.

The years passed, and both young men moved out on their own and began dating women. Brett was married for a time, and Avery took some classes at a trade school and then traveled for a while. But by the end of their twenties, Brett and Avery were living together again. It was slowly dawning upon them that they belonged together, though not in a romantic way.

Both Brett and Avery are Autistic, and they both have led difficult, often traumatic lives. In each other they've been able to find consistent support and commitment on a level that no other friendship or any romantic relationship has been able to provide. Right now they share a tiny one-bedroom in Seattle, which is all that they can currently afford. They pay the bills collectively from a joint savings account and sleep together in a shared bed. Avery drives Brett to work, since his friend can't drive himself, and Brett has Avery enrolled on his health insurance. Friends sometimes ask the men what they plan to do in the future, when their arrangement ends.

"Us no longer being close won't happen," Avery says with certainty. "We are family."

Brett and Avery are in a *queerplatonic partnership*, a close, committed, intimate relationship with no romantic or sexual component.

While Avery identifies as straight and Brett now identifies as queer and exploring, the two have found a relationship structure that transcends any option that's ever been presented to them. They've tried dating and tried partnering up with other people romantically, but no connection has meant as much to them as the devoted friendship they've formed.

A 2020 study found that Autistic people are more likely to practice nonmonogamous or otherwise unconventional relationship structures, compared to allistic people.[12] It may seem paradoxical from the outside, but as disabled people who often find being around other people to be exhausting, our needs for both support and space can be more intense than what neurotypical dating scripts teach people to expect. We have to navigate meeting our needs and finding acceptance and peace in ways that are completely our own, and that often means having a series of close bonds to other people with varying degrees of romance or sexuality involved in them.

Some Autistic people find that conventional marital roles do not suit their values or way of functioning at all. They may prefer to date numerous people independently from one another, or join a more complex, interwoven polycule where relationships can continually shift and re-calibrate. Other Autistic people discover that for them, sexuality and romantic partnership are not intertwined, and the people they wish to make a domestic commitment to aren't the same people they enjoy having sex with. Even within a committed monogamous marriage, Autistic couples tend to break the mold, dividing responsibilities, sharing care, expressing affection, and planning for the future in ways that might confuse their neurotypical friends or shock their older relatives. Maintaining separate residences, relying on a romantic partner for help with eating and bathing, raising children with one person while being romantically committed to another—the possibilities for loving and forming bonds as an unmasked Autistic person are truly endless. We just need the unconventional thinking necessary to recognize when we want something different out of life than what's been sold to us, and the unmasking skills to make it happen.

There are a variety of relationship structures that an Autistic person might choose to adopt, which have been thoroughly practiced and explored by nonmonogamous and queer people but are still not widely known in the straight, monogamous world. And to even place a label on some of these options is to make them sound more limiting than they actually are. In reality, every relationship is different because it represents the unique desires, abilities, limits, and chemistry of the people within it, and no relationship structure is guided by consistent rules. Still, it can be affirming to know just how many different options are out there, so here's a brief summary of some of the relationship models that exist.

Transgressing Relationship Norms
Alternatives to Monogamous Heterosexual Marriage[13]

Monogamish: A committed, emotionally exclusive romantic bond where either or both partners may enjoy occasional casual sex with other people.

Polyfidelity: A closed, committed relationship including more than two people, where all people involved are typically exclusive to one another.

Open relationship: A committed romantic relationship that is sexually nonexclusive; typically, partners are free to have sex with other people, and may develop romantic relationships as well, though usually the core relationship is considered "primary" in importance.

Hierarchical polyamory: A relationship structure where all partners may have sex with and date others, but various relationships differ in terms of their importance, commitment level, or centrality to a person's life.

Nonhierarchical polyamory: A structure in which numerous romantic and sexual relationships exist between various people, and no relationship is considered more important or core than another.

Poly-intimacy: Forming multiple close, meaningful bonds with other people that may or may not involve either romance or sex.

Solo polyamory: Maintaining multiple sexual or romantic relationships with other people while maintaining an independent or "single" lifestyle.

Swinging: A committed, romantically exclusive relationship where either or both partners sexually engage with others, typically with other couples who are in a similar arrangement.

Relationship anarchy: A fluid, nonexclusive approach to relationships that does not firmly differentiate between sexual, emotional, and platonic forms of intimacy.

Queerplatonic partnership: A committed relationship that is emotionally intimate and supportive, but not necessarily sexual or romantic, where partners are typically free to pursue sex or romance with others.

Nesting partnership: An emotionally close relationship that is often romantic or sexual, where both parties live together and share domestic responsibilities, but which is not exclusive.

Kitchen table polyamory: A series of nonexclusive relationships where all members can comfortably communicate and spend time with one another, including those they are not personally in a relationship with.

Parallel polyamory: A nonmonogamous relationship structure in which each relationship between two people is considered distinct and separate from any other relationship a person might have.

In addition to relationship structures that deviate from the norm, the nature and depth of an Autistic person's attachments can also challenge mainstream ideals of independence or self-sufficiency. Autistic people often attach in far more intense ways than neurotypical people do, leading our relationships to be mistakenly viewed as codependent or unhealthy. While it's certainly possible for us to be taken advantage of (and like all disabled people, we are at an elevated risk of abuse),[14] there's also nothing inherently wrong with leaning on other people and developing mutual networks of support.

To an outside, neurotypical eye, the bond Brett and Avery have is unacceptable. Brett has never been able to drive, and Avery's repeatedly had problems holding down a job. In hyper-independent capitalist society, adult men aren't supposed to need each other like they do. But in caring for and looking after each other, Brett and Avery have found a way to succeed without having to mask and negate themselves, and they experience unconditional love that's helped them recover from trauma-ridden pasts.

Similarly, some Autistic people find that they do not crave a wide social circle, and instead find fulfillment and connection through a small handful of relationships to close loved ones and partners. While taking a long time to get to know and trust someone is normalized in many cultures, in the United States it's considered a bit of a personality defect not to be a "people person" who opens up to new friends readily. Many Autistics are slow to adapt to change and unfamiliarity, and we've all been burned by people who rejected us for our differences in the past. It's completely fine if our primary social outlets are a spouse and a best friend, or the couple of people that we are intimately dating. For Autistics who do not communicate verbally or find in-person socializing to move too rapidly and confusingly, our online connections may be the most intimate and steadfast partnerships we have. So long as we feel understood, have people around who can assist us when needed, and are satisfied with the nature of our relationships, there is absolutely nothing wrong with relating in our own unique ways.

Some Autistic people are also *aromantic,* meaning that they do not experience romantic attraction or any desire to form love connections with other people. Like asexuality, aromanticism is quite widely misunderstood; the prevailing prejudice against aromantic people is that they are heartless and only wish to have sex without forming any kind of deeper commitment. The bias against aromantic people is caused by a social force called *amatonormativity,* which feminist philosopher Elizabeth Brake defines as "the assumption that a central, exclusive, amorous relationship is normal for humans, in that it is a universally shared goal, and that such a relationship is normative, in that it should be aimed at in preference to other relationship types."[15] It is amatonormativity that encourages young adults to grow more distant from their friends as they get older and partner off; it also leads many human beings to falsely assume that the unpartnered are incomplete and pitiable. Amatonormativity places a huge number of physical, emotional, social, sexual, sensual, practical, and psychological burdens on a single relationship, in spite of the fact that in the past, many would have relied upon a rich community of dozens of other people to meet all those needs.

It's unfortunate the mainstream culture preaches that a romantic relationship is the ultimate interpersonal achievement, because so much of forming a lasting bond is beyond a person's control. Even if we never find a singular person who fulfills all our needs, each one of us can search for meaningful comfort and connection in our lives. The ideals of amatonormativity are also ahistorical: throughout most of human history, marriages were not guided by love, and people did not expect to find fulfillment within them. Marriage served primarily as a legal and financial arrangement, and it largely regarded women as property or breeding stock to be exchanged. Historically, marriage was only a permanent commitment to the degree that a woman was legally incapable of escaping it; to hold up a long-term, exclusive marriage as the ultimate goal for all people is to distort a great systemic act of violence against women and romanticize it. Many neurodivergent people know better than that and instead seek connections in which all parties are free.

Sasha is an aromantic Autistic woman who says that she experiences romantic connections in much the same way that she experiences forced eye contact: it's too close, too intense, and too all-encompassing of a demand on her attention for it to ever be good for her. "People say I must be cold-blooded, but that couldn't be further from the truth," she says. "I feel too much." When she used to date romantically, she felt suffocated by her partners' need for closeness and quality time; they eclipsed her until she lost all connection to herself. Today, she has sex casually from time to time with a local friend-with-benefits who dislikes romance as much as she does. She mainly finds belonging in her friendships, her family, and her cats.

"The assumption that valuable relationships must be marital or amorous devalues friendships and other caring relationships," writes Elizabeth Brake. As we unmask, we have to actively push against these socially normative messages and values to determine the relationship dynamics that will work best for us. Even if we do wind up realizing we crave a monogamous marriage or enjoy grand romantic gestures, we have to be able to distinguish first between what we truly want and what we believe it's normal to want.

What does a valuable relationship look like for you? In the table below are some of the common emotional, physical, and practical needs that many people expect to get met in their relationships. Contemplate whether each of the needs listed applies to you, and if so, how you would ideally like to see that need fulfilled. For example, you may not desire romantic commitment at all, but need lots of physical affection. If that's the case, an exclusive, romantic marriage is probably not the right fit for you, but having close friends or a cohabiting partner who is open to cuddling might be. Any of your relationships can help you to meet your needs, regardless of whether they are explicitly romantic or sexual ones, so long as you communicate openly about your expectations, honor other people's interests and boundaries, and continually work on communicating and showing up for one another.

Creating Unmasked Relationships
What Do You Want from Your Connections to Other People?

Sex	Physical affection (e.g., cuddling)
Commitment	
Romantic gestures	Emotional intimacy

- Vulnerable conversations
- Unconditional acceptance
- Praise and verbal kindness
- Cohabitation
- Healing touch (e.g., a massage)
- Care when you are sick or injured
- Someone to grow with
- Regular company
- Quality time
- Financial support
- Sharing of chores
- Sharing of errands and daily obligations
- A traveling companion
- Reminders to look after your health
- Someone to care for and be generous with
- A "safe person" for social outings
- Shared finances or expenses
- Shared meals
- Emotional co-regulation
- Shared hobbies and interests
- Sharing of childcare or eldercare duties
- A biological co-parent
- A trusted advisor
- A secure attachment
- Someone to grow old with

Knowing what we want in our romantic or sexual lives is not the same thing as getting it. It's important for unmasking Autistics to clarify for themselves what they truly desire, so that they can communicate it to others and shake off the pressure to present themselves in the most blandly appealing, conventional way. However, a relationship is never a static object that can be acquired—it is an evolving dynamic that must be developed through consistent communication, quality time, and mutual generosity. And so, for the next section of this chapter, we will look at the foundational relational skills that make it possible for us to build relationships with others that reflect our preferences and our loved ones' desires equally.

Consent and Healthy Conflict

"I actually hate the word *consent*," Sarah Casper says with a laugh. "It's so ill-defined, yet it carries so much weight. Sometimes it means *permission*, sometimes it means *wanting*. Some people use it to replace the words *body autonomy* or *choice*." When working with clients or offering workshops on the topic, Sarah finds it more helpful to interrogate separately each of these aspects of what gets called consent, so that a person can express themself and collaborate with a partner effectively.

"A conceptualization I have been loving lately is that consent is the practice of navigating two or more people's boundaries and desires," she says.

So far we've spoken a lot about our desires for our relationships in this chapter—and this has naturally caused us to reflect upon what we *don't* want from a relationship, and therefore what some of our boundaries are. But how do we make sense of our needs when we are confronted with the needs of another person? When our desires and boundaries are potentially in conflict, how do we find a dynamic that works?

Autistic people commonly struggle with consent in a couple of ways: first, we may be unable to identify when our boundaries have been crossed, making it difficult for us to speak up and engage in conversations about consent in the heat of an encounter. On the flip side, because many of us cannot read facial expressions or nonverbal cues (particularly those of non-Autistics), we may also encroach on the personal boundaries of others without realizing it. Both of these issues are only exacerbated by masking: we may be afraid to confront a romantic partner who has hurt us because we're used to pretending to be as easygoing as humanly possible, or we may never trust ourselves to initiate sex for fear of missing a boundary. Numerous Autistic people avoid sex or romance entirely because we find rejection too threatening to accept, or because we can't tolerate the thought of ever making another human being uncomfortable. But expressing a desire is in no way abusive, and avoidance only prevents us from practicing our negotiation and consent skills.

The solution to all of this is to engage in explicit communication. If we wish for our relationships to be informed by our actual wants, we do have to be able to share them—and in order to feel safe enough with a partner to share sex, romance, or major life projects together, we have to trust them to express their wants and limits to us as well. Yet even naming what we want and do not want can seem taboo because in mainstream, neurotypical society, relationships progress along a predetermined path that is never to be questioned. Polyamorous writers and social scientists sometimes call this predetermined path the *relationship escalator*.[16]

Sasha explains it this way: "You're supposed to start with the talking stage, where you're texting and feeling one another out. Then you move on to dating, but you don't actually say that you're dating, you just have sex and hang out more. Then you define the relationship and are boyfriend-girlfriend. Then you move in, then the guy proposes, and then you get married and have children . . . and none of this is talked about barely at all." Sasha says that multiple men she's had sex with have tried putting her on the escalator without asking. They've simply started demanding more time from her and began getting jealous when she spent time with other men. As an Autistic woman who didn't want a serious relationship, she was puzzled—it was as if each man she dated was acting out the exact same role in a play that she'd never auditioned for.

In more short-term sexual encounters, many people also follow an escalator of expected activities. According to this escalator, sex begins with kissing, and then light touching under the clothes, and progresses to genital stimulation using fingers or the mouth, and it must culminate in penis-in-vagina intercourse that ends when the man ejaculates. Any person who is queer, kinky, or has a unique sensory profile is left out by this formula—and when our sexual partners follow it without even holding a discussion first, then feelings of dissatisfaction, disconnection, or even violation can easily occur.

The sex and relationship escalators move us forward effortlessly with only one potential destination no matter what we are feeling and where we wish to go. Standing perfectly still and allowing them to carry us forward can feel easy, and effortless, even while it traumatizes us and disconnects us from our bodies. In order to step off the escalator, we have to be willing to make the moment more difficult and awkward—and tolerate the distress of stating what we want, knowing that many other people's desires will not align with it. In the table below are a couple of ways that you can introduce necessary friction to the relationship and sexual escalators, so that you can slow down their forward momentum or step off them entirely.

Tolerate Discomfort

Phrases for Breaking Free of Existing Relationship Scripts

"How do you like to be touched?"

"What actions from a partner make you feel valued?"

"Can I tell you about sexual experiences that have felt good in the past? Do you want to share your own?"

"What does enjoyable sex look like for you?"

"What are some signs that your face or body give off when you're enjoying something? What about when you're not enjoying something?"

"What are you looking for in a relationship right now?"

"I really dislike anything to do with oral sex, or body fluids. What are some big turnoffs for you?"

"I'm happy to host you at my apartment for a date and potentially sex, but I'm not comfortable with having partners stay the night."

"I'm not comfortable with the way you're touching me."

"Please tell me directly when you are trying to initiate sex, I can't pick up on nonverbal cues."

"Let's have a conversation about our expectations before moving into anything sexual."

"I know my face may look really unemotional to you right now, but this is how I look when I am turned on."

"I get shy when I have a crush, please take it as a compliment."

"I'd really like it if we could share porn with each other, so we can each get a better idea of what turns each of us on."

"Tell me about a fantasy you've never gotten to realize. I promise I won't judge, even if it ends up not being for me."

Statements like these take nothing for granted—because quite commonly, Autistic people do not express our feelings of pleasure or discomfort the way neurotypicals do. According to research into the "double empathy problem," Autistic people are not actually worse at picking up on unspoken social cues than our allistic peers; rather, the groups are speaking separate languages, and routinely misinterpret each other's signals.[17] A decade of research now supports this idea, as numerous studies have found that pairs of Autistic people can communicate just as fluently and efficiently with each other as two non-Autistic people. Crucially, research finds non-Autistic people are even *worse* at reading Autistic people's nonverbal cues than Autistics are at reading theirs. When interacting with a diverse array of neurotypes, then, no meaning should be taken for granted. We need to ask other people how they feel—and share how we feel in turn.

Typically, allistic people manage questions of romantic or sexual consent by monitoring their partners' bodies for subtle indications of discomfort—scrunched shoulders, averted eyes, a flat facial expression, and so on—but for Autistic people, these exact same signals can sometimes be green lights because they reflect that we're no longer masking and trying to look normal. When we squint our eyes, shake from side to side, click our tongues, and fidget with our hands, we may seem as if we are nervous and uncomfortable, but actually we're engaging in the self-regulation strategies that make it easier for us to relate. Conversely, it is often when we are smiling, returning eye contact, nodding agreeably, and echoing our conversation partner that we are masking, in an attempt to make them feel at ease—and it may be impossible in such moments for us to practice ongoing consent. Simply put, we are free when we are allowed to seem off-putting, and we may be imprisoned when we're easiest to be around.

Clairborne is a kinky Autistic person interested in whips, floggers, and bondage, and they tell me they won't play with a potential sexual partner until they've witnessed firsthand that the person can confidently withdraw consent. "If a person says they have no limits, or that they like whatever I like, that is an enormous red flag," they tell me. "If they say that, I like to ask, *Oh, so you don't mind if I put my finger in your nose and dig around? You don't mind if I give your shoes to my dogs to chew on?* Everybody has boundaries. Each and every one of us has thousands of boundaries. We have to be able to talk about it. If you can't talk, you can't play."

There are numerous ways to broach these potentially nerve-racking topics. If we find that we can't speak up about our feelings in the heat of the moment, then expressing our concerns in a letter or a text message is equally fine. For partners who are newly delving into kink, there are even websites like We Should Try It, which allows both partners to privately fill out a list of potential sexual interests, and generates a report sharing only the activities that both parties said they were interested in.[18]

Learning to communicate more openly with our partners also means exposing ourselves to change, loss, and conflict. Sometimes an activity that we once enjoyed will suddenly lose its appeal, or we decide that we no longer wish to be in a relationship, and it is never wrong to express this. Our partners have the right to their own emotions about it, of course, but the possibility of disappointment, hurt feelings, or conflict is not a reason to conceal the truth. Conflict is productive when we engage in it mutually, in a spirit of good faith, and even a breakup can be a positive outcome when it reflects the best way of managing two people's needs. A relationship that fully respects our neurodivergence will work with the communication methods that are most accessible to us, and on the timeline that works for us, rather than forcing us to express ourselves with neuroconformist speed and convenience.

After we have begun developing the relationships that feel authentic to us, the complex work of nourishing those relationships begins. For masked neurodivergent folks, appreciating the value of conflict and accepting a partner's ever-evolving personality and outlook can be quite counterintuitive—for so long, our goal has been to seek constancy and make everyone happy with us at all times. But real relationships require a deep intimacy, which demands unmasking from all involved. Unfortunately, even if our loved ones are proudly neurodivergent and on board with unmasking too, we might encounter incompatible accessibility needs, miscommunication, and trauma triggers that set one another off. In the final section of this chapter, we will explore how to work on our relationships as time passes, express ourselves during moments of tension, and maintain deep connections even as we experience growth and change.

Maintaining Relationships Through Conflict and Change

"To love someone long-term is to attend a thousand funerals of the people they used to be," reflects psychology writer Heidi Priebe.[19] For many of us, it also means killing the imaginary versions of our partners that exist solely in our heads—the fantasies of who they "should" be that set us up for frustration, and the negative judgments we project onto them that echo everything we hate most about ourselves.

Masking is designed to keep other people at a distance. When we practice unmasking, we risk exposure of our least attractive habits, our most annoying qualities, our messiest emotions, our sorest spots, and the skills we never had the opportunity to develop. Nowhere is this exposure rawer and riskier than in our intimate relationships. But no matter how threatening it might be to reveal these sides of us, we have to keep pushing ahead and sharing ourselves with the people we love. The alternative is only a growing distance and resentment.

Here are some of the common struggles that Autistic people encounter as their romantic (or other intimate) relationships develop—particularly if those relationships involve cohabitation or some type of ongoing commitment:

- Hypervigilance: An inability to relax around your partner(s) because of the perceived need to mask any unwanted mannerisms, interests, and habits.

- Emotional self-censorship: Refusal to acknowledge negative feelings or thoughts about your partner(s), even at the expense of advocating for yourself.

- Over-justification: Compulsive explaining of all of your actions, needs, and emotions to your partner(s), not accepting that differing perspectives will sometimes occur between two people.

- Behavioral self-censorship: Avoiding activities, outings, or special interests that are not shared with your partner to prevent them feeling excluded, threatened, or irritated.

- Emotional surveillance: Constantly monitoring how your partner feels, or checking in with them for reassurance that they are satisfied, forcing them to feign happiness at all times because you perceive negative feelings as a relationship threat.

- Conflict avoidance: Pretending everything is "fine" and not discussing problems in the relationship or living situation, behaving as though a loving relationship is one without fights or selfishness.

- Denial of incompatible needs: Suppressing your body's own reactions, and treating your partner's needs as if they outrank yours, or vice versa.

- Over-processing: Discussing every incompatible want or feeling between yourself and your partner in a circular, repetitive way, attempting to "resolve" tension by discussing it to the point of exhaustion.

- Emotional victimization: Equating *feeling* unsafe with actually being unsafe; allowing the needs of the partner who is more visibly distressed to dominate all conversations.

- Boundary confusion: Attempting to control a partner's emotions through one's actions; attempting to regulate one's own emotions by placing conditions on how a partner should act.

These types of conflicts occur not because any member of the relationship is a "narcissistic abuser," "avoidantly attached," or less evolved than their partner, but because two traumatized people who haven't been listened to very often before aren't usually practiced in expressing hard truths. Behind each one of these behaviors, there is some unchallenged, unspoken belief that reflects the cultural messages we have been taught about our disability and about love. Here are some example beliefs, and the relational struggles they're most connected to:

- Hypervigilance: "It is my job to anticipate others' needs."

- Emotional self-censorship: "If I think or feel anything negative about my partner, it means I do not love them."

- Over-justification: "I need someone else to approve of my actions."

- Behavioral self-censorship: "Good partners share everything."

- Emotional surveillance: "I'm only safe if people are happy all the time."

- Conflict avoidance: "Fighting or disappointing another person is cruel/immoral."

- Denial of incompatible needs: "I can push through the pain, so I should."

- Over-processing: "My loved ones and I must be in complete alignment."

- Emotional victimization: "A bad feeling is an emergency that can and must be fixed."

- Boundary confusion: "What is good for my partner is good for me."

Behind all these beliefs lies a foundational myth about how relationships ought to work, which is even more potentially damaging:

If I do everything right, my partner will never leave me, and I will always feel secure.

In reality, we have no guarantee that our partners won't leave our lives one day, or that the nature of our relationship(s) won't dramatically change. We cannot control another person's feelings. In fact, we can't even control our own. The only thing that we have power over is our own *behavior*, and we must accept that our partners retain full control over their actions and how to manage their own emotions, too. Regardless of what happens, no relationship can ever promise us total feelings of security—we *will* feel insecure, unloved, left behind, not listened to, taken for granted, misinterpreted, and dissatisfied at moments, even if life blesses us with partners who care a great deal. Learning to accept these negative emotions in ourselves and others can free us to unmask. If it's not your job to make your partner(s) happy all the time, then you are able to give them the space to stew in their own resentments and anger when they need to without the world collapsing. You'll also be liberated enough to express your own anger or irritation when necessary.

Francisco and Crissy are a married couple in their twenties with two young kids. Francisco was diagnosed as Autistic as a young boy, though his mother never told him; he only learned the truth as an adult after dropping out of college. Crissy self-diagnosed as ADHD, OCD, and Autistic after seeking treatment for postpartum depression, along with the help of a therapist. The two have been in couples counseling ever since making these discoveries.

"We get under each other's skin," says Crissy. "I cry a lot and freak out about all kinds of things, and he—"

Francisco cuts in. "I think it's my fault she's upset and can't stand to see her cry, and I get so angry with myself."

"But then I see him calling himself stupid and doing all these things to make me happy, and then I feel like the bad guy, so now I feel bad about crying, and now it's like I can't tell him when I'm upset," Crissy finishes.

Patterns like these are quite common for neurodivergent couples to fall into. If every negative emotion is a threat, there's no room to just let a partner's difficulties just be. It might seem loving, but it's quite stifling.

I ask Crissy and Francisco what their therapist recommended. "He said we both need to be more selfish a lot of the time. It's not mean to stand in your truth, and feel what you're feeling," Crissy says.

Francisco explains what this sometimes looks like for him. "When the babies are crying it really hurts my ears. I am not a bad father if I need to go out in the yard and hit the bag for a while and calm down. I have a stressful job and home life is stressful and everybody needs their own space."

"That doesn't mean I don't get angry, either!" Crissy cuts in. "Sometimes I go out there and say okay, enough. You've been punching the bag a half hour. I need you to hold these kids because they're all over me."

The couple seems comfortable living in their messiness. They could both be too tired to be their best selves a lot of the time, and could make do through the yelling and complaining and worries about credit card bills. They don't expect their relationship to be endless happiness and romantic bliss—instead, they see each other as trusted companions through life's difficulties, and have humor about their flaws.

"Growing up in a Latino family, the mother is supposed to be this rock who cares for everyone," Crissy says. "It is unmasking for me to be like a *Malcolm in the Middle* type of bad mom."

"Not a bad mom," Francisco corrects.

"I'm a bad mom! Not *bad*-bad," Crissy says. "But I don't always want to be here braiding hair and changing diapers. I'll go to the bar with my friends. I'll tell my kids to shut up with the 'Baby Shark' [music]. I don't care."

Francisco rubs her back. "That's okay. That's good for kids to see."

Sustaining a long-term relationship requires that we accept the emotional mess, selfish impulses, heavy demands, and even the voice deep inside us that sometimes says we can't stand the way things are anymore. Though psychiatry pathologizes shifting emotions and complicated feelings as psychologically "switching" on our partners, or as harboring "disorganized attachment," we can learn to live with triggers, fears of abandonment, guilt, and the desire to sometimes flee, and move through them in a healthy way. In order to become more resilient and dynamic in the face of relationship changes and threats, try practicing acceptance of some of the following emotions.

Accepting Hard Emotions
Living with Complexity in Our Relationships

Here are some emotions that are completely normal to feel in a relationship, as well as some prompts to encourage you to consider how these emotions might be triggered by your partner(s). If you do not have a romantic partner, you can answer these questions about a housemate, close friend, or other person you are attached to.

1. **Anger.** The last time I felt angry with my partner was:

   What I did with that anger:

   Did I share that I felt angry?

   Is there anything I wish I had done differently?

2. **Annoyance.** The last time my partner annoyed me was:

What I did with that annoyance:

_____

Did I share that I felt annoyed?

_____

Is there anything I wish I had done differently?

_____

3. **Insecurity.** The last time I felt insecure around my partner was:

_____

What I did with that insecurity:

_____

Did I share that I felt insecure?

_____

Is there anything I wish I had done differently?

_____

4. **Resentment.** The last time I resented my partner was:

_____

What I did with that resentment:

_____

Did I share that I felt resentment?

_____

Is there anything I wish I had done differently?

_____

5. **Regret.** The last time I regretted being with my partner was:

_____

What I did with that regret:

_____

Did I share that I was regretful?

Is there anything I wish I had done differently?

6. **Ashamed.** The last time I felt ashamed to share something with my partner was:

What I did with that shame:

Did I share what I was ashamed about?

Is there anything I wish I had done differently?

If you find that you struggle to assert your own needs in your relationship(s), you can practice the skills of engagement and tolerating distress by finding small ways to permit yourself to be annoying, demanding, disappointing, or otherwise fully human. Here are some example behaviors to get you started.

Engage in Conflict and Tolerate Distress
Being Imperfect in a Relationship

- Watch a TV show or video that you know your partner doesn't like without apologizing for it or hiding it from them.

- Ask your partner to cover a chore that they normally assume you will perform.

- Ask for help with a task that you know your partner doesn't enjoy but can handle.

- Cry openly or express frustration without apologizing for it or expecting quick resolution.

- Take yourself on a solo date or spend time with friends without your partner(s).

- Make yourself a meal that you enjoy, even if your kids and partner don't like it.

- Tell your partner about a long-term goal or dream you have that might be difficult to achieve under your current lifestyle.

- Journal about what feels missing in your life, as well as what you're grateful for.

- Travel on your own or spend a night away from your house to remember how solitude feels.

- Warn your partner that you are going to stim or self-regulate in a way that they might find irritating and give them the opportunity to regulate their own reactions.

- Let your partner be sad, angry, or disappointed in peace, without trying to change how they feel.

- Ask your partner what they need, rather than assuming.

- Let your partner make choices you wouldn't make, without lecturing or trying to "save" them.

- Imagine how your life would look without your current partner(s). What would you be doing differently? Where would you live? How does thinking about this make you feel?

- Let a fight be unresolved if there's no easy answer. Affirm to your partner that you love them and support them, even if meeting both your needs is hard.

Like all other people, neurodivergent people are entitled to seek out love, pleasure, connection, and even discussions of consent that operate on our terms. We can be highly libidinal sexual beings with absolutely zero interest in romance, and we can be die-hard romantics and cuddlers who abhor sex. Sex can mean mutual masturbation, wearing a scuba suit, or worshipping someone's feet, and a worthwhile relationship can involve sharing financial and child-rearing commitments or living in a camper van and making music together. The most fraught conversations in our marriages can take place over a Discord chat, if we want them to, and joining a massive sixteen-person polyamorous polycule can be our life's greatest commitment. Every possible combination of interests and boundaries exists within our community in sizable numbers, and when we realize that all these options are legitimate, then we can wield our self-advocacy skills to finally start building the lives we want and deserve.

In the final chapter of this book, we will explore how unmasking Autistic people find true purpose and meaning in life. We've already gotten to throw out the neurotypical rule book and write our own guidelines for what friendship, family, work, and love can mean. But even after we've begun self-advocating in these massively important areas, we may harbor doubts about what truly fulfills us, and what we wish for our enduring legacies to be. Disabled people tend to approach the questions of aging, planning for the future, contemplating death, and thinking about our purpose on this earth a bit differently from how abled people do. The prevailing sources of life meaning that are given to nondisabled and neurotypical people might not appeal or be possible for us. And so, let's consider what it really means to unmask every element of our lives, from the hobbies and passion projects that shape our days, to our vision of what endures long after we are gone.

Life

In her essay "Redefining Safety," psychotherapist and clinical counseling supervisor Jessi Lee Jackson describes the moment when she first realized that there are two very different kinds of safety that exist in the world—the safety *from* immediate mortal harm and the emotional safety *to* actively venture out into the world in an empowered way.[1] Jackson first discovered this when working with a ten-year-old client, Sarah, who had a traumatic history of household chaos and familial neglect. When Jackson asked Sarah to describe a place where she felt safe, this is what the young girl had to say:

"Hiding under the car in the garage so that the bad men can't find me."

Jackson understood that Sarah had learned to prioritize protecting her body from an immediate physical attack. But in therapy, Jackson wanted her to feel more than just safety *from* danger; she wanted her to experience the inner security *to* open up, be emotionally vulnerable, and accept help. Eventually they arrived at an image of what the second, more relaxed and loved form of safety looked like for Sarah: cuddling with her mom on the couch, watching a movie and enjoying popcorn. Once the two of them had this comforting idea of positive safety in mind, they were able to return to it whenever Sarah felt dysregulated, and could move forward more successfully with her therapy.

"Whereas one definition of safety centers on figuring out how to respond to threats, the other centers on creating environments in which our needs are met and we feel valued," Jackson wrote.

When we mask our neurodivergence, we seek the first kind of safety: safety *from* ostracism, physical abuse, starvation, houselessness, and other forms of harm. We mask in order to avoid standing out, to prevent our natural responses from causing other people problems, and in hopes of ensuring that we're allowed into the social groups we rely upon for survival. We do not get to enjoy the liberty and joy of the second form of safety until we can regularly unmask ourselves around trusted others. A life that is centrally motivated by merely escaping danger is not a full life. In order to be recognized in the fullness of our humanity, we must have the ability to want things, to pursue goals, to feel valued, and to dream of a future that we could enjoy.

In the early days of the unmasking process, we remain quite focused on that first, more survival-based form of safety. We try to attend to our sensory needs in order to prevent horrific meltdowns, for example, or we attempt to find a way to stay housed and fed that won't exploit us or lead us into burnout. We learn to negotiate our boundaries and tiptoe around invalidating family members and our former abusers, slowly carving out for ourselves small safe havens and supportive communities where we can be ourselves. We're neuroconforming a whole lot less than we used to, but we're still just fighting to get by, and to be actively happy and enthused by our life might seem like a fantasy.

But after we have unmasked ourselves and our relationships a bit, we finally do have the skills necessary to dream of something better for ourselves. At this point, we can really be ambitious in creating the kind of existence we truly want and take steps to pursue it without apology. Where each Autistic person winds up at the end of this long road will be different, and for many of us finding our place in the world will mean beating a completely new path, unlike any that we've ever seen before. We get to be more than just safe from the pain of others' judgment. With adequate social support and self-advocacy skills, we are free to make for ourselves a radiantly, weirdly Autistic life.

Clover is an Autistic person in England who lives on a narrowboat within the country's vast canal system. They say that many people who used to squat in abandoned buildings or ride the rails have instead transitioned to living on boats in the canals in recent years.

"I love living on a boat and being closer to nature, but it could be a pain in the ass if you like having lots of electricity, or showering every day," they say. "You have to move your boat every couple of weeks, which can be isolating, and also stressful, if the engine breaks. People tend to be able to fix a lot of things themselves."

They say that many people living in the canals have anti-authoritarian, contrarian worldviews, which does make it easier to fit in. "Most people have part-time jobs like laborer, gardener, lorry driver . . . lots of neurodivergent people, but in the erratic, been-to-prison way than the [computer] coding way, if that makes sense. Basically people on the margins trying to quietly live their lives out of view and have control over their own homes."

Clover is careful not to idealize life on the narrowboat because many people watch overly sanitized "BoatLife" videos that can make the lifestyle seem a lot easier and more luxurious than it is. It's not for everyone, with the constant unpredictability and the tendency for most in the narrowboater community to be straight men. But, they say, "It can be really pretty and idyllic-looking, with swans knocking on your boats for food."

Clover says they love foraging, playing synth instruments, and being around nature, and at an early age they developed a distaste for being cooped up within schooling institutions all day. An English kid who spent their early years in Germany, they got accustomed to accidentally violating cultural norms without realizing it, during an era when it was impossible to google what normal behavior for any particular area was. Adopting a cheaper, more solitude-filled lifestyle has alleviated some of the pressure of capitalism's demands and reduced many of the world's conformity pressures, allowing Clover to create a more unmasked neurodivergent life. It's an existence that has no clear-cut formula, filled with challenge, isolation, but also moments of unexpected comfort.

"A lot of the canal where I live is by rail tracks, so I get to see lots of freight trains go by, including the train that measures the tracks and the royal mail trains," Clover shares. "During the most intense COVID lockdown I deliberately moored so I could see the trains going by because I thought it would be less lonely."

Over the years, I have encountered numerous neurodivergent people who have found their place beyond the bounds of conventional living. My friend Eric has a special interest in trains, and he's visited conventions for people who ride the rails and spent evenings out among their camps, listening to their music and storytelling. These are communal spaces where people leave behind unwanted gear and tools, make food in large batches for sharing with others, and provide one another with company and entertainment in a way that hasn't changed all that much over the course of the past century. Similarly, in his book *A Good Place for Maniacs,* Pacific Crest Trail hiker Chuck McKeever reports encountering numerous people on the trail who were neurodiverse, nonconformist, or simply uninterested in a life anchored by work, an apartment lease, and a static nuclear family. People who live in the woods or spend much of their years on the trail are often the types to use resources carefully, disconnect from the information overload of social media, and not worry about the pretenses of dress, style, and hygiene that can make neuroconformist life so punishing for Autistics.

Dio, who has spent a great deal of time out in the deserts beyond Vegas, confirms this: he says that if managing daily survival in the modern world alongside a job and other social obligations is difficult for an Autistic person, then camping can help reduce life to a manageable range of very practical concerns.

"Staying alive is much easier when I'm not watching a clock or remembering that I have errands and phone calls to make," he says. "All the rules are different, and my main priorities are making sure I have a place to sleep, food to eat, and to interact with my surroundings. Any people that are out there are also following the alternate rules and don't expect me to be 'normal.'"

It can be dangerous to attempt living outdoors alone without adequate supplies or skills. The neurodivergent people who will adjust well to such a living environment will typically have years of outdoor experience, and know how to work with tools, start fires, pitch tents, tie knots, and identify plants and water sources. My friend Emma, who is currently sleeping in a vehicle in Jaithmathang country in Australia, recently came to the realization that she's been in and out of homelessness all her life. The state of homelessness was so heavily stigmatized that she'd never put together that all the times she'd needed to exchange sexual acts for a place to sleep were, in fact, times she was unhoused. Now she's far more conscious about her position in life and the people she shares it with.

I envy the photos Emma posts of herself standing amid rolling hills of pineapple grass, though I feel ill-equipped to pursue it myself. The scratch of grass against my legs sends me into a sensory rage, and I get overwhelmed at times by the glare of the sun. I've long been the type of Autistic who finds their escape from the capitalist grind by holing up in a tiny, dark room they rent on the cheap, disappearing into the books that I'm reading and writing and connecting with other people online. Still, even if some Autistics like me can't live outdoors easily because of how we manage disability, we can still reap some of the physiological and social benefits of getting outside.

Some research shows that Autistic people experience less agitation and anxiety when we are in the presence of green spaces, and that time in nature can enhance our skill development and confidence[2]—and in this respect we aren't too different from most other human beings who benefit from regular activity in nature.[3] Nature gives us crunchy leaves and pieces of bark to tear apart as a form of self-stimulation without having to worry about causing a mess. The natural rhythms of the changing weather and the day-night cycle regulate our energy, and grant us an automatic permission not to be productive and moving all of the time. The rush of water and chirping of birds drown out less predictable honking horns and tinny speakerphones. The rolling surface of the ground can give our bodies feedback about how to position ourselves, and in the absence of vocal chatter or intrusive notifications and advertisements, we can grasp moments of peace. There's also the incidental social contact that happens when you step out and make yourself a part of nature; people are more community minded out there, quicker to share resources, grateful for the company, and less likely to judge you for how you dress or move your body.

When Autistics abandon the standards of neurotypical society to create a proudly disabled world of our own, we are rewarded with genuine relationships, fulfilling hobbies, new adventures, long-term stability, and a sense of purpose and meaning in our lives that was never accessible to us when we were masked. This final chapter of the book will explore how Autistic people use our skills to reorient our lives and find the safety to become the people we've always wanted to be. In the remaining exercises, we will each go beyond merely unmasking ourselves, and move on to unmasking our future lives and our worlds.

Pursuing Passions and New Hobbies

Autistic people are frequently shamed for having special interests, extreme passions that can register to non-Autistics as immature or obsessive. We're perceived as childlike and embarrassing when we show genuine excitement, and some of us were conditioned to "tone down" our hyper-fixations when we were children. This can make it difficult for us to pursue our interests and fully enjoy them out in the world as adults. But if we wish to be free from the strictures of the mask, we deserve to do more than simply tend to our necessary comfort and address our immediate physical needs. Our personal enrichment, deep-seated obsessions, and even passing fancies merit attention, too.

We can overcome some of the shame surrounding our passions by deliberately choosing to share them with others. Many Autistic people already find communities for discussing their special interests online and at conventions filled with other like-minded individuals, but we can also challenge ourselves to broaden our circle of openness and self-disclosure and get some of our other loved ones involved in our hobbies, too. By inviting a more "normie" friend to watch a favorite documentary with us or dragging a supportive relative to a comic book convention, we push back against the notion that what interests us is insufferably weird and impossible for others to understand. We can also express curiosity and interest in our loved ones' hobbies, and by asking them questions about the topics they find fascinating cultivate a greater sense of wonder in the world that will make it easier and more rewarding for us to try new things.

In the table below is an exercise to get you thinking about some of the positive changes involving special interests and new hobbies that you could introduce into your life, and some of the ways that you might involve other people in your passions to a greater degree.

Accepting Change

Making More Space in Life for Special Interests and New Pursuits

Expanding Existing Interests

- Is there anyone in your life who you wish understood your special interests better? Who are they? How might you include them in activities, or share some of your knowledge with them?

_____

_____

- Do you have any special interests that are currently quite solitary, but which you wish you could form community around? How might you find or create opportunities to connect over these interests?

_____

_____

- Do you have any special interests that you are still ashamed of? How could you slowly begin incorporating this interest into the time you spend around other people?

_____

_____

Life

- Do any of your special interests and passions feel neglected? How might you make more time for them?

Identifying New Interests

- Are there any crafts or hands-on skills that you want to learn?

- Are there any topics you wish you could learn more about?

- What are some local spaces that you've always wished to visit but been afraid to do so on your own?

- Have any activities ever felt forbidden to you because you were different, but which you've secretly always wanted to try?

- Are there any activities you've wanted to enjoy but fear that someone like you is not allowed to do?

In the introductory chapter of this book, we met Bill, a forty-five-year-old Autistic man who would love to try visiting punk rock concerts and receiving body modifications such as tattoos, but who feels that he missed the opportunity to enjoy such things because he spent so much of his life masking. Bill cannot wear pants comfortably—he wears only kilts or shorts with long underwear underneath—and he can't stand in one place without constantly twisting his hands and cracking his fingers. For a long time, he hid these facts about himself from others by simply staying at home. He's less embarrassed about these traits these days, but he is afraid of how they'll register to people he doesn't know at music shows, especially in light of his age.

"If I were to start going out, I would be the oldest person at these shows, and I'd feel really weird and out of place," he says. "I fear I missed my chance to have a normal, enjoyable life."

Bill absolutely would *not* be the oldest person at a majority of the music shows he wants to attend. As a later-in-life convert to visiting concerts and clubs myself, I can attest that a wide array of human beings routinely shows up, and that nobody is concerned with monitoring the ages of the people in attendance or forming any judgments about them. Like Bill, I used to avoid most public events, primarily because I did not trust myself to know how to act. As a result, I only ever went to the plays and comedy shows that my friends or romantic partners liked, including many that I didn't enjoy. Convincing other people to visit the gay bars and dance clubs I had an interest in was a chore; I felt like a pain for making such a request, and if my companion didn't enjoy the experience, I felt personally responsible. Until I was in my midthirties, I truly believed that people like me were somehow not *allowed* to go out on their own, dancing in the dark and chatting up strangers.

When I finally did venture out to clubs on my own, I learned my worst fears were totally unfounded. Nobody even noticed that I was in the space by myself, or thought I was a loser for it; plenty of people came on their own, and nobody was monitoring me. I was very far from the oldest or weirdest person there by a long shot: young twentysomethings in tank tops and wide-legged jeans danced alongside senior citizens in leather skirts and long acrylic fingernails, with middle-aged

Cubs fans in jerseys and suburban workers in suits and ties mixed in for good measure. It didn't matter whether I was in a gay bar, a warehouse party, or at a hard techno set: all kinds of people were around, moving their bodies with lovable awkwardness, some of them smiling and confident, others shy and nursing their drinks. There was nothing I could do that would mark me as particularly unusual. Humanity was plenty unusual on its own without me, and I only helped contribute to its beautifully diverse array.

Beq, an Autistic, trans, plus-sized wheelchair user, tells me that they similarly used to exclude themself from the fetish communities that they found appealing because they assumed that a person of their size and disability status would not ever be welcome. "I worried for months about how I would be received as a fat disabled trans person in a rope bondage class," they say. "And the reality is that there were already people like me there, and they were waiting for me to join them. Queer and kink spaces are far more welcoming than you could ever imagine, and they are also equally diverse."

I think that nearly all of us can draw some courage from Beq's observation: there are already people exactly like us in the spaces that we crave joining, and those people want us to find them and make ourselves a part of their lives. We aren't intruding by joining a space; we are helping make it what it is. A community is not a static thing; we *are* the community when we participate in it.

The first time I took myself out to a local club on my own, my eyes instantly locked onto a bald, androgynous person in their sixties who was wearing fishnet gloves and dancing vigorously atop a big black platform in the middle of the dance floor. All around us there were younger Millennials and Zoomers sipping cheap beer and barely moving their bodies to the music, but this person was a shimmering beacon of activity, and people came by to give them high fives, dance alongside them, or offer them a shot or a hit of poppers while they continued breezily doing their own thing.

I instantly felt more comfortable dancing once I saw this person, and all my concerns about being too visibly trans, or too old, or too Autistic to be there went away. It occurred to me that I could also be a beacon of relief to others the next time I went out. Now I am happy to be the first on the dance floor, and I'm not shy about flailing my arms or pacing the whole length of the room. If I'm the oldest or the most unusually dressed person there, then I know that someone else who feels self-conscious about their age or presentation is looking to me and feeling reassured. By remaining present and involved as a neurodivergent person I widen the scope of what's considered normal and acceptable—and I have nothing to feel apologetic about because I am improving the space for me and others like me.

When Bill pondered whether he was "too old" to start trying new things, he was expressing a common and understandable insecurity, but it's also a nonsensical question. There is no such thing as being too old to continue living one's life. The past is already over, and it cannot harm us. All that matters now is how we wish to spend our remaining days. Do we want to continue locking ourselves away from the communities and experiences we crave? Or do we want to live actively, trying new things and forever growing, whether that's for another forty years or for another four days? The social skill of accepting change teaches us that we only stop encountering new shades of human existence once we are dead. To be alive is to keep changing. We might as well do so in the directions we truly want.

Speaking with other people about our interests, forming communities around our passions, and pursuing new interests publicly are all incredibly challenging things for Autistics to do. But we can claim satisfying lives for ourselves, and a rewarding place within society, by practicing the skill of accepting unfamiliarity and change. We can also gradually build our tolerance for the distress that comes with all things scary and new. In the table on the next page are some distress tolerance–building strategies we can use to help ourselves push through those feelings of uncertainty, so we can remain present and involved rather than fleeing or masking ourselves away.

Tolerate Distress
Remaining Present and Grounded in Unfamiliar Places

Notice when you feel shaky, agitated, or as if you are not welcome in a space. Recognize how anxiety feels in your body, and how it changes the contents of your thoughts.

Distinguish between feelings of being unsafe and actual threats. Do you have any reason to believe that you are unwelcome in this space, or is your body just activated because of past experience?

Remind yourself that public spaces exist in order to have people use them, and your presence is actually desired. When you feel an urge to flee, recall the reasons why you have decided it's important to try new things.

Express gratitude to your body and your brain for trying to keep you safe by giving you these warning signals. Then dismiss the thoughts, reminding yourself that you are safe, even if you feel uncomfortable.

Imagine yourself in a place where you feel fully safe and loved, and free to be yourself as you are. Close your eyes and imagine moving about freely and happily without having to worry about how you look to anyone else.

Observe your surroundings. Try to take the focus away from yourself or what others might be thinking about you, and instead take an interest in *others*. What are other people doing? Who looks comfortable? Who looks uneasy or shy? What catches your interest?

Move toward activities, people, or features of the environment that interest you. Listen along to an engaging conversation and consider jumping in. Watch other people dancing or playing games and consider participating. Study the books on the bookshelves or find a cat in the corner to pet.

Check in with your body. Where are your anxiety levels now? Is there anything else you can do to make yourself more comfortable?

Through the consistent practice of these skills, we can bring ourselves out into the world more frequently and feel increasingly capable of coping with the unfamiliar. We will always remain disabled, with greater energy recovery needs than most people and our own ways of communicating, but that doesn't mean we have to write off any life experiences that are especially important or appealing to us. We can learn new languages, take up needlepointing, attend orgies, travel the world, go speed dating, take up rock climbing, or simply take ourselves out for a meal. Masking is driven by the belief that Autistic people do not deserve to be seen in public as we really are, but by venturing out into the world and tolerating the initial distress of the unknown, we can create a world where difference is familiar, unremarkable, and everywhere.

I find that the more often I use my self-advocacy skills, the more in control of myself and my surroundings I feel when I try something new. Whereas I used to hesitate and circle the block multiple times before even entering a bar on my own (sometimes giving up entirely and going home), now I can saunter right in, find a seat for myself, and even chat with a stranger about how their day is going or what they've been watching on TV. I really used to believe that was something I'd never be socially competent enough to do. It turns out I was just so debilitated by doubt that I wasn't letting myself claim any attention. I'm quite happy with the unusual person that I am these days, and so I don't mind revealing elements of that true self to people. Even if I say something awkward or misunderstand a person's joke, I will do so while remaining completely me and without having given up on myself, and that is a victory.

Part of building complete, enriching lives for ourselves as unmasked

Autistics is preserving our energy enough to be able to go after the things that we want, rather than burning it out on productivity or people-pleasing. Everyday life is uniquely exhausting to us for social, sensory, and accessibility reasons. Leading a fully unmasked, self-accepting life, then, may require that we do less and displease people more, preserving our energy for activities that actually matter to us. We can make peace with the fact that we will never be the hyperproductive people we once strived to be when we were masking, and that being ourselves will naturally require letting some people down. Let's take a look at how.

Coping Through Autistic Burnout

Aisha sometimes sleeps twelve hours or more per day. On the days when her kids are with her ex-husband, she spends a lot of her time in bed, simply recuperating from the duties of motherhood, and due to her past difficulties in her family and her unsatisfying marriage, she sees a therapist twice per week to work on trauma recovery. Sometimes that still isn't quite enough to help her hold everything together, so long breaks for meditation, journaling, and soothing her tensed-up muscles get figured in, too.

"I know it sounds like a lot," Aisha apologizes. "But that's what keeps me at my best when the children are around. I want to be able to keep a level head and be the mom that can help them with homework and fight for them when their teachers are not accepting, and not fall apart into tears."

Her eldest child's teacher believes that ADHD is made-up and over-diagnosed and won't give them the extra test time to which they are entitled by law. Aisha had to spend weeks lobbying her child's school to get them moved to a different, more accepting classroom as part of the child's individualized education plan (IEP).

"I had a migraine for two weeks afterward," she says. "I'm still barely able to function."

When Autistic people are overextended, we hit the point of Autistic burnout. Like the traditional form of burnout observed in exhausted nurses, doctors, teachers, social workers, and others in emotionally taxing jobs, Autistic burnout is characterized by a loss of skills, depressive symptoms, physical unwellness, greater dependence upon other people, and even a lack of hope for the future.[4] For Autistic burnout sufferers, the condition is also marked by a reduced ability to withstand upsetting sensory stimuli.[5]

Burnout is no light matter; many people who suffer from it lose all drive to participate in the activities that had originally led them to become exhausted in the first place. They may even lose any sense of emotional connection to others, or to the person they once used to be. In its most extreme forms, both Autistic burnout and conventional burnout are linked to an increased risk of self-destructive behaviors and thoughts of suicide. There is no rushing healing from burnout, either—the only healthy response once it has struck is to do far less, rest a whole lot more, and slowly find ways to spend one's time that are restorative and life-affirming rather than dreaded.

I first became interested in the study of burnout after I hit a nonnegotiable energy wall of my own, following years of masking as a competent, professional academic. After I became physically ill and incapable of working, I discovered that I had been Autistic all along. Other leading writers on the science of burnout, including one of the authors of *Burnout: The Secret to Unlocking the Stress Cycle,* Emily Nagoski, have subsequently found out they were Autistic as well.

"My diagnosis was an enormous relief," Nagoski writes, "because it gave me a coherent structure for thinking about all the things that are so very, very hard for me that other people do without effort."[6] I felt similarly about the discovery that I am Autistic. Knowing that I am disabled granted me the permission to stop smiling and physically mirroring other people all the time. Being Autistic, I am allowed to be flat-voiced, dim-eyed, unappealing, and uninterested in hanging out. I don't have to be cool or pleasant, I can just *be*—and if others are disappointed in my limitations, I can just as easily find their expectations disappointing.

While it is certainly the case that non-Autistic people experience labor exploitation, overwork, and the consequences of burnout at increasingly high levels today,[7] the demands that life places upon disabled minds and bodies lead us to reach that breaking point more easily, more often, and with even more dramatic effects. I have studied both conventional burnout and Autistic burnout thoroughly, and the literature suggests they are fundamentally similar. However, recognizing signs of burnout within Autistic people may be a challenge for most doctors and clinicians, as many of them do not know how to read our nonverbal signals, and we are less likely to open up to care providers when we are in pain. We conceal our suffering as part of our masking, and so we may be unable to admit to ourselves when we are having a difficult time. I certainly had no idea that I was burning out when I was spending twelve hours per day in my office working on my dissertation, only heading home in the darkness to complete a kickboxing video and heat up some food. I was singularly focused on completing my goals and saw other people and the needs of my body as an unwanted distraction. You don't have the mental space to care for yourself when you're in survival mode all the time.

In 2023, researcher Samuel Arnold and colleagues developed the first-ever statistically validated measure of Autistic burnout. Arnold and his team found that Autistic burnout had four key dimensions: heightened awareness of Autistic traits, cognitive disruption, exhaustion, and overwhelm, which were reflected by participants agreeing with the following statements.[8]

Dimensions of Autistic Burnout

Adapted from the Autistic Burnout Severity items by Arnold et al, 2023.

> **Heightened autistic self-awareness:** "I found some of the following more distressing than usual: sudden or loud noises, bright or flickering lights..."
>
> **Cognitive disruption:** "I had difficulty remembering instructions given to me."

Exhaustion: "I did not have the energy to carry out daily activities."

Overwhelm and withdrawal: "I had difficulties doing my usual work as well as I typically do."

What really distinguishes Autistic burnout from conventional burnout is that it's often caused by masking,[9] it reduces our ability to mask, and it has a higher extremity and longer duration. Some Autistic people require *years* of reduced demand in order to feel better following burnout, and a sizable number of us *never* return to the levels of productivity and overextension that brought us to burnout in the first place. In fact, some Autistic burnout sufferers report living out an endless cycle of being incapable of working, and then doggedly overcommitting themselves to a massive number of obligations in order to "make up" for lost time, only to then burn out again immediately thereafter, losing more abilities with each loop. This illustrates how misguided it can be to view burnout as a temporary loss of ability that can or should be restored: the true sickness of burnout is in the social conditions that lead a person to push their body beyond the brink again and again, not their body for failing to do the impossible.

For masked Autistics who have experienced burnout, unmasking is the only viable solution: research has found that engaging in self-stimulatory behavior, enjoying one's special interests, understanding oneself more fully as an Autistic person, honoring one's sensory sensitivities, and finding robust and authentic community support are all protective factors that can prevent and reduce the severity of the burnout.[10] Being able to withdraw from an overstimulating world and many major life obligations is also necessary, as is being believed when we say we need help and then receiving it.[11] Every single one of these defenses is impossible when we're trying to camouflage ourselves as nondisabled. And they're all massively taboo in a world that requires adult people to aim for full independence, and to constantly aspire to do and accomplish more.

In my interviews I have discovered that many Autistic burnout sufferers radically transform their lives following their own bouts with sickness, depression, and disillusionment. They are ex-therapists, once-practicing medical doctors, retired military members, former warehouse workers, ex-servers, and stay-at-home-parents who now rely upon their loved ones for help. They've dropped out of graduate programs, stopped cooking meals for unthankful spouses, sold their cars, downsized their homes, and walk everywhere but mostly stay at home. All kinds of sustainable, silly, slow lives are possible once we determine that life's core purpose is not productivity. Below is an exercise for practicing transgressive self-advocacy and preventing burnout in your own life.

Transgress Demands

Relieving External Pressure and Escaping
the Burnout Cycle

Keep track of how you spend your time for a full week. Do so without judgment, aiming to describe only how you actually spend your time rather than what you set out to accomplish.

Now assume that your current activity level actually represents the most that you will ever be capable of. How do you feel about that idea?

If this were true, what changes would you make to your life?

Lighten the load: Identify at least one life obligation that you can no longer manage. It might be a chore you can no longer do around the house, or an obligation someone in your life routinely expects you to fulfill.

Write down how you might tell this person that you cannot complete this task anymore. Try framing it as a request for help: "I am finding it very hard to be around large groups of people these days. Can you help me by picking the kids up from school?"

_____

_____

_____

How does making this request feel?

_____

_____

_____

Listen to dread: Are there any events on your calendar that you can't stop worrying about? Are there any tasks that you have agreed to complete that you feel resentful about or regret agreeing to? List some examples here.

_____

_____

_____

Assume for a moment that dread is a legitimate sign that you are in pain, and that resentment is a warning of your needs not being met. What do these two emotions have to teach you, if you treat them as teachers rather than enemies?

Dread teaches me:

_____
_____
_____

Resentment teaches me:

_____
_____
_____
_____

We can also practice transgression by thinking of society's dominant path, the one directed by values such as productivity, wealth, accomplishment, competition, and a desire to control the future, and visualizing how our own journeys diverge. Our unmasked path might instead be guided by values like self-acceptance, peacefulness, playfulness, curiosity, or healing—or any other value that we hold dear.

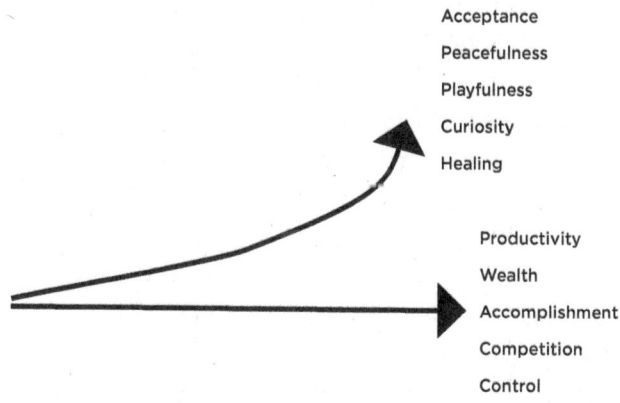

Although burnout often gets talked about in our culture as if it were just a temporary malaise, in reality, severe burnout can be a tectonic disruption of the very foundation of a person's world. True recovery from burnout is not a return to productivity, it's a rebuilding of a new life atop the jumbled remains of the past. And that rebuilding demands we make peace with the person we now are. As Autistic people grow older, we may continue to lose certain abilities and gain others, all while finding new ways that we need to honor ourselves and unmask. Accommodating our aging bodies and minds is a difficult subject that can make many disabled individuals feel hopeless, but it is possible to live well for the rest of our days while remaining unmasked. We just have to accept the reality of aging and plan for it.

Aging and Planning for the Future

The needs of the aging Autistic population are still not adequately understood by the scientific community, which has almost exclusively focused its data collection on the needs of families with Autistic children rather than those of Autistic people themselves. In 2022, only 136 peer-reviewed articles on Autistic older adults had ever been published, in contrast to the over 22,000 studies that had been published about children,[12] which primarily concerned themselves with the nondisabled parents of Autistic kids.

What we do know about growing older as an Autistic person is thanks to the work of a handful of researchers and some clinicians who serve our populations, but more than that, the efforts of older Autistic adults themselves. As is the case with so many other facets of the neurodiversity movement, the handbook for a successful life has never been provided to us, and we have had to invent our own solutions and construct stores of wisdom ourselves.

As they age, many Autistic people do appear to experience losses in their abilities.[13] We burn out more easily and require more rest following stimulating or demanding activities. Our sleep quality declines, our productivity levels reduce, and our ability to mask appears to diminish.[14] We experience epileptic seizures,[15] gastrointestinal conditions, and hypermobility conditions like Ehlers-Danlos syndrome at elevated rates,[16] and each of these risk factors makes it more difficult for us to lead autonomous lives in old age. Older Autistics have to cope with limited integration into supportive social groups, high unemployment and underemployment rates, and a risk of mental health problems such as depression, anxiety, substance use, and suicide ideation.[17]

Though the potential long-term outcomes for Autistics can sound bleak, with suicide being one of the leading causes of death for our population,[18] some critics have pointed out that the existing research tends to exclude Autistics who have strong support systems. Those of us who go on to make numerous friends, form a committed romantic relationship, or find a fulfilling job are sometimes barred from empirical research for supposedly no longer being Autistic. When Autistic people develop social skills, find belonging, or start to seem less emotionally disturbed, many psychiatrists and psychologists conclude that they simply can't be Autistic anymore, rather than believing that a person can be happy, interpersonally effective, and disabled.[19] What social science data does exist on the subject is unequivocal that having close social connections helps protect Autistic people from an early death, both because having close people in our lives helps us meet our material needs for food, shelter, and healthcare, and because the social and emotional support of good friendships reduces our risk of depression, excessive substance use, illness, and suicide.[20]

Growing older as an Autistic person is unquestionably perilous—so much so that our average life expectancy is six years shorter than average for men, and twelve years below average for women.[21] But at the same time, we also see data suggesting that Autistic people continue to develop broader social skills across the life span, growing and changing far more significantly than non-Autistic adults of the same age do.[22] Autistics over the age of fifty, for example, tend to be far better at predicting and understanding the thinking of other people than younger Autistics, likely because they've had time to accumulate a large body of experience and develop a framework for making sense of people. The way that society teaches us to read others (by looking at their faces and body language) doesn't work for us, but in time we create our own system that does work.[23]

Roughly 40 percent of Autistics report having improved social skills as they age, and 58 percent find it easier over time to verbally communicate.[24] Brain volume studies show that whereas young Autistic children have far larger brain volumes than non-Autistic children, with many more interconnected neurons, by the age of fifty our brains have pruned enough that they resemble non-Autistic brains in size.[25] Again, this doesn't mean that we have ceased to be Autistic, but merely that our brains have adapted better to the patterns of our daily lives.

Even our life expectancy difference relative to non-Autistics drops away with time: those of us who are privileged enough to make it to age sixty-five have life expectancies far more comparable to the rest of the population.[26] All of this fits with the categorization of Autism as a *developmental* disability: we tend to learn to walk, speak, write, name our emotions, and work with others at later ages than our nondisabled peers, needing to find our own unique ways of functioning on our own timeline. But we are also more mutable and varied in our ability levels than our non-Autistic peers are. Each Autistic brain varies so dramatically from the average non-Autistic brain in its neurological mapping that existing models of what aging even *means* in most other humans do not really apply to us, according to some neuroscientists.[27]

One final complicating factor impacting the lives of older Autistics that needs to be mentioned is just how few of us even get to know who we are. Fewer than 10 percent of Autistic children who would be diagnosed today were diagnosed as kids in the 1990s. If more than 90 percent of Autistics of my own generation went undiagnosed as kids, just think of how many Autistic elders have never gotten the benefit of understanding who they are or finding their people. As public knowledge about Autism continues to rise and the Autistic self-advocacy community expands, we will finally begin to see what it looks like for an Autistic person to grow up not viewing themself as defective but instead buffered by an entire culture of fellow disabled people who understand and support them. Who knows what the future of Autistic life and aging will be in such a world? We've only just begun to find one another and create the generational wisdom and living culture that help so many other marginalized groups endure.

At the international Institute for Challenging Disorganization conference in 2023, several clinicians told me that their senior Autistic male clients often present as "clean hoarders"; they keep overflowing collections of objects related to their special interests, are quite socially isolated, avoid seeking help, and are mild-mannered, unfailingly polite, and agreeable to work with. In the profiles of these older, late-diagnosed or undiagnosed Autistic men, I hear the telltale signs of the masked Autism profile: a tendency to downplay one's needs, intense inhibition, fear of public exposure, and a propensity to cling to one or two singular sources of available comfort. We can only begin to guess at the many other subtle ways older generations of Autistic adults compensated for their hidden disabilities. But by speaking openly about Autism, educating our loved ones, and taking great strides to unmask ourselves, we help create a culture where they can be recognized and receive help—and where our future selves can as well.

To sum up the data as accurately as possible: we know that Autistic people will need assistance with things like paying the bills, managing physical and mental health conditions, and looking after themselves as time goes on, but that Autistics are also a surprisingly flexible population who are capable of enjoying their older years if they have that necessary support. It is important, then, for Autistic people to plan for all the hard eventualities of our later lives—that we might become less independent, less capable of working, and more reliant upon other people as we grow old, but that we also might have a real hunger to connect and engage as we get to know ourselves better.

One older Autistic ADHDer that I spoke to, Vera, has been working as a digital nomad for the past two years and lives in a van that she's modified to include a full-sized bed and a desk with a hotspot for internet connectivity. The administrative duties she used to perform in person have now become possible to do online, since much of her company went remote due to COVID, and she now considers herself semiretired while she lives on the road.

"I can visit my grandchildren and children, but still have my privacy to do my own thing," she says. Her eight-pound dog, Jerry, also lives with her in the car. Before she found out that she was disabled, Vera used to be what she describes as a functional alcoholic, retreating to dimly lit bars to blunt her anxieties and meet people who wouldn't judge her for being unusual. "My kids still have many raw feelings about that," she says. "They may always have raw feelings. I can just love them and give them that space. I understand that they don't trust me in the house, after the ways I behaved."

Vera's life in a van allows her to split the difference between independence and interdependence, connection and solitude. She's always needed a lot of stimulation, which alcohol used to provide her during her dull, desk-job days. Now she has hiking, and taking Jerry to dog parks all across the United States, and sleeping in the open air in remote areas with perfectly darkened skies. She knows that it can't last forever, but she wants to feel freedom while she can—"When my body or my van breaks down, I have an old girlfriend in Arizona that will take me in. She's divorced and could use a little liveliness around." Vera is also well-connected to online communities for other van dwellers and people who live off the grid. She's met many of her pals from the forums in person, and they take care of one another, providing tips for how to live without a stable mailing address, and Venmoing one another money when tires burst or water pumps stop working. "It's the most accepting community I've ever known," she says.

Another older Autistic man that I spoke to, Craig, recently moved a few hundred miles, from a major European metropolis to a small house near his friends in the country. He says he's ready to downsize and be near the handful of people he's known and trusted nearly all his life.

"I'm in the spare bedroom of a married couple I've known since childhood," he says. "We live all together, share meals, do everything together. I've been thinking a lot about where I want to be, what is home to me. And these are the people I wanted to make sure I would be around when I grew old." In his younger life, Craig was a world traveler, fluent in four different languages. He went to school abroad in the United States, and then spent half a decade in South Korea teaching. Now he cannot handle the instability of travel anymore. He finds adventure by translating short stories and news articles into other languages and reading to his loved ones over communal meals.

"It is very bittersweet to be slowing down, and there are certain things I may never do again," he says. "The way you think changes. I used to be so hungry. Now I just feel very lucky to be near to my people."

Many Autistic people adapt to the challenges of aging by retiring early, moving into multigenerational, multifamily homes, modifying vans or tiny homes into livable structures, or by pooling resources together with fellow disabled people whose needs complement our own. Sorting out the practical concerns of life as an older person is one major challenge, but arriving at a state of acceptance with all that loss and change is also a major endeavor. One way we can cope is by thinking very intentionally about the life we wish to create for ourselves, asking key questions that reveal our priorities such as the ones in the exercise below.

Create a Plan for the Future
Reflections on Autistic Aging

Who do you want to surround yourself with in your later years?

_____

_____

_____

When you imagine yourself as an older person, what is your ideal location?

_____

_____

_____

Imagine yourself as an older person, going through the course of a typical day. What is your routine like? What brings you pleasure? How would you like each morning to begin, and each evening to end?

_____

_____

_____

Anticipate the needs you'll likely face as an older person. Do you have any existing medical issues you'll likely need help managing? How do you expect your financial needs, social support needs, and rest and recovery needs to change?

_____

_____

_____

When we are young, we are incapable of being productive or taking care of ourselves. Other people feed us, bathe us, look after our medical care, decide what is important to teach us, make sure that we get enough rest, include us in social activities, and try to surround us with the tools they believe are necessary to leading a full life. Some of us then experience what society considers "productive years." As we age, our ability to be productive and independent reduces, and we increasingly need other people around to address our basic care requirements and be mindful of what is important to us, too. Disability justice activists are always quick to remind abled people of these facts, to challenge the widespread notion that a human life can only be meaningful if it's lived alone. True freedom does not come from isolation or a lack of mutual reliance. Real freedom comes in being loved, understood, and looked after, and having others to look after in turn.

Forming a plan for the long-term future as an Autistic person requires that we engage meaningfully with other people to build the communities and support networks that all people require. You can use the next exercise to contemplate the roles that you'd like various people to play in the rest of your life, and how you might engage with them to have difficult, important conversations about life's changes and eventualities.

Engage with Others
Building Your Long-Term Support Network

Who would you like to provide you with close company as you grow older?

_____

_____

_____

How might you ask this person (or people) to serve this role in your life?

_____

_____

_____

Who would you like to handle legal responsibilities for you, such as serving as executor of your will or your legal power of attorney?

_____

_____

_____

How might you ask this person (or people) to serve this role in your life?

Who do you want to live near, or share housing with?

How might you ask this person (or people) to serve this role in your life?

Who would you like to serve as your medical advocate, or otherwise help you look after your medical needs?

How might you ask this person (or people) to serve this role in your life?

Who would you like to consider to be close family in the remaining years of your life?

_____

_____

_____

How might you ask this person (or people) to serve this role in your life?

_____

_____

_____

It is incredibly vulnerable to approach another person with requests like these. Many people are so uncomfortable with the realities of death and aging that they never even bother to speak about long-term plans, just assuming biological relatives will look after them or ignoring thoughts of illness and mortality until they have no choice but to face them. That is all too often the neurotypical way of things, looking away from unpleasant truths and pretending that we are not dependent upon others. But as proudly unmasked neurodivergent people, we can choose to shed a light on these topics and banish the fear that can make them seem so dark. If there is no shame in disability, then there's no problem with leaning on one another.

Another Autistic older adult that I'm close to, James, tells me that watching his own father die has made him acutely aware of his mortality. In his final months, James's dad had no room for future plans or dreams anymore; all he could do was watch cheesy Hallmark Christmas movies and dream fondly of the past. That experience motivated James to write openly about the subject of death, and to think about ways he can spend his remaining years that still have meaning.

"I'm over 60 now and in poor health," James writes.[28] "Despite having been a competitive amateur marathoner training for a triathlon only a few years ago, my mortality is fast catching up with me... So now I face some decisions. If I don't like where my life is right now, what will I do about it? Even if I only have 10 or 20 years left, tops, will I take action now to make those years as fulfilling and joyful as they can be?"

All disabled people are forced to author our own legacies. We've been written out of most history books and neglected by our governments as well as many of our families. Our most beautiful qualities and greatest strengths are left out of all the diagnostic guidebooks that treat us as a blight upon humanity rather than one of its many jewels. Yet in spite of it all, we have found one another, forged an understanding of our community, and risen up in a chorus of defiant voices demanding the justice that we are owed. Just as we have the ability to create our own identities, our own friendships and families, we also have the ability to craft our own enduring legacies. This is where the journey of unmasking for life will culminate: in no longer working to justify our existence, but boldly deciding for ourselves what we want life to be *for*.

Autistic Legacies

The project of unmasking is ultimately a question of values and priorities. Before we know ourselves as disabled, most of us adhere to a common set of values society has passed down to us: we believe our ultimate goal in life is to find gainful employment, live independently, achieve impressive things, be beloved by others, and create a legacy through the fruits of our labor and our families and kids. But after we've started to unmask, we may have to accept that we aren't capable of pursuing many of these supposed sources of life's meaning—and may find that we're not particularly interested in many of the rest anyway. Rejecting a limited perspective on life's purpose can be freeing, but an existential void opens up in its place. What does it mean to have a worthwhile existence? What legacy can we leave behind that we truly believe in? If we don't want to be the neurotypical people whom society long forced us to be, who do we really want to be instead, and how do we get there?

From the time I was eighteen until the time I was thirty-five, I never lived in an apartment for more than two years. I shuffled between studios, rented spare rooms, and one-bedroom apartments, each one plagued with leaky radiators, peeling tubs lined with black mildewy grout, and "landlord-white" walls that I could not decorate and contained lead-based paint. Each time that I moved, I threw more things out because I couldn't handle the stress of loading and unloading so many bulky items. I kept my clothing in a stack of milk crates, had almost no cutlery, and wrote at a tiny repurposed children's school desk that a friend had loaned me and that caused me back pain. I didn't cook, I didn't entertain, I just wrote and worked out in my apartment and otherwise tried to spend as much time as possible somewhere else. I found it depressing to be at home. There was nowhere for me to sit, nowhere to read, and the overhead lighting hurt my eyes and covered everything in unflattering shadows.

I was never comfortable. I didn't feel that I deserved to make myself comfortable. All my money and energy was devoted to the work that made it possible for me to stay alive as a disabled person. I didn't have it in me to maintain a full-time job, pursue my creative projects, and hold dinner parties or build furniture. Life as a well-balanced human was a task I kept putting off, like a bad tooth I was afraid of having pulled. I was certain that if I made a little space in my existence for "frivolous" pursuits like decorating or hobbies, it would consume too much of my attention, and I would no longer be able to hold my life together. I had never missed a deadline, never gotten a bad performance review at work, and never stopped looking for side-hustles and cost-cutting measures to keep me from going hungry. I couldn't let that start now. I was living, as my friend Jess would describe it, as if my apartment wasn't a place with an actual person living in it. Instead, it was a storage space for the tool that I used in order to make a living—my mind.

In the middle of my thirties, my outlook finally started to shift. When my friend Madeline was able to take in a friend who was suffering from a chronic illness, I felt a lovely kind of envy at her and her spouse's ability to be so kind. Every time I had gone to visit Madeline and Megan at their home in Michigan, they'd been able to offer a cozy guest room to me, the bed freshly made, the chairs overflowing with Squishmallow stuffed animals, another spare bedroom and a massive couch available for other friends to crash on, too. At their house, I'm always free to step away for some privacy without judgment or questioning, and warmly welcomed when I come back downstairs to join in the chatting and playing of games. I've had some of the most peaceful sleeps of my adult life in that guest room, blanketed in the warmth of their hospitality and secure in the knowledge that other close friends were just a few feet away, comfortable and safe too.

In my life, I have often felt like a terribly antisocial person because I need so much space from others to recharge my social batteries. I don't always have it in me to be lighthearted and conversational. I don't experience empathy, or feel many of the emotions that others do, and that's often led me to believe I don't deserve love. But I've never felt quite so whole as when I've been free to go dwell in my darkness and solitude while still being surrounded by loving people, knowing that I can rejoin their reverie at any time, even if there is nothing for me to say. It feels like all sides of me are being held—the dark and the light of me, the warm, overly sensitive bits and the cold, numb "robotic" elements that I've always had to apologize for. There I am free *from* stress and overwhelm, but also free *to* be my full self.

As I grow older, close friends of mine are making homes for themselves, adopting cats, raising children, moving to be closer to their families, nursing sick parents, starting rock bands, writing manifestos, and taking steps to form the queer anarchist communes of their dreams. I have finally found myself longing for a sense of permanence, a source of meaning that endures even as life is marked by change, loss, and disruption. I want to be able to offer a bed where others can lay their heads. I want a cozy nook in my home where anyone can curl up with a book. I want to carefully select the paint for the walls in a color that soothes my nervous system, to hang curtains that keep the drafts out and don't just attach with adhesive strips and Velcro. I want to be able to write and livestream with others from a workstation that does not hurt my back. I want to stop constantly fleeing from the places that I have lived in, out of complete distress, dropping all my possessions behind me as if they're dead weight. I *want* my life to have a weight to it, a substance; I want it to be able to take up space. I want to be comfortable, to offer comfort and belonging to others. And I want to finally be able to move slowly enough that every day doesn't feel like an emergency.

My friend Emilie is an Autistic trans woman living in Montreal, and I've noticed that she's been on a similar trajectory recently. Before she dropped out of graduate school, she was struggling with being misgendered and disrespected by her colleagues and professors nearly every day, and she worked herself to the bone while living in a threadbare, uncomfortable small apartment and drinking and doing drugs to cope with how miserable she was.

Once she left her academic program and moved away, though, she started gradually taking steps to properly care for herself. She lobbied for her doctor to up her estrogen dose so that she could start presenting in the ways that she wanted to. She bought clothing that she liked and started carefully lining her eyes with a single strip of white eyeliner that made her face light up. She spent a lot of time taking long walks outside, pondering her old life and the future she wanted. Emilie bought herself a giant stuffed whale to cuddle with, stopped self-harming with substances, started eating more, and for the first time took an interest in putting up fall decorations, candles, and other comforting items in her apartment.

Emilie's mental health seemed to take a nearly 180-degree turn thanks to her leaving a punishing academic environment and beginning to look after her happiness and health. She became obviously less obsessive about subjects that upset her, yet also more willing to cry openly the moment her soft feelings were touched. She became more playful and satisfied, as well as more earnest, losing the ironic shell that once protected her from abuse. Emilie has unmasked her entire life, throwing away the old goals and negative environments that kept her so restricted, just as she became more openly Autistic and came into her gender identity.

Having watched dozens of Autistic and other neurodivergent people embark on their unmasking journeys at this point, I fully believe that it must be a holistic process if it is to be successful: it's never as simple as just deciding one day to shake off all concealment and fear. Being resolutely unmasked is not a question of willpower so much as one of circumstances and resources. It is our environment and culture that require us to mask who we are: the fear of poverty, expulsion, and homelessness drive so much of our loathing and terror at the prospect of truly getting to know ourselves or to show ourselves to others. In our relationships, our homes, our daily habits, our plans for the future, and our means of survival, we cannot constantly have the mask of neurotypicality pressed back onto our faces. For most of us, escaping social pressure and systemic injustice entirely is not possible, but we do require a safe haven, a place of warmth and acceptance where we can fully be ourselves—and one of the great projects of lifelong unmasking is building out that safe haven until it covers a greater and greater expanse in our lives. We claim our safety with our self-advocacy skills and community support, as well as our choices. And the less we believe that our true selves are inherently shameful and broken, the greater inner clarity we develop about what it is that is best for us.

When we attempt to unmask our disabilities and unmask ourselves, we have to get acquainted with the values that we personally hold dear, and the ways in which those values contrast with society's dominant perspective. Much of my previous book on the subject, *Unmasking Autism,* asks readers to reflect on impactful moments in their past in order to discover what their true values are. These values might be things like curiosity, connection, passion, adventure, kindness, pleasure, nature, faith, solitude, meditation, music, loyalty, justice, beauty, wisdom, or any number of other powerful anchors that are unique to us. And as we move forward and work on unmasking our relationships, means of survival, and all the other external facets of our life, we get to start putting our values into practice.

At first, this can seem daunting because of course no person perfectly embodies all their personal ideals. Life will sometimes demand that our various values compete. However, by asking ourselves specific, grounded questions about how issues of values manifest in our lives, we can plan for these dilemmas and make decisions that lead us closer to reflecting the principles we believe in, rather than getting swept up in momentary concerns and social pressures and winding up with an existence that makes us unrecognizable to ourselves.

Here we will consider a final series of questions, which are designed to target our legacies and long-term future goals as unmasking people. Because I think these questions can seem intimidatingly large and abstract, I will be sharing some of my own responses, as well as examples from other neurodivergent people's lives, to give you an idea of just some of the possibilities. Throughout, remember that you are the sole expert on your experience, and that your answers can change over time as you further adapt and grow into yourself.

What matters most in life to me? This may sound like a massive philosophical question, but we can also answer it by simply observing what brings us the greatest pleasure and sense of rootedness in our current lives. Your life as a disabled person does not need to justify its existence with some higher purpose that would impress anybody else. You were not made "for" anything because you are not an object. Rather, you are a living being that *gets* to experience the fullness of being alive and interacting with reality. So which aspects of being alive interest you, motivate you, or bring you contentment? It might be activities like the following:

Enjoying my hobbies

Spending time in nature

Building things

Tearing things apart

Being around animals

Fighting injustice

Playing games

Making art

Helping people in my community

Looking after loved ones

Cuddling with my partner

Having vivid dreams

Trying new things

Or something else entirely

One Autistic person that I know, a wheelchair user named Olive, has found purpose in designing and sewing colorful patterned covers for wheelchair seats, armrest bags, and the handles of canes. Olive's physical disabilities and neurodivergence prevent them from working in the conventional, wage-earning sense, but they are an avid hobbyist with a loom for spinning yarn and a sewing machine that they use nearly all the time. So much of the gear that physically disabled people rely upon is mass-produced in drab shades of gray and beige that evoke the most depressing of medical environments, but Olive's handicrafts allow their friends to express their unique personalities with the items they carry around every day.

Olive and I first became acquainted because we were both friends with a nonverbal, intellectually disabled Autistic teenager who had trouble connecting with any peers of his own age. He was a lonely, easily frustrated kid with a big heart and a curious mind filled with questions, but because he couldn't speak verbally, he seldom got to interact with others. He rarely even used his adaptive communication device to express himself to his family, yet he loved sending Tumblr posts and chat messages filled with questions and reflections to his friends. Since I am not planning on having children, I have always longed to play an important role in the lives of a few young adults and teens. I found some of that gratifying connection through my friendship with this teen, and likewise through getting to know people like Olive, who made themself available to him at all hours of the night should he experience a meltdown or psychotic episode.

Olive and I both text with our teenage friend whenever he needs it, and we are in regular communication with his parents to let them know when he's in pain or grappling with difficult questions and feelings that he isn't sharing with them. It's an honor to be trusted by a young man who has been bullied relentlessly by peers and mistreated by some of his own caregivers. I know that being a presence in his life has mattered a lot to me, and that it has for Olive as well.

One of the things that matters most to me in life, I have learned, is simply being present for other people's stories, hearing them, supporting them, and learning through them a bit more about what being a human means. Though many Autistic people do "feel others' feelings" quite strongly, I do not: I can't look at a person's face and intuit their emotions nearly at all, and when something bad happens in another person's life, I do not automatically empathize. Instead, I'm relatively numb inside, and when I try to guess what another person might be thinking or wanting, my mind draws a blank, or I feel instinctively annoyed at the presence of a problem. Despite all of this, I do have compassion for my fellow human beings: I *want* to understand what moves them and how they cope, and I want to be there to help in whatever ways they need. But I have to actively choose to be caring, by learning more about what people are feeling and studying what most people find helpful when they are in need.

Through my close friendships with other people, and in the deep conversations I get to have about the inner workings of people's lives as a psychologist and writer, I have come to better understand how people feel, what they need, and what the common emotional reactions are to moments of loss, trauma, disruption, and unpredictability. Simply learning more about what makes people tick and what's going on inside behind their inscrutable faces is endlessly motivating to me, and getting to use that slowly growing body of knowledge in order to better help others is one of the most gratifying things I've done with my life. I have found that my tendency to be coolly analytical in the face of tough life moments can be helpful; I can jump into action by making phone calls and arranging doctors' appointments or meal deliveries while everybody is still panicking. But I also need to take people's feelings of sadness, grief, or anger into my calculations of what should happen next. I know how to be a really active, present listener because my own emotional reactions don't tend to emerge at all when other people are talking to me. Getting to know people deeply and learn more about how to best show up for others is one of the things that matters the most in life to me, and I happen to do it in a uniquely Autistic way.

Where does too much of my time currently go? When we know what matters the most to us, we can also identify the distractions and demands that keep us from enjoying our lives. In order to live more fully as ourselves, we may find that we need to cut back on some or all of the following:

Work

Commuting

Worrying about others' opinions of me

Pleasing my family

Maintaining my appearance

Keeping things clean

Trying to convince others to approve of me

Exercising

Trying to make my relationship work

Food prep

Questioning myself

So many of the neurodivergent people that we've heard from in this book have ultimately decided that in order to unmask themselves, they had to stop working so vigorously and sacrificing so much of their energy. Emilie and I are just two examples of Autistic people who stopped being workaholics as we began to unmask, and whose health restored after we finally ceased neglecting our well-being. Many of the Autistic parents and physically disabled people that I have spoken to have shared that holding life together has required getting more comfortable with messiness. And nearly all of us who mask pour far too much energy into maintaining relationships with the very people who provoke us to feel ashamed of our disabilities the most: invalidating parents, absent spouses, nitpicking friends.

Opening up space in our lives for the activities that matter requires that we also identify time wasters and drains on our energy that we are willing to cut out. By harnessing the skill of accepting change, we can skip out on weekly dinners with our parents, cancel our gym memberships, let our dirty dishes pile up, and begin searching for remote, part-time jobs in more affordable areas of the country as needed. Life demands so much of us, especially as disabled people. We have to practice recognizing when an expectation has been placed in our laps and then rejecting it because unfair demands will never stop appearing.

What do I want my legacy to be? This is a big question, and in mainstream capitalist society, the only worthwhile answers are ones involving massive, lucrative accomplishments. But when we think about our legacies as disabled people who challenge normative values, we can think instead about the ripple effects we want to see radiating out from our own humble existence. Our impact doesn't have to be enormous for our lives to have altered the world; merely being in the world as ourselves and interacting with others authentically and with integrity creates a meaningful mark. Here are just some of the legacies that we leave behind:

The people I've helped

The ways I've grown

The cycles I've stopped

The friends I've introduced

The home I have made

The community I've built

The children I've raised

The generation I've mentored

The elders I've cared for

The relief I have offered

The love I have found

The information I've compiled

The art I've made

The creators I've supported

The things I've seen

The places I've been

The harm I've stopped

The activism I've done

The strangers I've reached

The skills I've learned

The faith I've practiced

The books I've read

The problems I've fixed

The surprises I've had

The mouths I've fed

The joy I've felt

The tears I've dried

The wounds I've soothed

You'll notice that many of the legacies I've listed do not involve making or producing anything at all. Your presence alone is felt in the world, and choosing to be part of a space has a great impact upon it by itself. We interact with the world that surrounds us constantly, absorbing new messages and observations and putting out our energies and attention into our surroundings in turn. That itself has value.

Looking back on my own life, I can see that the person that I am is not defined by the words I have written; if anything, it is shaped more by the words I have read. Everything that I've ever thought, felt, believed, dreamed of, or concerned myself with has been thanks to the influence of thousands of other people's work. Anything that I've ever done has been the synthesis of experiences, learning, and inspiration that other people made possible for me. When I read a book or watch a film, it alters me slightly, and transforms me into a person unlike the one I was before that moment. The same thing happens after every single conversation I have with another person, and with every random street corner that I choose to wander down.

All the experiences and transformations we undergo in life aren't necessarily "for" any certain outcome; to live and to change is a purpose all its own. Our legacy is the unbroken line that passes through us and connects us to the lives of others. We do not have to force that connection so much as recognize that it's already there, and learn to appreciate it for what it is.

Which people and communities helped make me the person that I am today? One of the great remedies to worrying about the future is to cast our gaze backward, gratefully, to the past. When we contemplate the people who have influenced us in a positive way, and the communities that have made our lives possible, we experience a feeling of continuity. It puts our journeys into a greater context, so we can see we are already a part of something far larger than our own short time on earth. For disabled people and other marginalized groups, it's particularly important to locate our elders and learn our histories so that we better understand our own struggles in the present day, feel thankful about what gains we have made, and be stirred toward positive change for our shared futures.

I draw great strength from the queer people throughout history who have lived openly as themselves in spite of legal oppression and social condemnation. The silent film actor William Haines is a great inspiration to me: a former sex worker turned charming on-screen wisecracker, he was one of the first publicly gay actors, and openly lived in his home in Hollywood with his long-term partner, Jimmie Shields.[29] When film studios began cracking down on "moral violations" and forcing stars into the closet, William Haines refused, sacrificing his career and launching a new one as an interior designer so that he could continue to live on his terms. I am also deeply moved by the life of Peter Berlin, a gay filmmaker and exhibitionist whose 1974 art film, *That Boy,* is a tribute to unconventional, transgressive sexuality. Even within the queer world of San Francisco in the 1970s, Berlin was unique: he strutted up and down the streets of the city in handsewn leather outfits, posing for onlookers and cruising for attention, yet rarely consummating his flirtations with any actual sex. *That Boy* is a manifesto for gay, asexual eroticism: the main character revels in being the subject of every man's fantasies but doesn't actually want to be touched himself. As a queer person and an Autistic with my own unusual fetishes and a sense of detachment from others' bodies and feelings, I take immense solace in Berlin's proud artistic declaration of exactly what turned him on. His work helps me feel free to be the person that I am, and to never forget that I can make up my own rules about what sex, romance, and true connection mean.

Many neurodivergent people can find meaning through the study of our shared histories. Books like *A Disability History of the United States* by Kim Nielsen, *Disability Visibility* edited by Alice Wong, *Beyond Shame: Reclaiming the Abandoned History of Radical Gay Sexuality* by Patrick Moore, and *Body and Soul: The Black Panther Party and the Fight Against Medical Discrimination* by Alondra Nelson can orient our present-day fights within an enduring historical legacy and help us find the elders and ancestors many of us have been denied access to. In the fights for greater disability rights protections, AIDS research, and sickle cell anemia research that prior generations have fought, we can see that we are not alone, and that we do collectively have the power to change the social paradigm as disabled people. By getting to know our elders through volunteer work and participation in cross-generational communities, we can also see a vision of what our futures might be.

We can also find strength and self-knowledge by reflecting upon the close loved ones that did accept or affirm us, or even in the fictional characters that have empowered us to unmask. One Autistic person that I know practices pop-culture paganism and maintains shrines devoted to the deities from *The Legend of Zelda* games because she never grew up with any kind of conscious religious practice. The worlds of those games allowed her to escape when her home life was too overwhelming and disturbing, and the characters were unusual and wacky and resembled her own mannerisms as a disabled kid. Rather than bemoaning the lack of spiritual depth or connection that her childhood had, this friend of mine actively embraces her past as it was, and mines it for meaningful symbolism. We don't have to have any life but the one that we have: we are located at what often feels like the end of a long, rich timeline, but thankfully it will continue far past us—not only in any children we might have but also in the fellow disabled people, queer people, people of color, and other marginalized individuals and nonconformists who are our spiritual children.

Where do I still need to grow? A life that has not ended is a life where greater learning, growth, and creativity are still possible. Though aging and death are terrifying prospects, we do not have to resign ourselves to them so long as we have the ability to take in new information and think and behave in new ways. We can always become more free and more accepting of ourselves and other people.

Our unmasking journeys never really end because full authenticity is not really a static state. There is no singular true self lurking behind the mask of neurotypicality that we've been forced to wear: our selves are dynamic interactions between our past influences and our present surroundings, and that means we are constantly in flux. In the early stages of unmasking, we may be primarily focused on soothing our trauma responses and examining our innermost feelings. Over time, our gaze often turns outward, and we begin articulating who we really are to others, finding ways to love others more genuinely, and demanding the accommodations that we've long been denied.

Sometime after that, we may finally have emotional room to notice the harm we have unwittingly done to others and make amends for it, or see the ways in which we still hold on to prejudices and judgments that are not serving anyone. We eventually stop seeing ourselves as passive victims, instead recognizing ourselves as full, complex agents who can pursue what we desire, can manage our relationships, and have enough power to do both good and ill. No longer at the whims of other people's reactions to us, we get to take responsibility for many of our life choices, accepting that others may not always approve of them and that we will make mistakes, but continuing to engage with the world and express our values anyway.

Unmasking is an act of self-creation; who we are is shaped by the activities we engage in every day and the relationships we participate in with others. When we mask constantly, we feel as if we *become* the mask, but when we explore our deeper feelings and live more authentically, we actually develop greater depth as people. We can choose how to refine and alter ourselves for the better by selecting the skills we practice every day. Take a moment to reflect upon the core self-advocacy skills we have practiced throughout this book, and note for yourself the areas where you still have room to grow.

Accept Change, Loss, and Uncertainty

Areas where I still need to grow in this skill:

Where I will continue to practice this skill:

Engage in Conflict, Discussion, and Disagreement

Areas where I still need to grow in this skill:

Where I will continue to practice this skill:

Transgress Rules, Demands, and Social Expectations

Areas where I still need to grow in this skill:

Where I will continue to practice this skill:

Tolerate Discomfort, Disagreement, and Being Disliked

Areas where I still need to grow in this skill:

_____

_____

_____

Where I will continue to practice this skill:

_____

_____

_____

Create Accommodations, Relationship Structures, and Ways of Living

Areas where I still need to grow in this skill:

_____

_____

_____

Where I will continue to practice this skill:

_____

_____

_____

For my part, I know that I still need to improve upon my acceptance of change, particularly unwanted losses. One way that I practice building this skill is by turning toward honest conversations about loss, change, and death, rather than shying away from the disturbing feelings they provoke in me. I read about burial practices on forums for morticians, and I listen to my older friends when they discuss their end-of-life plans or growing medical concerns. In my home culture as a white midwesterner, awkward, morbid encounters like these are supposed to be defused with lots of joking and a rapid changing of the subject, but I refuse to mask the harsh reality because doing so is disrespectful to people's genuine suffering, and it will only weaken my ability to respond to it. When death strikes or even just when a simmering-hot romance suddenly begins to cool, I turn toward it and acknowledge that something is missing, and my relationships are better for it.

I also still need to grow in my ability to tolerate the consequences of standing by my values. At the time that I am writing this book, powerful pro-Palestinian resistance movements have begun to spread across the globe. In the past, I have been afraid to publicly oppose the apartheid against the Palestinian people because I feared that doing so would result in my losing my job or facing public censure, as so many other activists have experienced. But in order to live in accordance with my beliefs, I must be willing to make sacrifices. During a moment when so many innocent people are being displaced and dying, my own comfort and ease cannot be my priority. In future moments of injustice, I must be prepared to endure principled sacrifices, too.

I may be disabled and vulnerable, but I am also a person with morals, and a white man with a savings account and, therefore, with a job I can afford to lose. All my hard work and careful planning for an early retirement is useless if only I get to live stably while millions of others suffer. My well-being as a disabled person is indelibly tied to those of other people whom the world also regards as disposable, and I cannot be unmasked while keeping more controversial beliefs stifled in my throat. I am an abolitionist, and that truth has always been transmitted in my work; I'm also an openly queer person in a world where our lives are constantly under attack. If I believe in our liberation, I must speak out for the Indigenous people here in the United States and worldwide who deserve justice, not to be shunted away into restrictive reservations and prisons. With the free time and mental energy I have opened up by deprioritizing my career, I can become a more active force in movements for change.

At times, I am too fearful to contradict hateful speech in others, or to put my own body on the line to protect my broader community at a protest. I cannot tell others what path is right for them, or what they must do in order to enact their values. But I know that I can always take more concrete action, and give more of my money, my energy, my safety, and my time toward the causes that matter to me. One of the core unmasking projects of my life will be to continually push myself to stop turning away out of individualistic fear, instead folding myself into the larger movements and communities to which I can meaningfully contribute. To be interdependent requires sacrificing the selves that we cling to so desperately in our alienated privacy. Leaning on others and giving freely and with love is terrifying, but it is a love that we are powerful enough to choose.

For a group of people who have long been told that we are freakish, difficult to deal with, and too demanding, it can be terrifying for Autistic people to invent an entirely new life for ourselves. But by focusing on the practical aspects of managing our relationships, developing new skills, and eking out a living without sacrificing our well-being, we can embark on a bold act of self-creation that flies in the face of every ableist norm.

Ultimately, each one of us is the expert on our life circumstances and the areas of existence that we find the most meaningful and fulfilling. We may find our legacy in the work we've done to uplift and support other disabled people. We may take solace in the warmth we've provided to family and our cherished friends. Maybe we feel called to leave a mark on the world through our creativity, or by halting the cycle of neglect and abuse. Perhaps we see our lives as one great act of witnessing all that humanity is capable of, and simply being present for it will have been enough.

Whatever the answer, it is ours to decide, and with some of the self-advocacy skills we've developed, it is also ours to pursue. Leading an unmasked life is challenging, and it requires practical support as well as a whole loving community to lean on. But that life begins the moment we stop resisting the way our actual disabled bodies and minds are built, and begin accepting them as completely whole and worthy as they are instead. Nothing about us ever deserved to be masked. Every facet of us is brilliant, strong, and shimmeringly beautiful. We get to build the settings to hold the precious jewels of our personalities, to protect them, and carry them, and put them on display so that they might shine.

ACKNOWLEDGMENTS

Thank you once again to my wonderfully supportive editor, Michele Eniclerico, for continuing to advocate for my work, and for always asking questions that get my writing to open up more fully. *Unmasking Autism* has been able to contribute to the public conversation about neurodiversity in a significant way, and that wouldn't have happened without your vision for the book, and your support of my voice. Thank you to my agent, Jenny Herrera, for the philosophical conversations and level-headed reassurance when I am doubting myself; you are a powerhouse with an instinct for blending sharp thinking with softness and compassion that is unrivaled. Thanks to Annette Szlachta-McGinn and Loren Noveck for catching my errors and making my work look good; your meticulousness and clarity are so appreciated. I also want to express all my gratitude to everyone on the Harmony team who has helped my books get out into the world and find their readers: Ray Arjune, Jonathan Sung, Lindsey Kennedy, Maya Smith, Brianne Sperber, and so many more. Thank you to Amber Beard, Ethan Donaldson, Lynn Rondeau, Darlene Sterling, Scott Sherratt, Jade Pietri, and all of ARU Studios for continuing to adapt my writing into an accessible audio format that so many enthusiastic listeners have shared their appreciation for.

To everyone who has read and responded to *Unmasking Autism* in the past three years, I send my unending gratitude. This book would not exist without your emails, private messages, letters, reviews, questions at conferences, recommendations to other readers, Tumblr asks, TikTok reactions, random conversations on the street, and even reader translations. The neurodivergent people and our allies who have approached me to ask what comes next in the unmasking journey have inspired this work, and provoked me to make necessary changes in my own life. I also want to extend my thanks to every conference organizer and disability ERG member who has invited me to present my work at your organizations, often in environments that are quietly hostile to neurodiversity. Your advocacy matters, even when it has been unjustly punished. I have taken each of your stories to heart.

In the past few years, I have been blessed to be able to work with a variety of brilliant neurodivergent and queer video essayists who are shifting the culture's attitudes toward disability in a palpable way in real time. Their work has challenged me to remain optimistic and vocally critical of the status quo, even when I'm feeling hopeless. Alex Avila, your analysis of self-diagnosis on social media truly elevated the public consciousness on the topic. Elliot Sang, your videos on Autism, Narcissistic Personality Disorder, and other stigmatized neurodiverse identities have been deeply nourishing to me, and so necessary. Matt Bernstein, thank you for standing proudly in your "annoying queerness" and for making a space for all of us who diverge, be it because we are trans, or fat, disabled, or simply too strange for the average person to get. Each of you has given me so much faith in our collective power to build a better world.

Massive thanks to all of my Autistic author friends who have had my back on this journey: Eric Garcia, our books on Autism are siblings and it's been so meaningful to progress through our careers as authors together and share so many stages with you. I am so thankful for your work. Pat Loller, I cherish your authenticity and candor, and the strength of your artistic integrity. Your support of my work has meant the world, but even more than that, I am galvanized by your refusal to be ground up by the industry. Fern Brady, your memoir helped me to better understand myself in dozens of ways and I'm awed by your success, your realness, and your principles. Reese Piper, you have an incredible talent for narrative and spending time with you has always been effortless and comforting, which is all too rare for me.

There are so many other brilliant thinkers and advocates in my life that my writing owes an eternal debt to. Sarah Casper, your work and our conversation have enriched this book immensely. Ayesha Khan, your pro-Palestinian organizing and your writings about community have knocked the air out of my chest and made me get my shit together more times than I can count. Jesse Meadows, you eviscerate pseudoscientific ableism with a precision and heart that I can only hope to emulate. Marta Rose, you've gotten me thinking about entire aspects of my life that I'd never known how to look after before. Emma Barnes, I hope to one day share a long drive in the van with you. Your playful spirit is infectious and I love the way you think. Jersey Noah, thank you for showing us all what it means to give one's life to a righteous cause. Timotheus Gordon, your advocacy has made countless Autistic people in Illinois safer, and you light up every room or chat that you are in. James Finn, your writing and friendship provide me with a life-sustaining link to queer communities worldwide, as well as our shared history. Leo Herrera, your guides have taught me and countless other neurodivergent gays how to get out of our own heads and go cruise. Devon M. Price, so many of your reading recommendations have found their way into this book. Thank you for your sexual health work, and for all the learning you've shared with me. Emily Carrier, I have loved watching you grow. Your embrace of tenderness has made it easier for me to care for myself. Ana Valens, your perspective so often helps me feel as if I'm not alone, while expanding my horizons at the same time. Roxy, no one has an Autistic compendium of knowledge and wit quite like you.

Thank you to the book's many cited sources and interview subjects, and to the many friends who have generously allowed me to take inspiration in my writing from the lessons of your lives. Dio, thank you for showing me how to advocate for myself. August, thank you for all the long walks and contemplative conversations. Jess White, thank you for every rant you've ever dispensed on Facebook Messenger. Kelly Lenza, you've helped me expose the tender sides of myself that I've always believed that I could not show. Blair, thank you for being a prophet of self-acceptance and artistic zeal, and for illustrating to all of us that every moment that we share together finds its way into the work. Eva Mika, you've made my working life survivable and nurtured the lapsed psychologist in me. Melanie, I love you for your dryness, for the bullshit you hate, and for the people you'll choose to die on a hill to defend. To Tom and Joe the Anime Sickos, thank you for your friendship, for making podcasts that keep me company in my most drudgery-filled moments, and for ruining my vocabulary with your perfect turns of phrase.

Callisto, thank you for moderating my and Maddie's Twitch chats and our Discord server, and for demonstrating in that work what it means to be level-headed and responsible while still being a complete Autistic freak. To everyone who watches the Time Theft Today streams, thank you for contributing to such thought-provoking conversations. It has been a true lifeline in the past few years. Thank you to Megan and Maddie for opening up your home to me on countless occasions, for supporting me in one of the most rewarding and longest-running creative collaborations of my life, and for seeing me as a person worth approaching, long before I had any confidence or anybody knew who I was.

NOTES

Introduction

1. Tsang, V. (2018). Eye-tracking study on facial emotion recognition tasks in individuals with high-functioning autism spectrum disorders. *Autism, 22*(2), 161–70.
2. Brosnan, M., & Ashwin, C. (2023). Thinking, fast and slow on the autism spectrum. *Autism, 27*(5), 1245–55.
3. *Neuroconformity* is a term coined by the physician Dr. Dave Saunders in April 2022: X.com/drdevonprice/status/1513693021325434886.
4. Hull et al. (2020). The female autism phenotype and camouflaging: A narrative review. *Review Journal of Autism and Developmental Disorders, 7*, 306–17; O'Nions et al. (2023). Autism in England: Assessing underdiagnosis in a population-based cohort study of prospectively collected primary care data. *The Lancet Regional Health–Europe, 29*; Jones et al. (2020). An expert discussion on structural racism in autism research and practice. *Autism in Adulthood, 2*(4), 273–281; Bobb, V. (2019). Black girls and autism. In *Girls and Autism*. Milton Park, Oxfordshire UK: Routledge, 36–47.
5. Lockwood Estrin et al. (2021). Barriers to autism spectrum disorder diagnosis for young women and girls: A systematic review. *Review Journal of Autism and Developmental Disorders, 8*(4), 454–70; Constantino et al. (2020). Timing of the Diagnosis of Autism in African American Children. *Pediatrics, 146*(3), 2019–3629. doi.org/10.1542/peds.2019-3629; Lai, M. C., & Baron-Cohen, S. (2015). Identifying the lost generation of adults with autism spectrum conditions. *The Lancet Psychiatry, 2*(11), 1013–27; Daniels, A. M., & Mandell, D. S. (2014). Explaining differences in age at autism spectrum disorder diagnosis: A critical review. *Autism, 18*(5), 583–97.
6. Oredipe et al. (2023). Does learning you are autistic at a younger age lead to better adult outcomes? A participatory exploration of the perspectives of autistic university students. *Autism, 27*(1), 200–12.
7. Riccio et al. (2020). How is autistic identity in adolescence influenced by

parental disclosure decisions and perceptions of autism? *Autism, 25*(2), 374–88 doi.org/10.1177/1362361320958214.
8. Mogensen, L., & Mason, J. (2015). The meaning of a label for teenagers negotiating identity: Experiences with autism spectrum disorder. *Sociology of Health & Illness, 37*(2), 255–69.
9. Lei et al. (2023). Understanding the relationship between social camouflaging in autism and safety behaviours in social anxiety in autistic and non-autistic adolescents. *Journal of Child Psychology and Psychiatry 65*(3), https://doi.org/10.1111/jcpp.13884; Beardon, L. (2019). Autism, masking, social anxiety and the classroom. In Clare Lawrence (Ed.). *Teacher Education and Autism: A Research-Based Practical Handbook*, Jessica Kingsley Publishers.
10. Alaghband-Rad et al. (2023). Camouflage and masking behavior in adult autism. *Frontiers in Psychiatry, 14,* doi.org/10.3389/fpsyt.2023.1108110.
11. Miller et al. (2021). "Masking is life": Experiences of masking in autistic and nonautistic adults. *Autism in Adulthood, 3*(4), 330–38.
12. Forcey-Rodriguez, K. E. (2023). The risk factors and preventative methods of self-harm and suicidality for autistic people. *Canadian Journal of Autism Equity, 3*(1), 12–26.
13. Mandy, W., & Tchanturia, K. (2015). Do women with eating disorders who have social and flexibility difficulties really have autism? A case series. *Molecular Autism, 6,* 1–10.
14. Forcey-Rodriguez, K. E. (2023). The risk factors and preventative methods of self-harm and suicidality for autistic people. *Canadian Journal of Autism Equity, 3*(1), 12–26.
15. Valagussa et al. (2018). Toe walking assessment in autism spectrum disorder subjects: A systematic review. *Autism Research, 11*(10), 1404–15.
16. This rule has since been revised and reduced significantly—but not entirely—by the Biden administration. See: www.autisticadvocacy.org/2022/09/asan-statement-on-final-public-charge-rule/.
17. amnesty.sa.utoronto.ca/2023/04/06/dehumanization-archaic-immigration-policies-against-individuals-with-disabilities/.
18. www.theguardian.com/uk-news/2022/may/26/autistic-ukrainian-boy-timothy-tymoshenko-uk-grant-visa.
19. globalnews.ca/news/4142592/trudeau-liberals-overhaul-discriminatory-immigration-law-disabilities/.
20. Yu et al. (2020). Public knowledge and stigma of autism spectrum disorder: Comparing China with the United States. *Autism, 24*(6), 1531–45.
21. According to the American Psychiatric Association, 16 percent of Americans will experience major depression at some point in their lives, though we have reason to believe this underestimates the rate in populations that lack access to mental health insurance. According to the National Institute of Mental Health, more than 30 percent of people will experience anxiety at

some point in their lives. Finally, according to the Alzheimer's Association, 1 in 3 elderly adults will experience senility or Alzheimer's. www.psychiatry.org/patients-families/depression/what-is-depression; www.alz.org/alzheimers-dementia/facts-figures.
22. Milton et al. (2022). The "double empathy problem" ten years on. *Autism, 26*(8), 1901–03.
23. Sasson et al. (2017). Neurotypical peers are less willing to interact with those with autism based on thin slice judgments. *Scientific Reports, 7*, 40700. doi.org/10.1038/srep40700.
24. Sandoval-Norton et al. (2019). How much compliance is too much compliance: Is long-term ABA therapy abuse? *Cogent Psychology, 6*(1), 1641258.
25. Dudley et al. (2015). What do we know about improving employment outcomes for individuals with autism spectrum disorder? The School of Public Policy, *SPP Research Papers,* University of Calgary, Volume 8, Issue 32, September 2015.
26. Hedley et al. (2023). Cost-benefit analysis of a non-government organization and Australian government collaborative supported employment program for autistic people. *Autism, 27*(5), 1377–90.
27. López, B., & Keenan, L. (2014). Barriers to employment in autism: Future challenges to implementing the Adult Autism Strategy. *Autism Research Network,* 1–17.
28. index.medium.com/productivity-will-go-down-this-year-26f04e4a9455.
29. www.cam.ac.uk/research/news/one-in-three-young-people-say-they-felt-happier-during-lockdown; www.iser.essex.ac.uk/research/publications/publication-526161.
30. fortune.com/2023/02/16/return-office-real-reason-slump-productivity-data-careers-gleb-tsipursky/.
31. Brosnan, M., & Gavin, J. (2021). The impact of stigma, autism label and wording on the perceived desirability of the online dating profiles of men on the autism spectrum. *Journal of Autism and Developmental Disorders, 51*, 4077–4085.

Chapter 1

1. www.wgbh.org/news/local/2023-09-11/electric-shock-therapy-is-still-allowed-in-one-mass-treatment-facility-advocates-say-change-is-long-overdue; stopabasupportautistics.home.blog/2019/07/23/aversives-and-torture-in-aba/.
2. Sandoval-Norton et al. (2019). How much compliance is too much compliance: Is long-term ABA therapy abuse? *Cogent Psychology, 6*(1), 1641258; Shkedy (2021). Long-term ABA therapy is abusive: A response to Gorycki, Ruppel, and Zane. *Advances in Neurodevelopmental Disorders, 5*(2), 126–34.

3. Bellini et al. (2007). A meta-analysis of school-based social skills interventions for children with autism spectrum disorders. *Remedial and Special Education, 28*(3), 153–62.
4. Ibid.
5. Dubreucq et al. (2022). A systematic review and meta-analysis of social skills training for adults with Autism Spectrum Disorder. *Journal of Autism and Developmental Disorders, 52*(4), 1598–1609.
6. Taylor, J. L., & Gotham, K. O. (2016). Cumulative life events, traumatic experiences, and psychiatric symptomatology in transition-aged youth with autism spectrum disorder. *Journal of Neurodevelopmental Disorders, 8*(28), doi.org/10.1186/s11689-016-9160-y.
7. Rumball et al. (2021). Heightened risk of posttraumatic stress disorder in adults with autism spectrum disorder: The role of cumulative trauma and memory deficits. *Research in Developmental Disabilities, 110,* 103848.
8. Wood, J. J., & Gadow, K. D. (2010). Exploring the nature and function of anxiety in youth with autism spectrum disorders. *Clinical Psychology: Science and Practice, 17*(4), 281–92. doi.org/10.1111/j.1468-2850.2010.01220.x.
9. www.raptitude.com/2015/12/how-to-become-less-shy/.
10. To read more about this, I recommend Fine, C. (2010). *Delusions of Gender: How Our Minds, Society, and Neurosexism Create Difference.* W. W. Norton & Company; Fine, C. (2017). *Testosterone Rex: Unmaking the Myths of Our Gendered Minds.* Icon Books; and Jack, J. (2011). "The extreme male brain?" Incrementum and the rhetorical gendering of autism. *Disability Studies Quarterly, 31*(3).
11. Nuzzolo-Gomez et al. (2002). Teaching children with autism to prefer books or toys over stereotypy or passivity. *Journal of Positive Behavior Interventions, 4*(2), 80–87.
12. Lebenhagen, C. (2020). Including speaking and nonspeaking autistic voice in research. *Autism in Adulthood, 2*(2), 128–31.
13. Cook et al. (2023). Noncompliance. In *Handbook of Applied Behavior Analysis for Children with Autism: Clinical Guide to Assessment and Treatment.* Springer International Publishing, 313–38.
14. Cook et al. (2022). Self-reported camouflaging behaviours used by autistic adults during everyday social interactions. *Autism, 26*(2), 406–21; Cook et al. (2020). Camouflaging behaviours used by autistic adults during everyday social interactions; Barry, E. N. (2019). Exploring the female autism phenotype: Personal identity formation and well-being in autistic females; Weiss, J. A., & Fardella, M. A. (2018). Victimization and perpetration experiences of adults with autism. *Frontiers in Psychiatry, 9,* 203.
15. medium.com/autistic-advice/im-pathologically-demand-avoidant-it-rules-a034a4e20da4.
16. Kent, R., & Simonoff, E. (2017). Prevalence of anxiety in autism spectrum

disorders. In Kerns et al. (Eds.). *Anxiety in Children and Adolescents with Autism Spectrum Disorder*. Academic Press, 5–32.
17. medium.com/@attleehall/autistic-memory-foaming-2cfecfcb9e8c.
18. Aron et al. (1992). Inclusion of other in the self scale and the structure of interpersonal closeness. *Journal of Personality and Social Psychology, 63*(4), 596.
19. Pennisi et al. (2021). Autism, autistic traits and creativity: A systematic review and meta-analysis. *Cognitive Processing, 22*, 1–36.
20. Harvey, S., & Berry, J. W. (2023). Toward a meta-theory of creativity forms: How novelty and usefulness shape creativity. *Academy of Management Review, 48*(3), 504–29.
21. Gilhooly et al. (2019). Incubation and suppression processes in creative problem solving. In *Insight and Creativity in Problem Solving*. Routledge, 130–46.
22. devonprice.medium.com/the-biological-causes-of-mental-illness-cannot-be-separated-from-the-social-ones-e7609483c4fd.
23. Atchley et al. (2012). Creativity in the wild: Improving creative reasoning through immersion in natural settings. *PloS ONE, 7*(12), e51474.
24. Ding et al. (2014). Improving creativity performance by short-term meditation. *Behavioral and Brain Functions, 10*(1), 1–8.
25. Paulus et al. (2016). Getting the most out of brainstorming groups. In A. B. Markman (Ed.). *Open Innovation: Academic and Practical Perspectives on the Journey from Idea to Market*. Oxford University Press, 43–70. The recent literature does suggest some circumstances under which criticism can be used to improve creativity for non-Autistics; see: Curhan et al. (2021). Cooperative criticism: When criticism enhances creativity in brainstorming and negotiation. *Organization Science, 32*(5), 1256–72.

Chapter 2

1. Krämer et al. (2018). Social snacking with a virtual agent on the interrelation of need to belong and effects of social responsiveness when interacting with artificial entities. *International Journal of Human-Computer Studies, 109*, 112–21.
2. For an excellent primer on the research on parasocial relationships, as well as an exploration of what it means to relate parasocially in the social media age, check out Shannon Strucci's YouTube series Fake Friends: www.youtube.com/watch?v=x3vD_CAYt4g.
3. Sosnowy et al. (2019). Setbacks and successes: How young adults on the autism spectrum seek friendship. *Autism in Adulthood, 1*(1), 44–51.
4. Rowley et al. (2012). The experience of friendship, victimization and bullying in children with an autism spectrum disorder: Associations with

child characteristics and school placement. *Research in Autism Spectrum Disorders, 6*(3), 1126–34.

5. In fact, a 2016 meta-analysis of eighteen studies found that the majority of Autistic kids did report having a friend: Mendelson et al. (2016). Friendship in school-age boys with autism spectrum disorders: A meta-analytic summary and developmental, process-based model. *Psychological Bulletin, 142*(6), 601–22. doi.org/10.1037/bul0000041.
6. Orsmond et al. (2004). Peer relationships and social and recreational activities among adolescents and adults with autism. *Journal of Autism and Developmental Disorders, 34*(3), 245–56. doi.org/10.1023/b:jadd.0000029547.96610.df.
7. Grace et al. (2022). Loneliness in autistic adults: A systematic review. *Autism, 26*(8), 2117–35. doi.org/10.1177/13623613221077721.
8. Ee et al. (2019). Loneliness in adults on the autism spectrum. *Autism in Adulthood, 1*(3), 182–93.
9. Libster et al. (2023). Sex differences in friendships and loneliness in autistic and non-autistic children across development. *Molecular Autism, 14*(1), 1–12.
10. Mehling, M., & Tasse, M. (2014). Empirically derived model of social outcomes and predictors for adults with ASD. *Intellectual and Developmental Disabilities, 52*(4), 282–95. doi.org/10.1352/1934-9556-52.4.282.
11. Kelly et al. (2017). The impact of social activities, social networks, social support and social relationships on the cognitive functioning of healthy older adults: A systematic review. *Systematic Reviews.* doi.org/10.1186/s13643-017-0632-2.
12. Mazurek, M. O. (2014). Loneliness, friendship, and well-being in adults with autism spectrum disorders. *Autism, 18*(3), 223–32.
13. Pickard et al. (2020). Exploring the cognitive, emotional and sensory correlates of social anxiety in autistic and neurotypical adolescents. *Journal of Child Psychology and Psychiatry, 61*(12), 1317–27.
14. Ridgway et al. (2024). Camouflaging autism in pursuit of friendship and intimate relationships: A systematic review. *Autism in Adulthood.* www.liebertpub.com/doi/10.1089/aut.2023.0160.
15. www.hhs.gov/sites/default/files/surgeon-general-social-connection-advisory.pdf.
16. Sundberg, M. (2018). Online gaming, loneliness and friendships among adolescents and adults with ASD. *Computers in Human Behavior, 79*, 105–10. doi.org/10.1016/j.chb.2017.10.020.
17. Rosenfeld et al. (2019). Disintermediating your friends: How online dating in the United States displaces other ways of meeting. *Proceedings of the National Academy of Sciences, 116*(36), 17753–58.
18. Sasson et al. (2017). Neurotypical peers are less willing to interact with those

with autism based on thin slice judgments. *Scientific Reports, 7,* 40700. doi.org/10.1038/srep40700.

19. Cassidy et al. (2020). Is camouflaging autistic traits associated with suicidal thoughts and behaviours? Expanding the interpersonal psychological theory of suicide in an undergraduate student sample. *Journal of Autism and Developmental Disorders, 50,* 3638–48. doi.org/10.1007/s10803-019-04323-3.

20. Schneid, I., & Raz, A. E. (2020). The mask of autism: Social camouflaging and impression management as coping/normalization from the perspectives of autistic adults. *Social Science & Medicine, 248,* 112826; Hull et al. (2017). "Putting on my best normal": Social camouflaging in adults with autism spectrum conditions. *Journal of Autism and Developmental Disorders, 47,* 2519–34.

21. Abramov, E., *"An Autistic Man Lives Here Cops No Excuses . . . Oh Yes He Is Black Too": Cognitive Disability, Race and Police Brutality in the United States.* PhD diss., Columbia University, 2017.

22. opendoorstherapy.com/autism-in-women-why-speaking-to-a-medical-doctor-can-be-hard/.

23. Sasson, N. J., & Morrison, K. E. (2019). First impressions of adults with autism improve with diagnostic disclosure and increased autism knowledge of peers. *Autism, 23*(1), 50–59. doi.org/10.1177/1362361317729526.

24. Han et al. (2022). A systematic review on autistic people's experiences of stigma and coping strategies. *Autism Research, 15*(1), 12–26; Thompson-Hodgetts et al. (2020). Helpful or harmful? A scoping review of perceptions and outcomes of autism diagnostic disclosure to others. *Research in Autism Spectrum Disorders, 77,* 101598; Sasson, N. J., & Morrison, K. E. (2019). First impressions of adults with autism improve with diagnostic disclosure and increased autism knowledge of peers. *Autism, 23*(1), 50–59.

25. Griffiths et al. (2019). The Vulnerability Experiences Quotient (VEQ): A study of vulnerability, mental health and life satisfaction in autistic adults. *Autism Research, 12*(10), 1516–28; Pearson et al. (2022). "Professionals are the hardest to trust": Supporting autistic adults who have experienced interpersonal victimization; Hwang et al. (2020). Domestic violence events involving autism: A text mining study of police records in New South Wales, 2005–2016. *Research in Autism Spectrum Disorders, 78,* 101634.

26. X.com/AutisticCallum_/status/1592577994102833152?lang=en.

27. buynothingproject.org/.

28. chadd.org/wp-content/uploads/2016/10/ATTN_10_16_Emotional Regulation.pdf.

29. For a more thorough exploration of RSD through a neurodiversity-minded lens, see devonprice.medium.com/the-biological-causes-of-mental-illness-cannot-be-separated-from-the-social-ones-e7609483c4fd.

30. Miller, R. W. (2020). "How to Make Friends." In *The Art of Showing Up: How to Be There for Yourself and Your People*. The Experiment.
31. theanarchistlibrary.org/library/anonymous-prole-info-abolish-restaurants.
32. For a critique of executive functioning through a neurodiversity lens, see: devonprice.medium.com/being-socially-motivated-is-not-a-disorder-a5759bbece0a.
33. disorderland.substack.com/p/e02-kill-the-executive-in-your-head#details.
34. Uziel, L. (2007). Individual differences in the social facilitation effect: A review and meta-analysis. *Journal of Research in Personality, 41*(3), 579–601.
35. Elopement is a term for the common tendency among Autistics and other neurodivergent folks to wander, or to feel the impulse to walk away.
36. Weston, D. (2020). *Small Talk: How to Start a Conversation, Truly Connect with Others and Make a Killer First Impression*. Monkey Publishing.
37. www.tumblr.com/storybookprincess/751762323238191104/probably-my-most-powerful-interpersonal.

Chapter 3

1. Koomar et al. (2021). Estimating the prevalence and genetic risk mechanisms of ARFID in a large autism cohort. *Frontiers in Psychiatry, 12,* 668297.
2. Sauer et al. (2021). Autism spectrum disorders: Etiology and pathology. *Exon Publications,* 1–15.
3. Rylaarsdam, L., & Guemez-Gamboa, A. (2019). Genetic causes and modifiers of autism spectrum disorder. *Frontiers in Cellular Neuroscience, 13,* 385.
4. Taylor et al. (2021). Heritability of quantitative autism spectrum traits in adults: A family-based study. *Autism Research, 14*(8), 1543–53.
5. Gibson, L. C. (2023). Why Do They Make It So Hard to Want to Be Around Them? In *Disentangling from Emotionally Immature People: Avoid Emotional Traps, Stand Up for Your Self, and Transform Your Relationships as an Adult Child of Emotionally Immature Parents*. New Harbinger Publications.
6. Gibson, L. C. (2023). Why Do They Make It So Hard to Want to Be Around Them? In *Disentangling from Emotionally Immature People: Avoid Emotional Traps, Stand Up for Your Self, and Transform Your Relationships as an Adult Child of Emotionally Immature Parents*. New Harbinger Publications.
7. Gibson, L. C. (2023). Why Do They Make It So Hard to Want to Be Around Them? In *Disentangling from Emotionally Immature People: Avoid Emotional Traps, Stand Up for Your Self, and Transform Your Relationships as an Adult Child of Emotionally Immature Parents*. New Harbinger Publications.
8. Price et al. (2015). Open-minded cognition. *Personality and Social Psychology Bulletin, 41*(11), 1488–1504.
9. Ottati, V. C., & Stern, C. (Eds.). (2023). *Divided: Open-Mindedness and*

Dogmatism in a Polarized World. Oxford University Press; Ottati et al. (Eds.). (2002). The Social Psychology of Politics. *Social Psychological Application to Social Issues,* vol. 5. Kluwer Academic-Plenum Publishers.

10. O'Keefe, D. J. (2013). The elaboration likelihood model. *The SAGE Handbook of Persuasion: Developments in Theory and Practice,* 137–49.
11. Gibson, L. C. (2023). I'm Always Nervous about Angering or Disappointing My Adult Child. In *Disentangling from Emotionally Immature People: Avoid Emotional Traps, Stand Up for Your Self, and Transform Your Relationships as an Adult Child of Emotionally Immature Parents.* New Harbinger Publications.
12. McCleery et al. (2013). Motor development and motor resonance difficulties in autism: Relevance to early intervention for language and communication skills. *Frontiers in Integrative Neuroscience 7*(30). doi.org/10.3389/fnint.2013.00030. PMID: 23630476; PMCID: PMC3634796.
13. Gao et al. (2019). The language network in autism: Atypical functional connectivity with default mode and visual regions. *Autism Research, 12*(9), 1344–55.
14. Brown et al. (2021). Changing the story: How diagnosticians can support a neurodiversity perspective from the start. *Autism, 25*(5), 1171–74.
15. www.youtube.com/watch?v=15_9rHnJQFo&list=PLWuXLE5sEcwPc7xof8DZ4tek8-GuFi_a&index=2.
16. www.thechatner.com/p/finally-taking-my-own-advice-about.
17. janelied.wordpress.com/2018/04/30/my-metoo-tale-an-apology/.
18. Edelson, M. G. (2010). Sexual abuse of children with autism: Factors that increase risk and interfere with recognition of abuse. *Disability Studies Quarterly, 30* (1).
19. Ratanatharathorn et al. (2021). Polygenic risk for autism, attention-deficit hyperactivity disorder, schizophrenia, major depressive disorder, and neuroticism is associated with the experience of childhood abuse. *Molecular Psychiatry, 26*(5), 1696–1705.
20. Kildahl et al. (2020). Clinicians' retrospective perceptions of failure to detect sexual abuse in a young man with autism and mild intellectual disability. *Journal of Intellectual & Developmental Disability, 45*(2), 194–202.
21. Kallitsounaki, A., & Williams, D. M. (2023).Brief report: An exploration of alexithymia in autistic and nonautistic transgender adults. *Autism in Adulthood.* www.liebertpub.com/doi/10.1089/aut.2022.0113.
22. Zlotnick et al. (2001). The relationship between posttraumatic stress disorder, childhood trauma and alexithymia in an outpatient sample. *Journal of Traumatic Stress, 14,* 177–188. doi.org/10.1023/A:1007899918410.
23. Kallitsounaki, A., & Williams, D. M. (2023). Brief report: An exploration of alexithymia in autistic and nonautistic transgender adults. *Autism in Adulthood.* www.liebertpub.com/doi/10.1089/aut.2022.0113.

24. devonprice.medium.com/is-it-alexithymia-or-is-it-dissociation-fueled-by-trauma-f13cf5ae6d29.
25. Gibson, L. C. (2023). I've Cut Off Contact with Them, but I Still Think about Them a Lot. In *Disentangling from Emotionally Immature People: Avoid Emotional Traps, Stand Up for Your Self, and Transform Your Relationships as an Adult Child of Emotionally Immature Parents*. New Harbinger Publications.
26. slate.com/transcripts/R2JoRjM0RllObGtieWlWa3ByUFFhVVRVNnFITHEvNFQ5TC9wUGVVVzdPVT0=.
27. health.clevelandclinic.org/grey-rock-method.
28. www.thechatner.com/p/longer-than-you-think-dad.
29. www.newyorker.com/magazine/2023/03/13/agnes-callard-profile-marriage-philosophy.
30. X.com/AgnesCallard/status/1636394491228692480?lang=en.
31. harpers.org/archive/2022/03/the-eros-monster-agnes-callard/.
32. www.newyorker.com/culture/the-weekend-essay/the-case-against-travel.

Chapter 4

1. Scott et al. (2019). Factors impacting employment for people with autism spectrum disorder: A scoping review. *Autism, 23*(4), 869–901.
2. Doyle et al. (2022). Intersectional stigma for autistic people at work: A compound adverse impact effect on labor force participation and experiences of belonging. *Autism in Adulthood, 4*(4), 340–56.
3. Mai, A. M. (2019). Hiring agents' beliefs: A barrier to employment of autistics. *SAGE Open, 9*(3), 2158244019862725.
4. Chan, F., & Rumrill, P. (2016). Emerging issues regarding the employment and career development of Americans with disabilities. *Journal of Vocational Rehabilitation, 45*, 1–4. On the statistic that 27 percent of Autistics live beneath the poverty line: U.S. Office of the Assistant Secretary for Planning and Evaluation. (2014). *2014 Poverty Guidelines*. Washington, DC: U.S. Department of Health and Human Services. Retrieved from aspe.hhs.gov/poverty/14poverty.cfm.
5. Frank et al. (2018). Education and employment status of adults with autism spectrum disorders in Germany—a cross-sectional survey. *BMC Psychiatry 18*, 1–10; Lallukka et al. (2020). Unemployment trajectories and the early risk of disability pension among young people with and without autism spectrum disorder: A nationwide study in Sweden. *International Journal of Environmental Research and Public Health, 17*(7), 2486.
6. www.autism.org.uk/advice-and-guidance/topics/employment.
7. Brady, F. (2023). *Strong Female Character*. Brazen Books.
8. Halder, S., & Assaf, L. C. (2017). Employment and living with autism:

Personal, social and economic impact. *Inclusion, Disability and Culture: An Ethnographic Perspective Traversing Abilities and Challenges*, 295–311. Springer.

9. Fair Play Talks. (2020). 50% employers admit they won't hire neurodivergent talent. www.fairplaytalks.com/2020/11/03/50-employers-admit-they-wont-hire-neurodivergent-talent-reveals-ilm-study/; Mai, A. M. (2019). Hiring agents' beliefs: A barrier to employment of autistics. *SAGE Open, 9*(3), 2158244019862725.
10. Waldmeir, P. (2020). Overlooked workers gain appeal in challenging times. *Financial Times*. www.ft.com/content/ea9ca374-6780-11ea-800d-da70cff6e4d3.
11. Cleary et al. (2023). Autism, discrimination and masking: Disrupting a recipe for trauma. *Issues in Mental Health Nursing*, 1–10.
12. Miller et al. (2021). "Masking is life": Experiences of masking in autistic and nonautistic adults. *Autism in Adulthood, 3*(4), 330–38.
13. Arnold et al. (2023). Towards the measurement of autistic burnout. *Autism*, 13623613221147401.
14. Graeber, D. (2015). *The Utopia of Rules: On Technology, Stupidity, and the Secret Joys of Bureaucracy*. Melville House.
15. www.washingtonpost.com/magazine/2022/10/24/universal-basic-income/.
16. ascenddisability.com/disability-claims-denied-ssdi/.
17. www.disabilitysecrets.com/resources/how-long-does-it-take-to-get-disability.html.
18. Benevides et al. (2021). Racial and ethnic disparities in benefits eligibility and spending among adults on the autism spectrum: A cohort study using the Medicare Medicaid Linked Enrollees Analytic Data Source. *PloS ONE, 16*(5), e0251353.
19. Godtland et al. (2007). Racial disparities in federal disability benefits. *Contemporary Economic Policy, 25*(1), 27–45.
20. www.ssa.gov/benefits/disability/work.html#:~:text=If%20medical%20improvement%20is%3A,condition%20about%20every%207%20years.
21. www.cbpp.org/research/social-security/the-case-for-updating-ssi-asset-limits.
22. For a list of some of the disability policy reforms requested by advocates, see: www.forbes.com/sites/andrewpulrang/2022/04/30/whats-next-for-disability-policy/?sh=2f41e0bf26bd.
23. Jun, M. (2022). Stigma and shame attached to claiming social assistance benefits: Understanding the detrimental impact on UK lone mothers' social relationships. *Journal of Family Studies, 28*(1), 199–215.
24. Specifically, Sontag said that all people hold a passport to the kingdom of the well and to the kingdom of the sick, but the existence of people born with disabilities disproves that.
25. fortune.com/2023/02/16/return-office-real-reason-slump-productivity-data

-careers-gleb-tsipursky/; index.medium.com/productivity-will-go-down-this-year-26f04e4a9455.
26. hbr.org/2016/08/millennials-are-actually-workaholics-according-to-research.
27. www.cnbc.com/2023/07/06/the-job-market-is-still-favorable-for-workers-despite-cooldown.html.
28. www.insidehighered.com/views/2022/04/25/declining-tenure-density-alarming-opinion.
29. Larson et al. (2014). Too many PhD graduates or too few academic job openings: The basic reproductive number R_0 in academia. *Systems Research and Behavioral Science, 31*(6), 745–50. doi.org/10.1002/sres.2210. PMID: 25642132; PMCID: PMC4309283.
30. Whelpley, C. E., & May, C. P. (2023). Seeing is disliking: Evidence of bias against individuals with autism spectrum disorder in traditional job interviews. *Journal of Autism and Developmental Disorders, 53*(4), 1363–74.
31. X.com/etirabys/status/1763328890607677790/quotes.
32. Flower et al. (2021). Barriers to employment: Raters' perceptions of male Autistic and non-Autistic candidates during a simulated job interview and the impact of diagnostic disclosure. *Autism in Adulthood, 3*(4), 300–09.
33. Bijlenga et al. (2019). The role of the circadian system in the etiology and pathophysiology of ADHD: Time to redefine ADHD? *ADHD Attention Deficit and Hyperactivity Disorders, 11*(1), 5–19.
34. www.adagreatlakes.org/Publications/Legal_Briefs/BriefNo19_Update_on_Emerging_ADA_Issues_Disability_Harassment,_Retaliation_and_Constructive_Discharge.pdf.
35. webapps.dol.gov/elaws/eta/warn/glossary.asp?p=Constructive%20Discharge.
36. Hoffman, S. (2007). Settling the matter: Does title I of the ADA work. *Alabama Law Review, 59,* 305.
37. www.reliasmedia.com/articles/39413-here-8217-s-reassuring-news-most-lawsuits-under-the-ada-are-won-by-employers.
38. X.com/FractalEcho/status/1681632336771796992.
39. Lindsay et al. (2021). Disclosure and workplace accommodations for people with autism: A systematic review. *Disability and Rehabilitation, 43*(5), 597–610.
40. Szechy et al. (2023). Autism and employment challenges: The double empathy problem and perceptions of an autistic employee in the workplace. *Autism in Adulthood.* liebertpub.com/doi/abs/10.1089/aut.2023.0046?journalCode=aut.
41. Hayward et al. (2019). Autistic women long for belonging in the workplace, but seldom find it. "I would love to just be myself": What autistic women want at work. *Autism in Adulthood, 1*(4), 297–305.
42. Doyle et al. (2022). Intersectional stigma for Autistic people at work: A

compound adverse impact effect on labor force participation and experiences of belonging. *Autism in Adulthood, 4*(4), 340–56.
43. Romualdez et al. (2021). "People might understand me better": Diagnostic disclosure experiences of autistic individuals in the workplace. *Autism in Adulthood, 3*(2), 157–67.
44. eggybing.medium.com/you-are-disabling-me-af8d4cddb41.
45. eggybing.medium.com/you-are-disabling-me-af8d4cddb41.
46. www.bc.edu/content/dam/files/centers/cwf/research/publications3/executivebriefingseries-2/ExecutiveBriefing_EmployeeResourceGroups.pdf.
47. www.sequoia.com/news/sequoia-announces-2021_employee-experience-benchmark-report-findings/.
48. devonprice.medium.com/do-not-trust-employee-resource-groups-ergs-1c671b692039.
49. www.iza.org/publications/dp/12258/disability-and-the-unionized-workplace.
50. cepr.net/why-union-membership-is-good-for-workers-with-disabilities/.

Chapter 5

1. Yew et al. (2021). A systematic review of romantic relationship initiation and maintenance factors in autism. *Personal Relationships, 28*(4), 777–802.
2. Hancock et al. (2020). Differences in romantic relationship experiences for individuals with an autism spectrum disorder. *Sexuality and Disability, 38,* 231–45.
3. Strunz et al. (2017). Romantic relationships and relationship satisfaction among adults with Asperger syndrome and high-functioning autism. *Journal of Clinical Psychology, 73*(1), 113–25.
4. Sala et al. (2020). Romantic intimacy in autism: A qualitative analysis. *Journal of Autism and Developmental Disorders, 50,* 4133–47.
5. www.youtube.com/watch?v=i4psluyVv8A&t=9771s.
6. markmanson.net/fuck-yes.
7. Chen, A. (2020). *Ace: What Asexuality Reveals About Desire, Society, and the Meaning of Sex.* Beacon Press.
8. Elizabeth Weir, doctoral candidate, psychiatry, Autism Research Center, University of Cambridge, United Kingdom; Eileen Crehan, PhD, assistant professor, child study and human development, Tufts University, Medford, MA; International Society for Autism Research, presentation, online meeting, May 3–7, 2021.
9. Attanasio et al. (2022). Are autism spectrum disorder and asexuality connected? *Archives of Sexual Behavior 51,* 2091–2115. doi.org/10.1007/s10508-021-02177-4.
10. Warrier et al. (2020). Elevated rates of autism, other neurodevelopmental

and psychiatric diagnoses, and autistic traits in transgender and gender-diverse individuals. *Nature Communications, 11*(1), 3959; Weir et al. (2021). The sexual health, orientation, and activity of autistic adolescents and adults. *Autism Research, 14*(11), 2342–54; George, R., & Stokes, M. A. (2018). Sexual orientation in autism spectrum disorder. *Autism Research, 11*(1), 133–41. doi.org/10.1002/aur.1892. Epub 2017 Nov 21. PMID: 29159906.
11. nsfw.substack.com/p/ace-erotics-or-why-youre-thinking?utm_source=%2Fsearch%2Fasexual&utm_medium=reader2.
12. Sala et al. (2020). Romantic intimacy in autism: A qualitative analysis. *Journal of Autism and Developmental Disorders, 50*(11), 4133–47.
13. Some labels and frameworks here are adapted from Chapters 4–6 of Fern, J. (2020). *Polysecure: Attachment, Trauma and Consensual Nonmonogamy.* Thornapple Press.
14. Breckenridge, J. P. (2018). The Relationship Between Disability and Domestic Abuse. *The Routledge Handbook of Gender and Violence.* Routledge, 133–44.
15. Brake, Elizabeth. (2012). *Minimizing Marriage: Marriage, Morality, and the Law.* Oxford University Press.
16. Wauthier, P. Y. (2022). Stepping off the "relationship escalator." A spatial perspective on residential arrangements of consensually non-monogamous parents. *Sexualities,* 13634607221080515.
17. Milton et al. (2022). The "double empathy problem": Ten years on. *Autism, 26*(8), 1901–03.
18. www.weshouldtryit.com/.
19. This quote originally appeared in a poem Priebe posted online. www.goodreads.com/quotes/11067748-to-love-someone-long-term-is-to-attend-a-thousand-funerals.

Chapter 6

1. Jackson, Jessi Lee. "Redefining Safety." *Make/shift Magazine, 26,* issue no. 9 (spring/summer 2011).
2. Gaudion, K., & McGinley, C. (2012). *Green Spaces: Outdoor Environments for Adults with Autism.* Helen Hamlyn Centre for Design, Royal College of Art.
3. www.apa.org/monitor/2020/04/nurtured-nature.
4. To learn more about the causes, consequences, and treatment of burnout, you can read Nagoski, E., & Nagoski, A. (2020). *Burnout: The Secret to Unlocking the Stress Cycle.* Ballantine Books; Price, D. (2021). *Laziness Does Not Exist.* Simon & Schuster.
5. Raymaker et al. (2020). "Having all of your internal resources exhausted beyond measure and being left with no clean-up crew": Defining autistic burnout. *Autism in Adulthood, 2*(2), 132–43.

6. emilynagoski.substack.com/p/autistic-pride-day-22-06-17.
7. In 2022, United States Surgeon General Vivek Murthy declared a burnout epidemic, particularly among healthcare workers: www.hhs.gov/about/news/2022/05/23/new-surgeon-general-advisory-sounds-alarm-on-health-worker-burnout-and-resignation.html.
8. Arnold et al. (2023). Towards the measurement of autistic burnout. *Autism, 27*(7), journals.sagepub.com/doi/10.1177/13623613221147401.
9. Mantzalas et al. (2022). A conceptual model of risk and protective factors for autistic burnout. *Autism Research, 15*(6), 976–87.
10. Mantzalas et al. (2022). A conceptual model of risk and protective factors for autistic burnout. *Autism Research, 15*(6), 976–87.
11. Arnold et al. (2023). Confirming the nature of autistic burnout. *Autism, 27*(7), 13623613221147410.
12. Mason et al. (2022). Older age autism research: A rapidly growing field, but still a long way to go. *Autism in Adulthood, 4*(2), 164–72.
13. Happé, F., & Charlton, R. A. (2011). Aging in autism spectrum disorders: A mini-review. *Gerontology, 58*(1), 70–78; Wright et al. (2019). Autism aging. *Gerontology & Geriatrics Education, 40*(3), 322–38.
14. Jovevska et al. (2020). Sleep quality in autism from adolescence to old age. *Autism in Adulthood, 2*(2), 152–62.
15. Perkins, E. A., & Berkman, K. A. (2012). Into the unknown: Aging with autism spectrum disorders. *American Journal on Intellectual and Developmental Disabilities, 117*(6), 478–96.
16. Casanova et al. (2020). The relationship between autism and Ehlers-Danlos syndromes/hypermobility spectrum disorders. *Journal of Personalized Medicine, 10*(4), 260.
17. Howlin, P., & Magiati, I. (2017). Autism spectrum disorder: Outcomes in adulthood. *Current Opinion in Psychiatry, 30*(2), 69–76.
18. South et al. (2021). Death by suicide among people with autism: Beyond zebrafish. *JAMA Network Open, 4*(1):e2034018. doi.org/10.1001/jamanetworkopen.2020.34018.
19. For example, a 2023 study published in the *Journal of the American Medical Association* concluded that 37 percent of Autistics in their study sample no longer qualified as Autistic anymore because they had developed some social skills. Harstad et al. Persistence of autism spectrum disorder from early childhood through school age. *JAMA Pediatrics, 177*(11), 1197–1205. doi.org/10.1001/jamapediatrics.2023.4003.
20. Pelton et al. (2020). Understanding suicide risk in autistic adults: Comparing the interpersonal theory of suicide in autistic and non-autistic samples. *Journal of Autism and Developmental Disorders, 50*(10), 3620–37. doi.org/10.1007/s10803-020-04393-8.
21. Perkins, E. A., & Berkman, K. A. (2012). Into the unknown: Aging with

autism spectrum disorders. *American Journal on Intellectual and Developmental Disabilities, 117*(6), 478–96.

22. Bastiaansen et al. (May 1, 2011). Age-related increase in inferior frontal gyrus activity and social functioning in autism spectrum disorder. *Biological Psychiatry, 69*(9), 832–8. doi.org/10.1016/j.biopsych.2010.11.007. Epub 2011 Feb 18. PMID: 21310395; Lever, A. G., & Geurts, H. M. (2016). Age-related differences in cognition across the adult lifespan in autism spectrum disorder. *Autism Research, 9*(6), 666–76.

23. For additional theorizing on how differences in emotional recognition ends up influencing how Autistics think and process socially, see Gaigg, S. B. (2012). The interplay between emotion and cognition in autism spectrum disorder: Implications for developmental theory. *Frontiers in Integrative Neuroscience, 6,* 113.

24. Woodman et al. (2015). Change in autism symptoms and maladaptive behaviors in adolescence and adulthood: The role of positive family processes. *Journal of Autism and Developmental Disorders, 45,* 111–26.

25. Courchesne et al. (2011). Brain growth across the life span in autism: age-specific changes in anatomical pathology. *Brain Research, 1380,* 138–45; doi.org/10.1016/j.brainres.2010.09.101. Epub 2010 Oct 1. PMID: 20920490; PMCID: PMC4500507.

26. Perkins, E. A., & Berkman, K. A. (2012). Into the unknown: Aging with autism spectrum disorders. *American Journal on Intellectual and Developmental Disabilities, 117*(6), 478–96.

27. Torres et al. (2020). Aging with autism departs greatly from typical aging. *Sensors, 20*(2), 572. MDPI AG. Retrieved from dx.doi.org/10.3390/s20020572.

28. medium.com/prismnpen/im-gay-i-hated-red-white-royal-blue-but-my-dying-christian-dad-592c2037ca5b.

29. To learn more about William Haines, I recommend William Mann's excellent biography, *Wisecracker.*

INDEX

ableist bias, rethinking, 60–63
abuse, 4, 114–23, 192, 213
acceptance (of change, loss, and uncertainty), xxviii, xxx, 6–16, 23, 43, 52, 88, 93, 137, 172, 251, 256–58
   accepting change, 68–70, 94
   accepting uncertainty, 138
   building community at work, 19
   changing family dynamic, 97–98
   exercises, 14–15, 50–51, 68–69, 94, 97, 138, 177–78, 207–9, 218–19
   friendship, 7, 43, 47
   of hard emotions, 207–9
   job interviews, 153
   relationships, 177–79
   of special interests, passions, and hobbies, 218–19, 222
accessibility needs, estrangement and, 119
accommodations. *See* creation (of accommodations, relationship structures, and new ways of being)
ace erotics, 188
addicted and dissociated mask type, 91
aging, xxx, 211, 232–41, 255
AIDS research, 255
alexithymia, 116
allosexuals, 187
amatonormativity, 193–94

Americans with Disabilities Act (ADA), 158, 159
anger, 207
annoyance, 207–8
anti-Autistic biases, 46, 56–65, 152–53, 159
anti-gay conversion therapy, 3
anxiety, xxiii, 30, 223, 224, 233
   anxiety disorder, 29, 169
Applied Behavior Analysis (ABA) therapy, xviii, xxv, 3, 4, 6
ARE (anchor, reveal, encourage), 81, 82
Arnold, Samuel, 227
aromanticism, 193–95
Art of Showing Up, The (Miller), 75, 77
Ascend Disability, 141
asexuals, 187–88
Ask an Autistic series (Schaber), 101
assistive devices, 107
augmentative and alternative communication (AAC), 108
Autism
   diagnosis of, xvii–xviii, 85–86, 102–3
   "discovered" by Bleuler, 16
   education and, 98–100
   five core skills for unmasking. *See* acceptance; engagement; creation; tolerance; transgression
   genetics and, 87

Autism (cont'd)
  misdiagnosis of, 88
  PDA (pathologically demand avoidant) profile, 17–18
Autism journal, xvii, 45
Autism in Adulthood journal, 136
Autism Speaks, 100, 109
Autistic Burnout Severity items, 227
Autistic Instagram, 44
Autistic Self Advocacy Network (ASAN), 50, 99, 110
Autistic TikTok, 44
Avila, Alexander, 101
avoidance, 30, 93, 116, 197, 203
Avoidant/Restrictive Food Intake Disorder (ARFID), 86

Barnes, Emma, 166
Bellini, Scott, 5
Berlin, Peter, 254
Beyond Shame: Reclaiming the Abandoned History of Radical Gay Sexuality (Moore), 254
bias, 46, 56–65, 141–42, 152–53, 159
Bipolar Disorder, xvii, 116
Blanc, Eric, 171
Bleuler, Eugen, 16
blogs, as resources, 101–2
bodily boundaries, 104, 111
Body and Soul: The Black Panther Party and the Fight Against Medical Discrimination (Nelson), 254
Bones (television show), 133
books, as resources, 101
BookTok, 143
Borderline Personality Disorder, xvii
bottom-up processing style, xii, 22
boundaries, 197
  bodily, 104, 111
  digital, 124–25
  emotional, 125
  identifying and maintaining, 66–68, 106
  older relatives and, 104
  setting, 47, 70–73
  social, 125
  space and, 105
boundary confusion, 204, 205
Bradbury, Alexandra, 171
Brady, Fern, 101, 135
brain volumes, 234
Brake, Elizabeth, 193–95
Brenner, Mark, 171
Brown, Jenny, 171
bullying, 8, 45, 47, 58, 133, 156, 249
burnout, xx, 133–36, 140, 142, 149, 166, 176, 213
  coping through, 225–29
  dimensions of, 227–28
Burnout: The Secret to Unlocking the Stress Cycle (Nagoski), 226
BuyNothing group, 69

Cain, David, 12, 13
Callard, Agnes, 126–27
capitalism, 49, 136
career discernment, 147–50
Casper, Sarah, 103–4, 111, 118, 183, 184, 187, 197
Cassidy, Sarah, 58
Center for Economic and Policy Research, The, 170
challenge zone, 11
change, acceptance of. *See* acceptance (of change, loss, and uncertainty)
charity, 139
childcare, 144
  estrangement and, 119
Citizens Advice (UK), 139
clothing, 110–11
  job interviews and, 154–55
  in workplace, 160

Index

co-napping, 80
codependent mask type, 91
Cognitive Behavioral therapy, 34
Cognitive Processing journal, 36–37
cognitive reframing, 34
collective loneliness, 46
colonialism, 49
comedy clubs, 50
commitment, sources of, 130–31
community centers, 51
community mutual aid, 139
Comprehensive Consent, 103
conferences, 51
conflict, engagement in. *See* engagement (in conflict, discussion, and disagreement)
conflict avoidance, 203, 204
conflict resolution, 47
conformity, 25
consent, 197–201
consistency, 10
constructive dismissal, 157–58
contact improvisation, 37
conventions, 51
conversation, 64–65 *See also* meeting new people
  ARE (anchor, reveal, encourage), 81, 82
  initiating, 18
COVID-19 pandemic, xxvi–xxvii, 44, 48, 52, 148, 159, 168, 171, 214, 235
Craigslist, 69
creation (of accommodations, relationship structures, and new ways of being), xxxi, 7, 36–43, 78, 88, 137, 172, 235–37, 243–45, 258
  of aging and the future, 237–38
  building community at work, 171
  exercises, 40–42, 79–80, 163–64, 195–96, 237–38
  of family, 126–32

job interviews and, 154
  needs from connections to other people, 195–96
  tips for, 39–40
credit card debt, 137
Criminal Minds (television show), 133
crowdfunding, 137
cry parties, 81
crying, 95

Dale, Laura Kate, 101
dating, xxix, 10, 52, 173–81, 198
Dear Prudence advice column, 114, 115
death, 211, 241, 255, 258, 259
Deconstructing Neuro (Pogue), 101
deep shallow friendships, 76–77
DeleteMe, 125
demands, transgression and. *See* transgression (of rules, demands, and social expectations)
depression, xxiii, 4, 233
DIAL (Disability Information and Access Line), 139
dietary requirements, 104
digital boundaries, 124–25
digital technology, 44, 48
disability benefits, xxi, xxix, 137, 139, 141–144
Disability History of the United States, A (Nielsen), 254
Disability Studies Quarterly, 116
Disability Visibility (ed. Wong), 254
disagreement, engagement in. *See* engagement (in conflict, discussion, and disagreement); tolerance (of disagreement, discomfort, and being disliked)
Discord channels, 49, 51, 63, 153, 211

discrimination, 158–59
discussion, engagement in. *See* engagement (in conflict, discussion, and disagreement)
dislike. *See* tolerance (of disagreement, discomfort, and being disliked)
distress, tolerance and, 7, 29–36
distress-regulation tools, 53
distress tolerance toolbox, 35
Divergent Design Studios (Rose), 101
Divergentdesign.substack.com, 101
Dodson, William, 71–72
domestic violence, 116
double empathy problem, 200
dread, 230–31

education, 8, 98–100, 225
Ehlers-Danlos syndrome, 233
eldercare, 144
electric shocks, 3
elopement, 80, 274
embarrassment, 12
emotional boundaries, 125
emotional surveillance, 203, 204
emotional victimization, 204, 205
Employee Resource Groups (ERGs), 167–70
engagement (in conflict, discussion, and disagreement), xxx, 7, 16–22, 172, 257
  articulating discomfort, 21–22
  building community at work, 19
  with co-workers, 161–62
  exercises, 21–22, 55, 65–66, 70–71, 100, 143, 161–62, 180–81, 209–11, 239–41
  friendship, 47, 54–56
  imperfection in relationship, 209–11
  job interviews, 153
  listening to no's, 68–70
  long-term support network, 239–41

  in productive conflict, 70–73
  relationships, 180–82
epileptic seizures, 233
estrangement, 115, 117–18
  analysis of parents, 123–24
  grieving and mourning, 125–26
  maintaining no-contact with relatives, 124–25
  navigating, 114–26
  planning for, 119–21
Etsy, 167
eventbrite.com, 50
executive dysfunction, 78–79
executor of will, 239
exercises
  affirmations for growing away from family, 94
  affirmations for unmasking interactions, 65–66
  alternate sources of stability, 146
  alternatives to monogamous heterosexual marriage, 191–92
  areas of growth needed, 256–58
  articulating discomfort, 21–22
  being imperfect in relationship, 209–11
  breaking free of existing relationship scripts, 199–200
  building long-term support network, 239–41
  changing social dynamics, 14–15
  choices for survival, 138
  distress tolerance toolbox, 35
  education of loved ones, 100
  ending interactions, 83
  engagement with social group, 55
  finding neurodivergent-friendly ways to interact, 79–80
  finding no's, 68–69
  letting other people be wrong, 73–74

Index

living with complexity in relationships, 207–9
long-term masked Autism, 91–92
maintaining boundaries, 106
maintaining no-contact with estranged relatives, 124–25
maintaining values and authenticity, 155–56
making space for special interests, 218–19
needs of accessibility features in workplace, 163–64
needs of relationships, 195–96
noticing feelings of sexual activities, 184–86
pondering relationship needs, 177–79
reflections on aging, 237–38
reimagining routine, 40–42
relationship dynamic changes, 97
relieving pressure and escaping burnout cycle, 229–31
remaining present and grounded in unfamiliar places, 223–24
requesting financial aid, 143
rethinking ableist bias, 60–63
scripts for expressing romantic or sexual interest, 180–81
seeking understanding in workplace, 161–62
setting boundary, 70–71
stimming in public, 26–28
using five core skills for job interviews, 153–54
values for parenting, 112
visiting new events and places, 50–51
expectations. *See* transgression (of rules, demands, and social expectations)
explosive mask type, 91

eye contact, xvi–xvii, xxii, 3, 80, 194, 201
eye-tracking technology, xi–xii

Facebook, 110
Facebook Marketplace, 69
familial support, 139
family relationships, xxviii–xxix, 46, 82, 84, 85–132 *See also* parenting
 change and, 105–6
 communication of needs, 102–3
 creating, 126–32
 diagnosis of Autism and, 85–86
 education and, 98–100
 establishing new patterns and, 98–107
 estrangement and. *See* estrangement
 masked Autistic, 89–98
 navigating abuse and estrangement, 114–26
 older generations, 89–90
 role in health management, 103–5
 unmasking relationships, 93–96
fetishes, 182–83, 186, 188, 221, 254
FetLife, 186
finances, estrangement and, 119
financial support, sources of, 129–30
five core skills for unmasking. *See* acceptance; engagement; creation; tolerance; transgression
flextime, 163
flirting, 175, 179, 181
Flower, Rebecca, 152
food stamps, 137, 139, 140
forgiveness, 86
found family, 128
friendship, xi, xiii, xxviii, 10, 11, 13, 44–84, 233, 249 *See also* meeting new people
 deep shallow friendships, 76–77
 deepening and asking for help, 75–79

Index

Garcia, Eric, 101
gastrointestinal conditions, 233
gender, 7, 20–21
genetics, 87
Gibson, Lindsay, 94–96, 104–5, 118, 124
Glassdoor, 150
Good Doctor, The (television show), 133
Good Place for Maniacs, A (McKeever), 215
government aid, 139
Grace, Kana, 45
Grandin, Temple, 16
grey rocking, 120
gyms, 51

Haines, William, 254
Hall, Atlee, 30
Hancock, Grace, 173
headphones, xix, 164
Health and Human Services, Department of, 140
health insurance, 141
health issues, 46, 72, 233, 240, 259
hierarchical polyamory, 191
Hiki, 181
hobbies, xxx, 217, 218, 243
holidays, 119, 126, 128, 129
hot sauce, 3
houselessness, 72, 213, 215–16
housing, 144, 146 *See also* creation (of accommodations, relationship structures, and new ways of being)
  estrangement and, 119
How to Deal with Emotionally Explosive People (Bernstein), 121
How to Jump-Start Your Union (Bradbury et al.), 171
hypervigilance, 203, 204

I Overcame My Autism and All I Got Was This Lousy Anxiety Disorder: A Memoir (Kurchak), 101
Ido in Autismland (Kedar), 101
I'm Glad My Mom Died (McCurdy), 32
improv, 38
Incite! Women of Color Against Violence, 171
Inclusion of Self in the Other Scale (IOS), 31
individualized education plan (IEP), 225
information security (InfoSec), 121
Institute for Challenging Disorganization, 235
institutional injustice, 155–56
Intellectual and Developmental Disabilities journal, 46
interpersonal difficulties, in workplace, 156
intimate loneliness, 46
Issendai, 123–25
Issues in Mental Health Nursing journal, 136
Itzel, 77, 81
IZA Institute of Labor Economics, 170

Jackson, Jessi Lee, 212
Jaffe, Sarah, 171
job interviews, xxix, 134, 147–57
Journal of Autism and Developmental Disorders, 152

Kanner, Leo, 29
Kedar, Ido, 101
Kelly, Orion, 101
Kelsky, Karen, 149
Khan, Ayesha, 78
Kids & Comprehensive Curriculum, The (Casper), 103

Index

King-Lowe, Philip, 101
kitchen table polyamory, 192
Klein, Naomi, 145
Kurchak, Sarah, 101

labor unions, 169–71
Lavery, Danny, 114–15, 118, 125
Laziness Does Not Exist (Price), 144
legacies, xxix, xxx, 242–60, 260
letter boards, 107
life changes, 14–16
life expectancy, 233, 234
LinkedIn, 150
living accommodations. *See* creation (of accommodations, relationship structures, and new ways of being)
living outdoors, 215–16
loneliness, xx, 44, 45–46, 48, 72, 95
long-term masked Autism, 90–93
loss, acceptance of. *See* acceptance (of change, loss, and uncertainty)
Lovaas, O. Ivar, 3–4
love. *See* relationships

Manson, Mark, 186
marriage, 190, 194, 195
McCurdy, Jennette, 32
McKeever, Chuck, 215
Meadows, Jesse, 78, 101
Medicare and Medicaid, 139, 142
meditation, 38
meeting new people, xxx, 10–13, 44, 48–56, 221, 224
    boundaries, identifying and maintaining, 66–68
    creating connection, 79–83
    engagement with others, 55–56, 65–68
    events and places, 50–52

meetings, 163–65
Meetup, 50, 110
Mehling, Margaret, 46
Mel's Rule, 53–54
meltdowns, 10, 86, 89, 109, 213
memory-foaming, 30, 32, 33, 66
Mental Health (Moskowitz), 102
mental health problems, 233
Mentalhellth.substack.com, 102
mentorship, 153, 163
messages and gifts, exchanging, 80
Miller, Rachel Wilkerson, 75–77
misdiagnosis of Autism, 88
Moneysmart (Australia), 139
monogamish, 191
Morrison, Kerriane, 63
mortality, 241–42
Moskowitz, P. E., 102
multigenerational contact, 129
museums, 50
mutual aid funds, 137

Nagoski, Emily, 226
Narcissistic Personality Disorder, xvii
narrowboats, 144, 213–14
National Social Assistance Programme (India), 139
National Social Investment Programme (Nigeria), 139
Nature, 116
nature, time in, 38, 216
needs, denial of incompatible, 203, 204
neighborhood groups, 51
Nelson, Alondra, 265
nesting partnership, 192
Neurodiversity Network, 110
neurotypicality, defined, xxii–xxiii
new ways of being. *See* creation (of accommodations, relationship structures, and new ways of being)
New Yorker, 126, 127

Newson, Elizabeth, 17–18
Nielsen, Kim, 254
Nike, 167
no-conversation hangouts, 80
no-eye-contact conversation, 80
nonconformity, 23, 26
nonhierarchical polyamory, 191
no's, finding, 68–70

Obsessive Compulsive Disorder (OCD), xvii, 169
OkCupid, 181
online communities, 235, 236
online dating, 52
online social opportunities, 44, 49, 52
open relationships, 191
opinions of others, disregarding, 31–33
Oppositional Defiant Disorder, xvii
oral sex, 184, 186
Orsmond, Gael, 45
ostracism, xix, xxiii, 23, 30, 40, 45, 156, 213
over-justification, 203, 204
over-processing, 203, 204

Palestinian people, 259
pandemic, xxvi–xxvii, 44, 48, 52, 148, 159, 168, 171, 214, 235
panic, 71
parallel play, 79, 110
parallel polyamory, 192
parasocial relationships, 45
parenting, 37, 87–89, 98, 146, 190
  for neurodiversity, 107–12
  telling children about their neurodiversity, 109–10
  values and, 111–13
park districts, 50
passions, xxix, 217–19, 222

passivity, 17, 18
PDA (pathologically demand avoidant) profile, 17–18
Pennisi, Paola, 37
people-pleasing, xix, 30, 33, 66, 104, 154, 225
performance venues, 51
phobia rate, 29
places of worship, 51
planning for future, 211
play, 38
  parallel, 79
playdates, 110
podcasts, as resources, 101–2
Pogue, T Jamaica, 101
politeness, 7, 47, 235
poly-intimacy, 191
polyfidelity, 191
positive connection, 130
Post-Traumatic Stress Disorder (PTSD), 4, 9
power of attorney, 239
Prahlad, Anand, 101
prejudices, 47, 87, 158
pretend games, 24
Priebe, Heidi, 202
productivity, 41, 225, 228, 229, 232, 238
  productivity accountability, 80
  productivity circles, 78, 79
Professor Is In, The (Kelsky), 149
public gardens, 50
public libraries, 50, 51
public spaces, decline of, 48
public sporting spaces, 51

quality of life, in workplace, 156
queer exchange, 69
queerplatonic relationships, 189–90, 192
questions, asking, 19–20

r/SocialSkills subreddit, 64
racial bias, 141–42
racism, 88
RAINN (the Rape, Abuse, and Incest National Network), 122–23
Real Social Skills (Regan), 102
Realsocialskills.org, 102
Red State Revolt (Blanc), 171
reddit.com, 51
"Redefining Safety" (Jackson), 212
Regan, Rabbi Ruti, 102
regret, 208–9
rejection, 9, 10, 29, 31, 49, 66, 87, 133, 188, 193, 197
rejection sensitive dysphoria (RSD), 38, 71–72
relational loneliness, 46
relationship anarchy, 192
relationship escalator, 198
relationships, xii, xvii, xx, xxix, 13, 173–211, 251
　alternatives to monogamous heterosexual marriage, 191–92
　consent and healthy conflict, 197–201
　dating, xxix, 10, 52, 173–81, 198
　family. *See* family relationships
　flirting, 175, 179, 181
　maintaining through conflict and change, 202–7
　romantic, xvi, 9, 46, 172, 174, 180–81, 191, 194–95, 203–4
　sexual activities, 182–88, 198, 199, 201, 211
relaxation, 41
rent support, 137
rental assistance, 139
repetitive-thinking patterns, 38
resentment, 208, 229–31
resilience, 10, 11, 16, 31, 40

Revolution Will Not Be Funded, The (Incite! Women of Color Against Violence), 171
rigid and controlling mask type, 91
role-playing, 38
romantic relationships, 9, 46, 172, 174, 180–81, 191, 194–95, 203–4
Rose, Marta, 78, 101
rules, transgression and. *See* transgression (of rules, demands, and social expectations)

safety, 212–13
Salesforce, 167
Sang, Elliot, 101
Sasson, Noah, 63
Schaber, Amythest, 101
schedules, 42
Schizophrenia, 116
@schizophrenicreads, 144
scripted and structured interactions, 80
Secret Life of a Black Aspie, The (Prahlad), 101
self-advocacy, xv, xxviii, xxxi, 5, 17, 20, 47, 56, 69, 93, 114, 117, 137, 172, 174, 181, 211, 213, 224, 234, 246, 256, 260
self-censorship, 203, 204
self-consciousness, 12
self-denial, 99
self-disclosure, 157–62, 166
self-harming, xx, 108, 245
self-realization, 102, 103
self-soothing, xx, 24–25, 29, 31
self-stimulation (stimming), xiv, 3, 26–28, 38
sensory issues, xix, 9, 16–19, 29, 78, 86, 89, 104, 111, 116, 144, 160, 161, 164, 166, 167, 172, 198, 213, 216, 225, 226, 227

292 Index

sex work, 146
sexual abuse, 115
sexual activities, 182–88, 198, 199, 201, 211
sexual connection, 46
shame, xxix, 183, 209
shared experiences, 130
shared wandering, 80
Shields, Jimmie, 254
Shock Doctrine, The (Klein), 145
Shuherk, Nathan, 143–44
shyness, 12, 13, 20, 48
sickle cell anemia research, 255
sign language, 107
Signal, 121
Slate magazine, 115
Slaughter, Jane, 171
sleep-wake cycles, 41
Sluggish (Meadows), 101
Sluggish.substack.com, 101
social anxiety, xx, 4, 11, 13, 44, 46, 108
Social Anxiety Disorder, xvii
social boundaries, 125
social connections, forming, xxix, 44–48 *See also* meeting new people
social dynamics, changing, 14–16
social expectations, transgression and. *See* transgression (of rules, demands, and social expectations)
social facilitation effect, 79
social isolation, 46, 93
Social Motivation Theory, 47
social pressure, 23–24
social responsiveness, 6
Social Security Administration, 141
Social Security benefits, 139, 141
Social Security Disability Insurance (SSDI), 142
social skills training, 3–7

social snacking, 44
social welfare benefits, xxix, 139–40, 146
Society for Neurodiversity, 110
solo polyamory, 192
Sontag, Susan, 143
spaces, 78, 105
  rearranging, 69
special interests, 217–22, 228
specific compliance, 120
speech, loss of, 17, 107–8
starvation, 72, 213
stoicism, 99
Stop Gatekeeping Mental Disorders (Sang), 101
Strong Female Character (Brady), 101, 135
Strunz, Sandra, 174
substance abuse, xx, 71, 92, 93, 233
suicide, 4, 8, 136, 233
Supplemental Security Income (SSI), 142
support swapping, 80
support systems, xviii, 233, 235
swinging, 192

tabletop gaming stores, 50
Tasse, Marc, 46
Taylor, Lizzie, 110
Telecommunications Relay Service, 139
Telegram, 121
television shows, 133
texting, 107
That Boy (film), 254
theaters, 50
Thresholds, 140
TikTok Gave Me Autism: The Politics of Self Diagnosis (Avila), 101
Tinder, 181
Tjamaicapogue.com, 101

Index

Today's Autistic Moment (King-Lowe), 101
Todaysautisticmoment.com, 101
tolerance (of disagreement, discomfort, and being disliked), xxx–xxxi, 7, 29–36, 43, 88, 137, 172, 258
    breaking free of existing relationship scripts, 199–200
    building community at work, 171
    of discomfort, 73–75
    exercises, 35, 73–74, 106, 124–25, 155–56, 199–200, 223–24
    friendship, 47
    imperfection in relationship, 209–11
    job interviews, 154
    maintaining boundary, 106
    maintaining no-contact with relatives, 121–25
    of unfamiliar places, 223–24
    in workplace, 165
traditions, 119, 126, 128, 129
Transformative Justice Law Project of Illinois, 141
transgression (of rules, demands, and social expectations), xxx, 6, 7, 22–29, 53–56, 78, 88, 128, 137, 172
    alternate sources of stability, 146
    building community at work, 170–71
    escaping burnout cycle, 229–31
    exercises, 26–28, 60–63, 83, 112, 146, 184–86, 191–92, 229–31
    friendship and, 7, 43, 53–55, 47
    job interviews, 153
    of neurotypical norms, 83
    sexual expectations, 184–86
    transgressing, 60–63
trauma, 116, 117, 142
Trump, Donald, xxi
211 telephone number, 122, 139

uncertainty, acceptance of. *See* acceptance (of change, loss, and uncertainty)
Uncomfortable Labels: My Life as a Gay Autistic Trans Woman (Dale), 101
unemployment, xxvi, 72, 133, 134, 142, 233
unemployment benefits, 139, 140
unfamiliar, as threat, 9, 10
unfamiliar spaces, xii, 53, 223–24
Unmasking After Late Autism Diagnosis—Embracing Authenticity (Kelly), 101
Unmasking Autism: Discovering the New Faces of Neurodiversity (Price), xiv, xxv, 36, 57, 246
usefulness, 38

vaccines, 111
Valens, Ana, 188
values, 31, 33–34, 111–13, 231, 246, 259, 260
    alignment of, 155
video interviews, 152
videos, as resources, 101
volunteering, 49, 51, 121, 129, 130, 154, 166, 168, 254

watch parties, 80
We Should Try It, 201
websites, as resources, 101–2
We're Not Broken: Changing the Autism Conversation (Garcia), 101
Weston, Diane, 81, 82
Winslow, Samantha, 171
wisdom and advice, sources of, 130
withdrawn mask type, 91
Wong, Alice, 254

work, xxix, xxxi, 132–72, 250, 251
  alternatives to, 138–39, 144–46
  career discernment, 147–50
  constructive dismissal, 157–58
  disability benefits, 137, 139, 141–44
  engaging with co-workers, 161–62
  job interviews, 134, 147–57
  masking and, 135–36
  neurodiversity initiatives and labor organizing at, 167–72
  problems of, 133–34
  requesting financial aid, 143
  securing accommodations, 162–67
  self-disclosure, 157–62, 166
  socialization, 163–65
  surviving under capitalism, 137–45
  types of positions, 150–52
  unemployment, xxvi, 72, 133, 134, 142, 233
  work-from-home, 163
  work hours, 41
Work Won't Love You Back (Jaffe), 171
workaholic mask type, 91
written interviews, 152

Xerox, 168

Yew, Rui Ying, 173
YouTube, 110

ABOUT THE AUTHOR

DEVON PRICE, PHD, is a social psychologist, a professor, an author, and a proud Autistic person. He is the author of *Unmasking Autism, Laziness Does Not Exist,* and *Unlearning Shame.* His research has appeared in journals such as the *Journal of Experimental Social Psychology, Personality and Social Psychology Bulletin,* and *The Journal of Positive Psychology.* Price's writing has appeared in outlets such as the *Financial Times, HuffPost, Los Angeles Times, Slate, Jacobin, Business Insider, LitHub,* and on PBS, NPR, MSNBC, and the BBC. He lives in Chicago, where he serves as a clinical associate professor at Loyola University Chicago's School of Continuing & Professional Studies.

drdevonprice.substack.com

Instagram: @drdevonprice

ABOUT THE TYPE

This book was set in Minion, a 1990 Adobe Originals typeface by Robert Slimbach. Minion is inspired by classical, old-style typefaces of the late Renaissance, a period of elegant and beautiful type designs. Created primarily for text setting, Minion combines the aesthetic and functional qualities that make text type highly readable with the versatility of digital technology.

'I didn't realize how much I masked. An incredible book'
DR CAMILLA PANG

DR DEVON PRICE

UNMASKING AUTISM

THE POWER OF EMBRACING OUR HIDDEN NEURODIVERSITY

'A remarkable work that will stand at the forefront of the neurodiversity movement'
DR BARRY M. PRIZANT

"This book brings shame into the light where it can be faced, embraced, understood and ultimately, healed."
CELESTE HEADLEE, AUTHOR OF *WE NEED TO TALK*

UNLEARNING
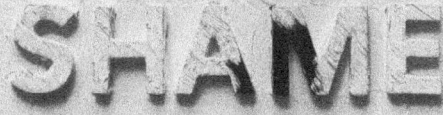
SHAME

**HOW REJECTING
SELF-BLAME CULTURE
GIVES US REAL POWER**

DR DEVON PRICE
AUTHOR OF *UNMASKING AUTISM*